About *Unlocked*

Unlocked follows twenty-one-year-old Isabelle Vasquez as she loses hope after encountering repeated obstacles. Through personal therapy and the support of trusted friends, Isabelle discovers the value of living in her true self.

More praise for *Unlocked*

Dr. Andrew Carey is a rare and compelling amalgamation of academic scholar and astute storyteller. I am so pleased *Unlocked* readers will be privy to his exceptional ability to give voice to the internal challenges faced by people who struggle with mental disorder.

As a novelist, Dr. Carey introduces us to characters so rich and complex that readers cannot help but empathize with their struggles, their pain, and to celebrate their triumphs.

On a personal note, having worked side-by-side with Andy as counselor educators for more than 20 years, I've witnessed his insistence that counselors-in-training and his professional peers see each client fully: listening to all of their complexity long before diagnostic codes and academic or social labels were ever considered or uttered.

Dr. Kurt L. Kraus — *Professor Emeritus in Counselor Education, Shippensburg University of Pennsylvania*

Cover art by Jeremy Ruby

Copyright 2025
Charles Bruce Foundation
ISBN 979-8-9921607-1-0

UNLOCKED

Andrew Carey PhD

Carlisle, Pennsylvania

Dedicated to those who work tirelessly to unlock
doors of hope for many who suffer alone.

Prologue

Oblivious to the rest of the world, she stared at the gravestone. The engravings blurred and wavered.

Her voice pleaded. "Grandma, please help. I don't know if I can go on." Tears streamed down her cheeks and fell to the ground.

"He did it again." She gasped for air between sobs. "I thought he'd be there for me, but I always end up on my own."

The young woman sat and rocked, writhing in pain. Then the anguish billowed up and erupted again. "I try so hard. But no one's there for me. You're gone. Dad's gone. Mom was always gone. What the hell's the use?"

Seeing no hope, no way forward, she shook her head. "I don't understand. Is it me? Am I cursed? Why is life so messed up?"

Strands of black hair stuck to her tear-stained face as a butterfly flew past and landed on a rose by the gray, porous stone. But she didn't care.

"I don't know if you can hear me, Grandma. But I need you. I need someone. I'm not religious like you. Can you put in a good word for me? I don't know what to do."

Nothing. Only a puff of air. A faint breeze blowing that scarcely cooled the humid, autumn day.

Then she heard a distant directive that lingered in the stillness: "Give her a start."

She looked around, not knowing where the barely-audible words came from. If they were in her head, or if they existed at all. Her heart pounding, she listened and waited.

Then she heard a car grinding, trying to turn over. The engine coughed and revved. A man cheered. "Told you we'd get her going."

Realizing that the voice had come from the service station beyond the edge of the graveyard, her shoulders shrunk again. She hung her head in defeat.

Up until an hour earlier, she had managed to keep her mounting devastation under wraps. An abusive mom, never there for her. A dad, finally able to show care, suddenly tortured and stripped from her by cancer. Her main pillar of support, Grandma, likewise was stolen from her in a time of need. And now, betrayed. By someone close—as close as she'd let anyone get. She usually hid the distress, even from herself. Until today. The universe's hideous jokes had finally escalated too much for her to hold back the avalanche of pain.

"Life's just a big freakin' game. What's the point?"

Wobbling as she arose and wiping her eyes, she staggered out of the cemetery.

Whispered Directives – Gene

Out walking Button later than usual on a Saturday night, I saw a woman face down at the edge of a dark alley, seemingly unconscious. She reeked of alcohol and vomit. *Probably came from Sap's Bar.*

The right thing to do? Help her. But after a long day, I didn't want to get involved. The heat smothered me. The humidity dripped from my body like the condensation from a cup of ice water sitting in the sun. I just wanted to go back to my air-conditioned place and watch another rerun of *M.A.S.H.* before going to bed. I tried to convince myself that she'd be fine, rationalizing that I got plastered as a teen, along with my friends. We all survived.

I could only see a silhouetted body in the dark but there was something about her, something I couldn't put my finger on that made me curious. Still indecisive, I watched as she became quieter. Her breathing sounded strained. Panicked now by her labored breathing, I called 911. With an ambulance on its way, I let out a long breath, knowing that she'd be helped and I had done my part. I felt sad for her. *Did she drink herself into oblivion? How did she end up in this dark alley all alone?*

The thought struck me: *Check her purse for identification.* I resisted, *Are you serious?*

I talk with myself. A lot. Worse yet, I hear answers. Maybe from counseling too many clients about paying attention to how their thoughts influence them. As I've conveyed to clients, certain thoughts help and others don't. Some are logical while others aren't. And logic doesn't always equate to helpful. Right now, logic told me to kick back on the recliner to old-fashioned humor!

These personal and hopefully-not-noticed-by-others conversations happen all the time. Sometimes out loud. Other times just in my head. Over the years, I've noticed that some thoughts are like gut instincts that go beyond the laws of logic. This time was like that. And I usually found that following my inner sense—what I call GUS, for Gut Understanding and Sensitivity—paid off.

With the woman lying half-dead in the alley, GUS chimed in without me asking. He first nudged me to stay and take action. Then he got more blatant, his whispered directives pressing me to discover her identity.

I sighed. *Yeah, I see the wide-open purse sitting beside her. But someone might think I'm stealing.*

GUS pushed harder. *Check to see who she is!*

Crossing my arms, I spoke aloud, hoping no one heard or witnessed this invisible debate. "It doesn't matter who she is. I did my part calling the ambulance. I'm exhausted and I want to go home and relax."

Standing there with my head tilted, I listened and waited. Only silence, other than Button, who whimpered and tugged at the leash again. He seemed determined for me to remain with this woman, too.

I gave in. *Apparently logic's not enough for you, GUS.*

Hesitating, I glanced around to make sure no one from the street would see me and walked over to the woman's purse. Moving back to the edge of the main road, I held her driver's license up to the light. "Isabelle Vasquez. Holy shocker! I knew something seemed familiar but I didn't recognize her in the dark. Thanks for persisting, GUS. As usual, you knew something I didn't."

I talk with GUS like he's a best friend. It started not long after my wife, Hanna, died. I lost hope when she passed on, unsure of how to continue without the woman who mattered more to me than anyone else in the world. But, one day, I stopped fighting with life about what *should have been* and yelled into the air exactly how I felt: "I feel cheated. Empty. All alone. I can't go on without her!"

After screaming out my raw experience instead of keeping a lid on it, the distinct thought bubbled up from somewhere deep inside: *Let me be your friend.*

That was it. Just a simple statement that resonated throughout my whole body. I had never thought about friendship with my gut like that—with that inner guidance that comes from somewhere in my core. After hearing those unforgettable words over six years ago, I said, "Well, GUS, it looks like it's you and me." Following that inner sense gave me peace and led to better decisions. Like how it happened tonight. I would have called 911 either way. But I'd have kept my distance and taken off as soon as they arrived. I wouldn't have crossed paths with Isabelle again. *Perhaps we're meant to reconnect.*

Button and I stood waiting as the siren grew louder and the ambulance came around the corner flashing its unsettling lights. I pointed toward Isabelle. The driver came to a screeching halt and backed into the one-way alley, blocking my view. It filled the narrow street with only a little space on each side, barely enough room for the paramedics to get out.

Scarcely able to form words, I approached the tall, skinny driver as soon as his feet hit the pavement. "She's still breathing, but, it's fainter!" The darkness swallowed him up as he went to the back of the vehicle. I couldn't stand not knowing, so I squeezed by the big mirror and moved to the rear corner of the truck to watch. In the dark, I could hardly make out the one paramedic checking Isabelle for a pulse while the thin guy pulled a gurney from the ambulance.

The woman with Isabelle suddenly turned toward the driver. "Let's get her in. Now! We're losing her."

I went numb as I watched the paramedics lift Isabelle's motionless body into the back of the vehicle. Then I moved to the sidewalk on the main street so the driver had room to return to his seat. I handed him my card with my name and number on it in case they needed information. He speed read it. "Eugene Singleton. Okay. Gotta run."

As quickly as they came, they slammed the doors and sped away into the night, blaring their siren. I stood there alone, my mouth open. I wanted to wake up from this nightmare, one of those where I'd find myself sweating, then thankful it wasn't real. But the siren's sound pierced me with its seriousness, causing me to turn in an all-out run to my home, if you could call it a run at age 68.

The dark night taunted me while I ran, as if gloating about its victory over Isabelle. *You didn't do enough when her grandma died.* My old nemesis, guilt, welled up as I fought for breath. Reaching the door to my house, I put Button inside and hurried to the car. My jittery hands fumbled with the keys and dropped them as I came around the front of my old blue Ford—the same car Hanna had driven. Leaning down to pick up the keys, I saw the dent in the front fender, reminding me of when she had backed into it with our riding mower. She had wanted to mow the grass to feel useful on one of her better days. I had never been able to get rid of the old jalopy or fix the dent. Finally, I unlocked the door and jumped in. Dreading the worst, I made my way through the back streets to Landsburg General Hospital.

As I drove, I pictured Isabelle on that gurney, my heart aching about how life had seemed stacked against her. I let out a scream, half to GUS and half into the evening air.

Memories — Gene

My old Ford raced toward the hospital like a toy car in a slotted track, having taken my wife there many times. Landsburg, a small city of 65,000 people, offered a reputable hospital, a university, progressive companies and schools, and considerable culture and diversity for its size. But slums, like weeds, weaved their way into the mix, too. The city sat in a valley nestled between forest-covered mountains. Well, small mountains or big hills, depending on who you asked. I liked living here. It provided enough culture to satisfy me while only being a fifteen-minute drive from good hiking.

During the not-knowing silence of the drive, memories rumbled inside like a flu bug. After retiring, my counseling background and passion for learning life's mysteries found an outlet in speaking about meaning-of-life issues at Landsburg's Friends of Family Community Center. Sophia, Isabelle's grandma, and her best friend, Camila, routinely ate lunch with me afterward at the center's outdoor picnic tables. Through Sophia's prodding, Isabelle had eventually joined us.

Every time our group ate lunch, Sophia sat to my left and Isabelle and Camila across from us. I smiled as I remembered Sophia saying, "Gene, you have such a gentle spirit. You touch people, like a butterfly visiting one flower after another." Isabelle, who feared her abusive grandpa and had been watching Sophia admire me, told her, "Grandma, you two look more like a couple than when you're with Grandpa." Sophia blushed. Isabelle sat there with a grin that could melt the Grinch's heart. Attractive, with long dark hair, her glowing face showed that she loved her grandma above all else.

After that day, Isabelle began calling me Grandpa Gene. The name stuck. Later, she called me "G" for short.

That thought warmed me as I turned down Magnolia Drive, about a mile from the hospital. But my mind still whirled with other echoes from the past.

Not long after Isabelle started picnicking with us at the pavilion, we crossed paths at a street corner. I remember her spontaneous, off-the-cuff way of relating. "Hey, G. You look like you're out in the ozone again. What the hell kind of crazy things are you learning about now?"

"Lately? I'm contemplating surrender during difficulties. Surrendering helps me be present and to learn more in the moment."

"Whoa. That's deep. You hear voices, too, don't you? That's what people at the center say."

I cringed. "I'd say that I pay attention to certain kinds of thoughts—to my gut sense of things. My gut usually picks up on things that regular logic doesn't."

"You mean like intuition, right?"

I gave a big nod. "Yeah, that's a good way to say it."

She laughed and snorted. "Well, don't use that voodoo shit on me, and we'll get along just fine."

Tears trickled down my cheeks as I thought about that day. She had become comfortable enough to tease me, but she had grown fond of me, too. She gradually spent more time with me and showed interest in whatever life lessons I was learning during my "bizarro" (as she called it) contemplative journey. She saw me as a grandfather. As family.

When her mom got overly abusive, rather than sleeping at a friend's house, she asked to stay at my place. She'd have stayed at Sophia's if not for her grandpa. But, next to Sophia, Isabelle trusted me more than anyone.

Our friendship blossomed the following two years—me as family support for her, and Isabelle as the child that Hanna and I never had. I finally got to experience, to a small degree, being a parent.

I clenched my teeth. "I had that with Isabelle!" Then grief bubbled up from inside as I drove up the hill toward the hospital's expansive brick building. The fifteen-floor monstrosity sat on a hill overlooking Landsburg like a fortress towering over its kingdom. I shuddered as I looked at the many lit windows and an ambulance sitting at the entrance.

I parked my car and paused before going in. My shoulders hunched.

Maybe I should've done more after she shut me out. After she shut everyone out when Sophia and her dad died! How horrible, losing the people who cared the most. I wanted to be there for her. We were family. But it slipped away. I hope she makes it.

Wiping my eyes, I let out a big breath from all the stress. *Okay, let's go see how she made out.*

Before opening my car door, GUS whispered, *She'll be okay.* Relieved and thankful, I felt ready as I turned toward the intimidating building. Well, readier. I hated hospitals.

I brushed the sweat off my forehead with my shirt sleeve as I walked through the front doors. Hospitals always flooded my mind with thoughts of sickness. *Hanna's* sickness—her agonizing battle with Lou Gehrig's disease.

I fidgeted as if I had hives when I approached the receptionist. Maybe just memories of Hanna. But I grew anxious that Isabelle's condition remained critical.

Savior Complex — GENE

The receptionist said that Isabelle had been moved from the emergency room to the fourth floor. As I walked away from the desk, I talked with GUS, trying to settle myself. "Well, at least she's out of the emergency room. You said she'll be okay." I glanced around to make sure nobody could see this invisible conversation.

I went to the elevators and pressed the up button. The door opened and a woman staggered out, sobbing and blowing her nose as if she had just received horrible news. I rolled my eyes after the elevator door closed and pressed button four as I spoke to GUS. "Great, just what I needed to stay positive." I told myself to get a grip, my stomach going in circles. "You said she'd be fine, didn't you?"

After the door opened, I spotted a nurse I knew sitting behind a desk at the hub of several hallways. I hadn't seen Glenda for half a year. With the same short, red hair and freckles, she gave a big smile when she saw me. She and I had talked after several of my presentations at the Friends of Family Community Center. She came across as competent and had a big heart, which probably made her a great nurse.

"Hello, Glenda. Good to see you. I'm here to visit Isabelle Vasquez."

Her eyes brightened when she saw me. "Hi, Gene. Glad to see you, too. It's been a while. But, I'm sorry, only family will be allowed to visit after she's moved to a regular room."

"My guess is that you haven't reached Isabelle's family, and that even if you did, no one plans to visit."

Furrows showed between her eyebrows. "How would you know that?"

"The few people who cared for Isabelle passed away, and the others who should care won't come even if you contact them. You remember her always sitting together with me at the center's pavilion? She has no family but me." I had stretched my point, making it sound like Isabelle and I still had that kind of friendship. She'd be twenty-one years old now.

She could be a whole different person. But unless her life had changed drastically in just over two years, she had no one close but me. She walked alone anytime I spotted her on the street, although I had seen her less frequently the last year and a half.

Glenda's eyes opened slightly, as if something registered—she had probably remembered me with Isabelle in the past, or maybe she had, in fact, encountered the lack of caring response from her family that I described.

I breathed a thankful sigh when she answered in a hushed voice. "Only because I trust you, I'll let you know when we move her to a regular room where family can visit."

I sat by the nurse's station for about fifteen minutes, growing anxious and sending healing thoughts and prayers Isabelle's way. I stared at the stark white wall in front of me. The longer I sat, the more Glenda's words about moving Isabelle to a regular room plagued me. That meant she *wasn't* in a regular room.

I glanced over at the wider hallway with the double doors. My stomach churned as I read above the entrance: ICU. *I don't remember Glenda telling me that.*

After I confirmed that Isabelle was there, I sat back down, now less able to stop the avalanche of negative thoughts. I pleaded, *Give her a second chance.* I reminded GUS, *She shouldn't be in danger. You said she'd be fine!* From experience, I trusted GUS' insight, even about the future. But sometimes outcomes popped into my mind that I simply wanted, rather than intuitive ones from him. Wanting something badly clouded my judgment at times. Fear did the same.

Several more minutes passed. The hallways reeked of silence. Normally, I found stillness rejuvenating. But something felt wrong.

Jarring me out of the silence, a beeper sounded and a code came across the intercom. I jumped to my feet. Through the double doors' small windows, I saw ashen faces on the doctors and nurses who ran from all directions, making their last-minute preparations as they entered a room to the right.

My whole body lurched. I knew Isabelle's life teetered on the brink of one door closing and another opening. I longed for her to get a second chance to live life to the fullest. My heart pounded like a violent intruder attacking the inside of my chest. With ferocity, I gazed through the little square panes and listened for clues about what was going down. Standing motionless, I heard a woman, probably the head doctor, barking out orders with authority to the staff. Then the door to the action-filled room closed and the flurry quieted down to muffled sounds. I strained to hear anything that might alleviate my fear of Isabelle dying.

Alarmed, I asked GUS in a voice louder than I intended, "Did I hear you wrong? I thought you said she'd be okay." The couple sitting across the room gave me a startled look, but quickly turned away when my eyes met theirs. No answer cut through my imagination that was running wild like a bucking bronco. I hated getting little to no direction from him when I encountered crises. I tried to quiet myself, but still got nothing.

Walking in circles, waiting felt excruciating. Finally, cheers and congratulations reverberated down the hallway. In some weird combination of relief and leftover shock, I collapsed into my chair and must have passed out. An hour later, Glenda shook me by the shoulder. She looked around to make sure nobody saw her and pointed toward one of the hallways. "You didn't hear this from me, but they moved Isabelle to room 404. The doctor still hopes that family will come."

"Thank you. Family will be there." I gave an assuring nod.

I poked my head around the doorway to Isabelle's room and saw her sleeping. Flashbacks of Hanna streaked through my mind when I noticed all the gadgets and monitors. *Just breathe,* I told myself, trying to focus on the reunion with Isabelle instead of the many past medical emergencies.

After sitting down in a chair, I watched her lying there. Her face showed no strain, as peaceful as an angel. *How did she survive the last two plus years? What did I miss in her life?*

I hoped that the crisis wouldn't cause any lasting issues, and that she'd learn to let people help her. I prayed similarly over two years ago when she had cut everyone off—that she'd pull down her walls and make good friends. I still liked the idea of mentoring Isabelle to be herself rather than being who others expect.

Friends had previously criticized me about having a savior complex, which was better than being accused of hearing voices. The counseling profession, in part, inclined me toward saving everyone from their pain, and hindsight showed that those tendencies grew to unhealthy proportions after Hanna died. Without knowing it, guilt had pushed me to rescue others to make up for not saving her.

I thought I lived with more balance now. Just in case, I checked with GUS: *Something seems right about renewing our friendship, or is this about me still wanting to be a rescuer?*

Chaos Before Peace — Isabelle

Laboring to put one foot in front of the other, I squinted as I battled the fierce winds. Every movement felt excruciating, like I was hauling all my belongings in a huge wagon with no wheels. I stopped and looked around, not recognizing the street. Shaking my head, I couldn't remember where I was going or where I had come from. *How do I keep gettin' myself into these freakin' messes?*

Distant screeches and howls, human ones, soared in the swirling air similar to violins playing creepy horror music. The violent gusts almost toppled me when I started off again. Chaos gyrated around me, forcing me to dodge trash and empty barrels hurtling like tumbleweeds across the pavement. Only getting glimpses of shadowy silhouettes through the fog and rain that now blew sideways, I shielded my eyes with my arm to see what people were screaming about. Their shrieks seemed directed at me. As I slowed to listen, these chilling voices, more pronounced now, slashed through the roar of the gale, although the words remained muddled. But, undeniably, spikes of anger and disgust sliced through the mayhem and penetrated me like hot arrows, each one lodging deep inside. The wounds burned. Groaning in agony, I strained harder to hear what I must have done wrong. When I couldn't, I clenched my fists at my side and cried out. "What do you want? What did I do?"

Coming to a halt, I watched and waited. No one answered. I still couldn't see who was harassing me or understand why they wouldn't stop. After half a dozen more gray shadows circled closer, the barrage of ear-splitting screams increased. Not yet distinguishing these predators' words, I braced for an inevitable all-out assault that I could feel was building dramatically—outrage and degrading attacks now beating me down under their heavy weight. I looked around for cover but saw no help or safety.

Weaving through several unfamiliar streets in some unknown city,

I forged my way ahead, hardly able to swallow the lump in my throat after seeing clusters of no-trespassing, go-back, and do-not-enter signs on many of the dilapidated shop doors and windows. I freaked out when a roar of voices from behind made me jump. I spun all at once, my feet moving before they hit the ground. Trudging onward and glancing back at points, I yelled: "Why are you doing this? What have I done?" Despite the torrent of pelting rain and the occasional dim street lamp, one look at the distorted faces hunting me showed hunger. Shaking violently, I spotted a labrador huddled against a building with boarded-up windows and a door with a large X on it. The attached leash snapped violently in the air while the dog trembled. *They might catch me, but I can't leave him there all alone. He might run and snag the line on something. He could choke.* I worked my way over to the abandoned pet, grabbed the flailing cord, and kept going as I heard more threatening sounds close at my back. "Come on boy. We'll make it."

Toiling through the elements whipping against me and my new companion, I came to a fork in the streets. *What if I go the wrong way?* Waiting for a moment, I panicked at the rustling behind me. The dog yelped and leapt forward with a jolt, tearing the collar and running off. I felt my shoulders sink, knowing that he would now be on his own. *There's no time to be sad.* Forcing myself through the relentless gusts, I veered to the left, hoping I made the right choice. The shivering labrador came into view on the sidewalk in front of me. Approaching it to help again, I gasped as it transformed before my eyes, doubling in size and glaring at me. Its teeth protruded several inches as it salivated streams of blood, and his menacing eyes followed my every movement. Giving it a wide berth and grinding incessantly through the sheets of rain, I encountered another Y.

My eyes widened when I spotted my social work professor, Dr. Sailhammer, holding a door open to a bigger, solid structure that appeared more likely to withstand the tempestuous uproar and bloodthirsty scavengers that followed me. *Finally, help!* But a momentary change of direction in the turmoil thrust me away from the building, safety now out of my grasp. Her face showed no expression when I sailed beyond her reach, the turbulence taking me toward the left. The one-lane street appeared darker and more deserted than the others. The tops of the desolate, charred buildings leaned out over me. Everything bleak, I slowed down and searched as far as my eyes could see. I couldn't keep going. I peered through the blackness without hope, unable to catch my breath. Quickly shrinking to a tiny alley, my surroundings had become utterly dark and I knew why. Ahead stood a great wall, barely visible—a dead end. I studied it, my eyes adjusting. No doors or windows in it. Panic-stricken, I looked at the buildings along each side. The same. Trapped and alone, with no help in sight and no escape from the unavoidable doom, I turned to face the ravenous mob moving toward me in a cloud of destruction. Fear suffocated me, pushing me backward until my head hit the wall. With no energy to fight anymore, knowing I only had moments left, I shut out the world and closed my eyes. My mind and body gave up. I felt myself sliding down the hard surface as awareness faded away.

Eyes still closed, my whole body felt lavished in peace and saturated with love, similar to a soft, deeply penetrating comforter warming and protecting me on a cold winter day. I couldn't make sense of the soothing experience at first. Everything had changed from earlier—from a nightmarish, windblown existence to an almost dreamlike fantasy world, yet utterly real and tangible to my senses. The wholeness, rest, and safety I experienced made me feel as if I was floating. I felt no hint of fear.

Finally opening my eyes, I looked around. My vision stayed blurry at first. I couldn't make out anything. Then everything got absolutely vivid and clear, and I simultaneously recognized that I had always lived with some kind of haziness. With a lack of clarity. I found myself, without fear, looking down from the ceiling at several doctors and nurses hustling into a room where I lay motionless on a treatment table. They turned toward the head doctor for orders as several staff began working on me. Behind her black-framed glasses, I saw stress lines on the forehead of the doctor in charge. *Why is she so afraid?*

The room and the people started to fade, not because I stopped watching but because intense bright light engulfed me. Surrounded by this shining brilliance and clarity, I buzzed with excitement and expectation. I felt more alive than I ever had. The light connected to and permeated everything, including me. It reached to my core, expanding me somehow. It dawned on me that maybe I had died and was experiencing the afterlife, although I had never believed in one. But I wasn't afraid. I felt as light as air and free, too. Beyond anything I could've dreamed.

Love and safety encompassed me in the form of a beautiful white cocoon. Feeling drawn to stay here forever, endless glimpses of my past began whizzing by my eyes. Similar to observing a fast-paced high-definition movie, and feeling no shame, I witnessed my repeated unwavering goal of pleasing the people around me—reacting to them as if my acceptance, maybe even my existence, depended on their approval. I acted like I had no value and no choice. Only a shadow of me existed, except when I was with Grandma and Grandpa Gene. But with everyone else, I hid. I lost myself, my connection with myself and my direct connection to the light! *How sad that I let fear of judgment and rejection stop me from living!*

Taking in what I had seen, I heard an urgent voice. "Come back, Isabelle. Stay with us!"

Aware that the doctors and nurses in the room wanted me to rejoin my body, I shook my head. *I don't want to go back. I want to stay here.*

They kept pleading. "Come back!" I felt sad for them, which pulled at me to leave my cocoon. I somehow knew that I'd lose this incredible clarity and comfort if I returned, and also the fact that light connected everything, here and there. But I sensed the importance of returning. I vowed that regardless of fear, I'd live authentically wherever safety allowed for it.

Then my body jumped with a jolt, and like a film reel snapping free from the projector, my exhilarating, yet serene, reality disappeared.

Second Chance — Gene

After long periods of silence and another nurse making her rounds, Isabelle stirred. *How might she greet me after over two years of no contact?*

The previous nurses hadn't questioned me and, if anything, seemed pleased to see a visitor. The new nurse in the room kept glancing at me as she worked. Her movements, measured and precise, told me that she rarely deviated from standard operating procedure. Now standing erect, she reprimanded me just as the physician entered. "Only family members are allowed to visit."

We both glanced at the tall, slender doctor with a sharp jawline. Her striking hazel eyes were enhanced by the multi-colored frames she wore. I didn't know what to make of her yet. Dr. Hamilton, according to her gold-plated name tag, stopped and studied me. She tilted her head and appeared inclined to follow up on the nurse's comment when Isabelle spoke. "Grandpa Gene. How did you know I was here?"

We all turned in surprise toward Isabelle. Her jet-black hair told a story, matted in places and sticking out in others. She struggled to focus, or possibly to remember how she ended up in the hospital.

Dr. Hamilton observed her for a moment. "You seem to be doing well, given the touch-and-go night you had."

"My head's throbbing, but I guess that's what I get for being lit like I was."

"You're fortunate that's the extent of the damage." Dr. Hamilton's pressed lips shifted slightly. "The drinking pushed you to the edge, and then some."

Isabelle's eyes brightened. "You changed your glasses since the other room."

The doctor's distinguished jaw dropped. "How could? You must have seen me previously." Still puzzling over it, she shook her head and turned toward me. "Hi. I'm Dr. Hamilton."

I reached out and shook her hand. "I'm Gene. Pleased to meet you."

Everyone waited in silence as she checked Isabelle's vital signs. Then putting a hand on her hip, she looked directly at Isabelle. "Your situation was life-threatening, but I'll wait to share the details until you're more rested."

Isabelle nodded.

The doctor's tone became sterner. "I'd like you to make an appointment with the hospital's psychiatrist to talk about whatever led to this."

Isabelle reacted as if she had expected to be admonished. "I know I need to come clean, but I'm not seeing some hospital shrink. I'll find somebody else to chat with."

Dr. Hamilton looked at me with a make-sure-she-follows-through look. I gave a slight nod. Then she and the nurse left.

"G, it's crazy that you're here, but you're supposed to be." Her words sounded far off, making me think that something more had happened. She also came across softer than in earlier days despite her headache. I had never seen much beyond her tough exterior and street-smart ways.

I smiled, glad that she appeared happy to see me. "Yeah, our reunion seems more than coincidence. I'm relieved that you made it through last night. What happened to Dr. Hamilton's glasses?"

She changed the subject. "You still act like a lame mother hen. Who told you I was here?"

Now that's the Isabelle I remember. "I saw you lying in an alley. Your breathing got worse so I called 911. I've been here since." I decided not to press her about the glasses.

"Maybe I'd be playing some harp or carrying a freakin' pitchfork if you hadn't. You won't be railing me about seeing the shrink, will you?"

I shook my head. "At some point you ought to talk with someone about what happened, but I won't pressure you."

She took a deep breath. "I, I'm sorry that I shut you out after Grandma died. I didn't show it, but I knew you wanted to help. Beyond her, and maybe my dad for his last few months, you were about the only good thing in my life."

Again, she appeared gentler, even though she still razzed me. I couldn't remember ever hearing her apologize before. It warmed me to know that she remembered our friendship as good, because I questioned it when she had thrown me away as easily as a worn out pair of shoes. "I wish you would have let me be there for you."

She frowned. "I knew that's what you wanted. You always had a thing about saving people. That's stuck on you like peanut butter."

I grinned.

She let out another breath. "I didn't want to be saved. A bomb went off—nothing made sense. I wanted to stay mad and wouldn't let anyone in. But I went through hell 'cause of it."

"I'd say that you're still in that battle." I hoped that she'd open up about what happened.

Her whole body sagged. "More of the same. It just sucks." Her voice broke. She fought to contain the emotions that insisted on coming out. Her sobbing melted my heart. Something about almost dying must have changed her. She had shown anger and emotional reactions before, but never vulnerability. I had never seen her cry.

After catching her breath, she stayed silent rather than finishing her thought. Then she shifted focus, speaking in a soft voice. "Did I put you through hell last night?"

Her compassion, different from the past, triggered the stress from the last six or seven hours. My eyes watered, in spite of trying not to show anything. "It's just that I never got to say goodbye when you cut me off. I was afraid that things would end that way."

"I'm sorry." The pain-filled sadness in her eyes told me that she meant it. Squiggling in the bed, she grimaced, as if fighting a headache or struggling to stay awake.

"You don't need to talk. It might be better to rest."

Eyes only slits now, she slurred her words, barely understandable. "Alrigh' mother hen. I could use some shut eye." A hollow voice hung in the air and eventually gave way to the sound of beeping and humming medical gadgets. She fell asleep in less than a minute, her deep breathing joining the chorus of hospital sounds.

I sat until daybreak, nodding off occasionally and wondering what she wasn't telling me. I moved from one position to another in my chair over the next few hours. For now, I felt relieved that Isabelle seemed out of her yet-to-be-revealed sinkhole. But spending time in a hospital still made me restless.

Around noon, a nurse saw Isabelle stirring and went to get the doctor. Dr. Hamilton entered the room and told me that she first wanted to talk to Isabelle in private, and then to me in the hallway.

After the doctor came out and described the night's events, I reentered the room. Isabelle sipped water, her forehead crinkled as she readied to speak. "Doc gave me the thumbs up but pressed me again to see the shrink. When I didn't fold, she asked me to take it seriously. She told me I had cardiac arrest in the ambulance and had flat-lined in the hospital."

I lowered my head slightly. "Yeah, she told me, too."

"She hassled me about pushing things past the limits—beyond what it looks like on TV—saying that people rarely make it after flat-lining. She wanted me to know how lucky I was and to work through my issues so it doesn't happen again. She said to make use of this second chance. That's what she called it."

"I second that."

"Something happened," she hesitated. "I want to get free from things. I'm just not sure what that looks like."

Isabelle stopped midstream, her voice halting abruptly, making clear that she was holding back again. I prodded her. "Feel free to say whatever you need. I'm sure you have more churning around in you after what all you've been through."

She shrugged and continued, her tone conveying total detachment. "Nah, not really. Just random things."

I almost pointed out her obvious and sudden break in thought. That she was hiding something. But GUS intervened. *Give her space.*

I objected to GUS' input. *But her past pain will keep sabotaging her life unless she deals with it.*

A few seconds passed. *True, but give her time.*

I decided to talk casually. "We have a lot of catching up to do. I don't know what's happened in your life since we stopped talking over two years ago."

"Yeah, sweet." Her words sounded empty as she flicked her hair back. She spent several minutes describing her work at Books & Facts Warehouse, known as B & F, as a mindless job for hauling in the bucks.

She rolled her eyes and dragged out her words. "I package millions of boxes for shipment and place them on a conveyor belt."

After a pause in conversation that sounded like small talk she'd made a thousand times, I looked at my watch. "I need to head home to let my dog out. Do you need anything before I go?"

"No, I'm cool. I'll be back on my feet in no time. I'll give you a call as soon as I'm out of here. They might cut me loose tomorrow."

I doubted she'd call but didn't know why. GUS told me to leave it alone.

Restart Button — Isabelle

I felt brain dead about "regular" life after the hospital, like I had checked out. Focusing on my assistantship and school work at Landsburg University was all but a wash. LU mattered, but not compared to my ultra-high-resolution experience when I had flatlined. Not knowing what to make of it yet, I obsessed over it. The implications blew me away and threw a wrench into life as I knew it. I couldn't shake it and, for some reason, I didn't want to.

Questions kept running through my mind after what happened: Does more exist behind the scenes than I can see? Is there greater purpose even during all the struggles and messed up situations I go through? And who am I, really?

Give it time. That's what I told myself. Which isn't me. I hate waiting. I want order and to know what's up. To be the captain steering my ship into sunny days. But, lately, that equated to grasping rays of sunshine coming through gaps in the clouds. Crashing and burning after Sap's Bar made that clear. I needed to hit a restart button. To start life over and be who I'm meant to be instead of acting like a robot ruled by everyone's expectations. I wanted an easy button, and I knew the path forward would be anything but.

Monday morning after the hospital, my mind reeled with regrets. My biggest one was waking up every day with Dean next to me—well, with him beside me *most* mornings, depending on whether he had hooked up with someone or not. I never imagined things could get this bad.

I had called Val, my friend from high school, about meeting over coffee early this morning before she went to work. I needed to talk with someone about the hospital and Dean. I slid out of bed quietly. His snoring never wavered as I got dressed. *No wonder. You never got in from your night escapade until 3:33 A.M.*

Ten minutes later strolling into Expresso, a small shop specializing in espresso and trendy coffees, I spotted Val sitting at a booth. I hadn't seen her in a while, but she greeted me with high energy, as if we had just spent an awesome day together yesterday. "Hey, Izz. What's happenin'?" She talked as if words would evaporate if she didn't say them fast enough.

"Hey, Val. I got lots to talk about but wanted to check first about how you're doing."

Rapid fire, she took off and finished before I felt awake. "You know me, always staying busy. Gardening, out with our group at Fitzpatrick's on Fridays, and still working at MedCheck."

I leaned forward, trying to clear the fog in my head. "You seeing anybody?"

"Not a chance. I'm having too much fun as a single. Don't want anyone to answer to."

She flipped the focus before I could ask anything else. "How's it going with Dean?"

"That's what I wanted to talk about. I feel betrayed. He's been cheating on me the last few months and has no intention of stopping. Last Wednesday night I went to Sap's Bar 'cause I couldn't deal with it. Ended up in the hospital. Flatlined and everything."

"What a load of shit! No guy's worth that. That's why I'm single. I heard rumors that he was on the prowl but didn't want to believe it. Thought he adored you. What happened?"

"You cool if I get right into it?"

Her words rattled off like they were on fast forward. "Good to go."

"Everything felt so right in the beginning, like we were made for each other. Three months after high school graduation, I met friends at Strikers Bowling Alley. I had finally connected with them again after cutting everyone off when my grandma and dad died. I asked them about the new guy standing at the counter. Joey glanced over at him while lacing his shoes. He said he met Dean at Fitzpatrick's and that he had graduated from West Bank a year before us."

Val usually interjected a lot during conversations, but she just nodded and listened.

"We had a blast that day. Dean looked comfortable with himself. Confident, quick-witted, and funny. He hit it off with the group. Unless

I imagined it, his brown eyes lingered a little each time he looked at me. My legs got weak when I watched him. I don't know if you've seen him. Tall, dark hair, and insanely built with a square jaw. He came across as friendly, good with people. Everything I had dreamed of. While leaving Strikers that day, he asked me to go for a picnic the following Saturday afternoon at Landsburg Park. I tried to play it cool but got tongue-tied.

She just smiled and shook her head.

"I met him at the park, not knowing what to expect. The grounds were packed with people: joggers, walkers, picnickers, and kite flyers. I had never seen it that crowded, but we found space under a sycamore tree by the lake. We sat on a blanket, ate subs, and shared a bottle of cabernet sauvignon. I fidgeted under his gaze. Then he scratched his chin and said, 'You're quieter than you were at Strikers.'"

Val jumped in. "See, that's how things always start out. They take notice of you. Then, later, they act like you're hardly there. But go on."

"I hadn't realized that I was quieter because of my mom attacking me earlier in the morning about something senseless. I tried not to show anything but my eyes filled with tears. I couldn't help it, with him showing concern and studying me. I told him my mom had picked a fight again for no reason, as usual, and that my dad did what he always does. Said and did nothing 'cause he's terrified of her."

"Yeah, I remember that your mom's like that."

"Then my eyes got big as a wave of sadness washed over Dean's face. I saw him gulp, and pain filled his voice when he told me his dad was the same as my mom. That he never knew when his dad would erupt. He put his big arms around me and said he never wanted me to feel that way again. He just held me for a while. I felt protected. Maybe for the first time. He showed a tenderness I could never get from my mom."

Val tilted her head as words shot forth in a flurry. "I see how you would've fallen for him. But how'd it change?"

"We got hitched after four months of bliss—talking meaningfully, going everywhere together, discussing future dreams. Then, as planned, we met at his parents' place for a dinner invite. They seemed cool with me previously, so I thought they'd be excited about our news. But after his mom swung the door open with a blank, frozen face, I turned and saw both big men standing toe-to-toe. Dean's six-foot-three dad, almost as big as him, knocked him against the wall and screamed into his face. 'Eloped? How could you be so stupid?' I'll never forget those words."

"Yeah, that would do that, make an impression."

"The words echoed throughout the room. I wanted to disappear. But just as Dean got to his feet, a fist shot into his stomach, and he staggered. I watched in shock as he collapsed, out of breath. It felt as if everything had stopped. Then Dean suddenly lunged like a bull, fists flying nonstop. His dad had no chance. If his mom and I hadn't both heaved at his belt from behind and pleaded with him to stop, he'd have killed his dad. He told me the next day that he had felt guilty for years because of doing nothing when his mom took the brunt of those attacks."

She wagged her head. "It's amazing what some people live with."

"From that point on, Dean was filled with hate. That messed-up day tormented him but he wouldn't talk about it. I never saw sensitivity again. Thoughts about his dad, and my mom, consumed him—they'd come out in his occasional outbursts. Based on how self-destructive he got, I'd say he despised himself the most. The rub was, ever since then, he strutted around with a chip on his shoulder. As if life owed him something."

Val shrugged. "That sucks. I don't know what else to say, Izz."

"Then my social work program's homework assignments, which centered on me dealing with my issues and closest relationships, threatened him. Big mistake for us. I needed help to make sense of life and to heal. But he wanted no part of it. I didn't pressure him. I only asked once. But he cursed the program incessantly after that."

She made a pained face. "Well, some people have a hard time when it comes to therapy."

"I realize that. But studying social work gave me hope, despite Dean tearing down the profession. My coursework showed how clueless I had been about myself, especially about my knee-jerk reaction to marry him so soon after meeting. I had wanted someplace safe to land that wasn't with my mom. Spending long hours at LU to get away from her didn't cut it. I still never felt safe. I didn't let people in. Anyone. Except him. Until after the earth-shattering incident with his dad, when anything I said about my pain triggered his. Then I stopped sharing that stuff." I took a breath after unloading.

She stood up. "I wish I had more time to talk, but I gotta split for work."

"Oh, I didn't realize how much time had flown by." We hugged. "Thanks for listening. I'm gonna finish my last few sips before I head to LU."

"You know me. I'm practical. Not a touchy-feely person. A friend of mine went for therapy once. Seemed like a shitload of mind games to me."

After she took off, I just sat and stared at my cup. Her last statement stung. It slammed my whole career choice. I tried to regroup, reminding myself that Val had always been logical, science-oriented, and sometimes blunt. Now that I thought about it, she had never been one to talk personally or share her feelings. She had been a loyal friend, but today her callous statement hurt. Getting to unload my story felt satisfying, but in the future I wanted to stay clear of talking with her about my profession and personal struggles.

Sliding into my car, I grunted as I realized I hadn't brought my backpack for school. *Where was my head at? I don't want to go home and face him this morning. Just be stealth.*

Returning to our tiny, two-bedroom ranch, I wished Dean or I would have oiled the front door hinges. The last I remembered, swinging the door open quickly squeaked less. Holding my breath, I turned the knob and pushed the door fast. No such luck. The sound pierced the silence with a volume equivalent to a blood-curdling scream in a horror flick. I rolled my eyes, hoping beyond hope that Dean wouldn't awaken.

Last evening, his hook-up was Jessie. Not the first time. That's who he spent most of the night with when I was out of commission in the hospital. Two friends gave me the scoop: him and her slobbering all over each other at Fitzpatrick's Pub. The worst part is, he knew that I knew and didn't give a shit. A big, fat zippo. Dean always got what Dean wanted—the new normal ever since he almost beat the life out of his dad. Like he felt justified to *take* what he wanted in life after that day. Including women, although I didn't suspect that for a while.

His voice boomed from the bedroom. "Where are you going?"

Here we go again. I marched to where I could see him through the doorway. "Shouldn't I be asking you that? About last night? I don't have to answer when you don't give a rip about me. I know who you were with. The same as when you didn't come to the hospital."

"Well, if you'd just give me the respect I deserve, we'd be cool."

I shut down. "You're a piece of work. You didn't even flinch about sleeping around. I can't do this."

He fired back. "Took the words right out of my mouth. Something's gotta give."

"I won't even pretend that I give a damn when you just stay on the hunt without looking back. I'm going to LU to do work. And to chill."

"Yeah, go running to your advisor, your mommy replacement. That's the problem. You spend all your time with those freakin' crazy profs."

I shook my head and turned to leave.

The accusatory blast hit me from behind. "See. You're the one who bails instead of talking."

"I've made clear that I'm ready to talk things out together with a counselor and, if you're not willing, our future doesn't look good."

His brazen voice reverberated off the walls with anger and finality. "I'm not confessing our personal shit to some idiot. There's no chance in hell!"

I knew to keep walking when the jackhammer kept pounding. Same as with my mom. I grabbed my backpack and split.

Trying to hold it together, I walked into Bigler Hall, the two-story grey stone building where the social work faculty taught. I didn't exactly feel jazzed to be back at school or to answer people's questions about my absence. While stuck in the hospital, I had missed two of my assistantship days carrying out administrative work and research for Dr. Burns, the research coordinator. I also missed three classes and needed to get my head back in the game. I had caught up with homework assignments apart from answering half a dozen questions for today's theme on interviewing skills.

I sat down in the student study room. With nobody else there, I couldn't hold the hurt in any longer. The wave of emotion poured out as self-pity tried to overtake me. Battling with it for several minutes as I kept glancing at the doorway to make sure no one else was coming in, I didn't want to give way to wallowing about Dean again. *I just want to learn to be me, but damned if I know how.*

Shifting to school work, I plodded through material that seemed trivial or at least didn't capture my interest today. Several times I found myself staring at the display on the front wall about mindfulness while my thoughts alternated between the morning fiasco and the exhilarating cocoon during my time in the ICU. I shook my head at the irony of the poster about being mindful and present while my thoughts journeyed to two different worlds, neither of which were in the room. I still finished with half an hour to spare.

Exhausted, I zoned out, lost in thought about my decision over two years ago to be a social worker. I wanted to help people. At first I didn't know why. Later I realized it stemmed from watching Mom need help and never knowing how to reach her.

I remember the first time I came into Bigler Hall for an info session about the program. The profound sayings on the walls pointed toward being part of something bigger, and the faculty emphasized how gratifying it felt to make a difference in people's lives. Dr. Sailhammer, the chair of the department, presented for part of the meeting and spoke with an air of confidence I wished I had. After several faculty members answered questions from the audience, they gave frequent glances at her as if for a nod of approval. That day seemed imprinted on my mind. Everything clicked, despite my fear about whether or not I could do the work.

By the beginning of the second year, I gained confidence. Well, maybe a false confidence because I had loaded up early on all the content-heavy courses. For some reason, the idea of taking the experiential ones in the last half of my curriculum—where the rubber met the road—freaked me out. Other than friends describing me as super observant, I still wasn't sure why I chose being a clinician as my specialization.

Our clinical track went beyond most other undergrad social work programs. They required entry level students to sign up for one of three profession-enhancing experiences: receiving personal counseling from a clinician in training, conducting research with faculty, or volunteering to be a participant in a study. As a clinician in training, I should have opted for receiving personal counseling to better prepare me for the clinical role in my final year. But I didn't. I chose to do research.

Even worse, I should have been looking forward to counseling during our Interviewing Skills courses I and II. But I'm not. Now in the fall semester of my third year, I'm taking the first part. We use in-class role-plays as training for working with clients, and for the second one in the spring, we will counsel first-year students. I feel the pressure to be on point in these classes, and no one teaches them except Dr. Sailhammer, my advisor. She intimidates me, as she does most students. She acts like she expects perfection.

Startled by students coming into the study room, I looked at the clock. "Damn, eight minutes until facing my professor. Back to reality." I tried to shake off my apprehension about class, and headed to room 133. There stood Sailhammer with shoulder-length black hair graying at the fringes, her eyes intense as she talked with one of my classmates. Her stern demeanor made my heart jump as I went to my seat.

Efficient and serious, she always cuts to the chase. "Let's get started." It only took ten seconds for people to find their seats and turn their eyes toward her. "I've assigned each of you a partner and would like you to take turns as clinician and client, role-playing one of the scenarios in the handout. Treat the sessions as real, beyond the role-play practice earlier in the course. We've already talked about confidentiality. I'd like you to videotape the sessions so I can give feedback, which stays between you, your partner, and me as your instructor. Although, this feedback can be used to evaluate your suitability for clinical internships in your senior year."

In dread, I looked over at Susan McGonagal, my partner. I genuinely liked my classmates, but, for some reason, she irritated me. She constantly nailed the answers to Sailhammer's questions, overkilled the projects and assignments, and always seemed to have a blinding look-at-me spotlight shining on her. I initially thought that I alone saw her that way. But a few classes ago, I had noticed other students rolling their eyes and making faces when her arm shot up time after time. Sailhammer kept her jack-in-the-box hand under a lid with responses like, "Let's see if anyone else has thoughts about this."

Today, Susan's wide eyes showed excitement about doing the role-plays. I felt dread. Fear kept whirling around in my stomach while several students asked logistical questions. My heart kept thumping wildly as the performance expectations mounted. I got mad at myself. *Enough! Stop acting like someone's gonna take your head off. Get a grip!*

Role-Plays and Reality — Isabelle

A jumbled mishmash of harrowing "first-timer" stories whizzed through my mind while I sat waiting for our professor's directions about where to carry out the assignment. My peers had been terrifying one another with traumatic accounts of past students' initial taped interviews...of epic proportion. Rumor had it that Sailhammer abruptly halted one session ten minutes in and asked the person's best friend to escort them to the university counseling center. Other individuals were apparently told after their sessions to call for an appointment to deal with personal issues and also to explore whether or not social work was an appropriate profession. Similar recent classmate discussions had centered on preference of being counselor or client first, with most agreeing that demonstrating interviewing skills in front of Sailhammer felt equivalent to jumping from a plane without a parachute. That's why consensus was to start as clinician and get it over with.

After our professor gave final instructions, half the students went in pairs to another large classroom for space to do their role-plays, and half of us stayed in the same room. War still going on in my head, I sighed. *Ugh, getting taped...just breathe. You can do this.*

After Susan and I found our place, she asked if I cared who counseled first. Her bright, eager face showed her choice. I shrugged and, as expected, she jumped on being the counselor.

Looking at my client scenario, I related to the topic of career indecision and being unclear about what I wanted to do in life. Susan introduced the session as we had been taught, emphasizing confidentiality and informing me about recording the interview. After she turned on the recorder, I started.

"I'm stuck about direction in my life. I went to college for history and can't find a job. The only ones I found are teaching positions, and I don't want to teach. I'm not even sure I like history."

She focused on me like a hawk watching the lay of the land for anything moving. If I had been the counselor, I would have asked, *Why choose history?* Instead, Susan responded to my feelings. "That's scary when you put all the work into your major and then question if that's what you really want."

Her statement nailed how I felt. Maybe because I had personally been living with not knowing what I wanted to do for a year or two, I reacted spontaneously.

"Yeah, it's scary. I feel like I'm wandering in a fog, not knowing where I'm going."

Her tone conveyed intense curiosity to understand my experience and sounded more like a question. "And you feel like you're wandering because you're not sure what you most value and where you fit."

"That's it. I don't know what's important to me." My mouth hung open about the truth of my words. Only a role-play. But it felt relevant to my life. Susan had already hit a bull's-eye.

After a long pause, she leaned forward and showed genuine interest. "In a way, you seem to be wrestling with not knowing where you fit, possibly because you don't know or understand yourself?"

Damn. She's nailing this, too. How can you know where you fit if you don't first understand yourself and what's important to you? I sat reflecting during the quiet. Then I got afraid, not knowing if I could counsel this well. I studied her for a moment, noticing that she appeared relaxed. No fidgeting or strain on her face, as if she knew her response hit home and wanted to give it time. Textbook pacing—I couldn't do that. I hated silences.

After allowing considerable time, she continued with the issue I presented. "It's difficult not knowing what you're passionate about." She sat, patiently waiting.

During the space, something registered in my mind about Mom. I couldn't know what I really wanted when she constantly told me what I *should* be doing. I tried to stick to the role-play but just started saying whatever came to mind. "I felt like I had to please everyone, especially my mom, and I didn't ever pay attention to what I wanted."

In the five minute break for transitioning roles after our twenty-minute talk, I shook my head. I had learned not only about how to counsel a person on career indecision, but also realized why I didn't know what was important to me—always bending to Mom's overbearing voice, then to Dean's. I gladly would have paid for the session. As we sat down in our chairs for the next scenario, I told her what I thought. "Susan, you killed it. As the client, it felt beyond simple role-play. You were spot on." She beamed and thanked me.

A lump formed in my throat as I prepared to counsel. Doubts raced through my mind, especially after Val's words earlier this morning about counseling being a shitload of mind games. I tried to shake it off. *But I just experienced therapy's impact only minutes ago with Susan, a trainee only doing a role-play!*

Glancing down at the client situation that Susan chose, my eyes suddenly zoomed in on the topic. Loss. My mind went hazy. I could barely breathe. The pressure felt unbearable and made me afraid of having another panic attack, which had increased to almost once a week after marrying Dean. I sank in my seat. *I'd give a week's pay to be able to counsel half as good as Susan.*

Holding my breath, I turned on the recorder. I tried to cover up my fear while introducing the session the way we had been taught. Compared to Susan, I felt like a snail trying to run, let alone walk. After seeing her ace the therapist role, I mostly wanted to avoid looking like an idiot.

Susan started slowly as the client. "I, hmm, lost my mom."

I fidgeted in my seat, feeling hot. Starting twice, my voice broke. "Do you? Do you mean? She passed away?"

Scarcely nodding, she stared at the floor, not saying anything for at least half a minute. Instead of responding, I clenched my teeth and pressed my lips together to allow her time to continue. Silently I congratulated myself for waiting through this unexpected, and what felt like oppressive, black hole.

Finally, a sound—as if each word came out from under a rolling pin. But, at least, something. "She got pneumonia. It went downhill from there." Then, nothing except the air conditioner fan. I couldn't even see her face because she hunched over and wouldn't look up at all.

Caught off guard by this never-ending void, I froze. I tried not to get frustrated with her for giving me next to nothing to go on. *At least I talked as the client.*

"That's gotta be difficult," I managed, finally remembering to show empathy.

She let out a tiny puff of air and sat motionless without adding anything. *Is she overdoing the role-play, or am I paralyzed by the topic?*

Not knowing what else to do with the silence, I wanted something to happen. "Are there other things in your life that help you to feel better when you're down?"

She looked glum, shrugged her shoulders, and sounded like Eeyore letting out a long sigh, pronouncing the word, piano as "Pe an o."

My whole body revolted in frustration at the relentless, miniscule disclosures, and my voice shot out with no censorship. "Piano?" Trying to regain composure, some of our interviewing skills whirled through my mind: paraphrasing, probing, summarizing. If you ask questions, ask what and how questions rather than why. *Okay, Isabelle, use your inside voice!*

With a controlled tone, I asked, "What do you like about piano? How does it help?"

She let out a breathy, "It makes me feel better." I wanted her to provide more details so I could learn what she needed, but nothing else came. In my mind, I could have guessed better if she had been doing sign language, which I had never learned!

I don't remember how we ended, but I left class more agitated than when I arrived. Already dreading next week's meeting with my professor about the session, I moseyed to my car mumbling sarcastically to myself. "Well, I can't wait to hear the warm fuzzies about my stellar job. I just don't want to be one of those failures calling the center to discuss other career options!"

A week later, I sat down with Dr. Sailhammer to discuss her critique of my counseling videotape with Susan. She had already sent the feedback. Her stern eyes bore down on me, treating the role-play as real. "What did you think of the session before you saw my comments?"

"I knew I hadn't nailed it but thought Susan embellished the acting. That added to the difficulty."

She nodded and narrowed her eyes, which scared me. "I realize that it's difficult as a beginning clinician to respond well to considerable silence."

I wanted to say, *Considerable silence? That's calling a freakin' bottomless pit a little hole!* But I softened it. "That's for sure." I made big eyes and tilted my head to emphasize my point.

Responding in a matter-of-fact tone, her stern face never changed. "Let's watch the beginning." After pressing play, she stopped it immediately when I hesitated twice. "What were you feeling when your voice cracked?"

Her direct approach put me on my heels even though I sat in a chair. "Maybe uncertain about what direction to take."

"Let's look at your face again." She replayed it.

After reviewing it, I saw her point. "Afraid, I guess."

"When I study your face, I see someone who looks terrified. Frozen from fear. The tremor in your voice conveys that, too. Your reaction happened right when she mentioned losing her mom."

Like a kid caught in a lie, I fessed up, at least to part of it. "Yeah, afraid fits, especially when she stayed so silent."

With no letup, my professor seemed to grow bigger before my eyes. "Your reaction happened before she became quiet. And her silence was consistent with how grieving clients often present." She paused and put her hand to her chin. "One of your responses as you continued, which acknowledged the difficulty of losing her mom, showed empathy. Good. But you could have gone more into the loss for her to feel understood there instead of directing the session away from her pain. Let's watch it again." She played through that part and stopped it right after I asked Susan what she does to feel better when she's down.

I shrunk after watching it, still having no clue about what I should have said or done. "How could I have gone into it further?"

"Good question. Keep asking that in future sessions. You could have explored her experiences about losing her mom instead of leading her away from the pain. She showed more emotional energy there—the grief. Clients need to be understood and cared for about that anguish, but you redirected the session away from it. That tells me, as I've mentioned before to you in class, that you likely have unresolved loss and possibly mom issues."

Tensing, and on the verge of an all-out panic, I wondered if she'd direct me to the university center to consider another career. But her face softened, probably after seeing terror on mine. "It's normal for clinicians to have unresolved issues in their lives, so it's okay. But it needs attention. Being evaluated on the role-play may have added to the fear, but your tone of voice and reaction showed bigger attached experiences. Probably from childhood. If you don't address the pain, as you're aware, it hinders your work with clients."

She waited on a response. I just nodded and stayed quiet. I hated showing weakness and my feelings—I always had to be tough growing up with a mom like mine. But that didn't seem to be in the cards anymore. I couldn't hold things together like I used to.

"You're in the clinical track, so you would've already had Dr. May's class that focuses on countertransference, which addresses how your own issues cloud your perceptions of clients, and can even cause harmful responses at times."

My hands went numb, clenching the arms of the chair. Trying to act casual, I let go and put them on my lap. "I remember her talking about that."

She plodded along. "That class also covers the stats indicating that therapists-in-training experience greater mental health issues than the average person. The research also shows that students usually avoid talking with anyone about their pain. Is that ringing a bell?"

I gave a nod, waiting for the hammer to drop. I wanted out from under her gaze.

She tilted her head, her eyes still locked onto mine. "You'd think that students in social work would be more at ease with getting personal therapy. But that's not the case. They usually listen to their friends' struggles, and, if anything, they're uncomfortable with the opposite direction—sharing vulnerably about their own weaknesses."

She had pegged me. I despised talking about loss and my mom. About anything personal. Feeling sick to my stomach and squirming in my seat, I expanded, hoping that she'd stop pressing. "Yeah, a few other students and I talked after that class. I know I need to deal with grief. I just wasn't sure if it was that or if things would have been cool had Susan given me more to go on."

She studied me before speaking. "Let's put it this way. My instincts tell me that your issues hindered not only this role-play but also the informal ones earlier in the course. A pattern shows. This session indicated loss as a starting place, but I'm sure there are other attached issues. Particularly with your mom."

I knew to agree with her when she insisted. "Yeah, I'm sure counseling would help."

"Over the years, I've watched clinicians' personal issues cause all kinds of reactions, sometimes big ones—impatience, fear of silence, and giving quick advice that shuts down client awareness. That's why I recommend personal counseling for you. Even if your own struggles hadn't interfered today, therapists always benefit from addressing their unresolved pain."

I still felt tense and out of control. I thought she might ease up if I appeared more willing, but I didn't want to admit that both my grandma and dad died the same year—she'd never stop pressuring me to get counseling. I tried to sound matter-of-fact. "Yeah, my grandma died at the end of high school. I'll definitely consider getting therapy."

She didn't buy it.

"Loss is difficult. I hope you more than consider it. If you want to be selected as one of the six students during your senior year to do a clinical internship at Landsburg Health Services, our top site, personal counseling makes all the difference. You're very perceptive. Your comments in class show that. You have the makings of a solid clinician as long as you deal with your baggage."

Her encouragement meant a lot—she didn't give it out often. But almost having a panic attack and the thought of facing the harsh reality of my past sucked the life out of me. I thought I had been all-in when I initially asked Dean to go for counseling with me. Today showed otherwise. Both of us were terrified of our past.

Guardian Angel – Gene

My morning contemplation, as usual, filled me with peace. Being still and present in the moment, rather than striving for some outcome, often awakened fresh thoughts. Today I heard GUS say, *opportunity*. I waited to hear more, but nothing else came. After finishing coffee and mowing the grass, I took Button for a walk while staying alert about GUS' word. Near noon now, the sun's rays broke through an opening in a patch of white clouds. Beauty abounded everywhere. The low humidity made the small mountains in the distance appear blue instead of green. Few cars moved about on my quiet back street, one with little activity other than walkers. I admired the lamp posts and the hanging flower baskets in front of the shops that added color and life.

As I strolled up the next street, my stomach whirled, despite my earlier peace. "What's up, GUS?"

He didn't answer. But Isabelle came to mind shortly after I asked. With weeks having gone by without word from her, I had given up hope about reconnecting. I had felt led to leave it in her hands and she hadn't called after my hospital visit. *She's shutting me out again and won't let people help her. She won't make healthier decisions if she doesn't allow support.*

I looked at my watch. Ten minutes after noon. Probably a good time to catch her. "GUS, I think you're nudging me to call Isabelle." I proceeded down a street parallel from mine, planning to make the next right and head home. Approaching the upcoming intersection, the words *Oak Street, North,* filled my mind. I shook my head. "That's away from home." But inside, a surge of energy compelled me to turn as GUS had directed. After starting that direction, I heard yelling in the distance. Two people stood face to face, arguing—a tall, chiseled man and a small woman.

Is that Isabelle? My eyes didn't focus as well as they used to.

The guy towered over her, torquing a wrist and splashing what looked like a take-out container of chili onto her. She shrieked in pain. "Dean. That's hot. You're hurting me!"

With no let-up, the overpowering brute forced her wrist back farther. His booming voice echoed down the street. "I can make it hurt a hell of a lot more!"

Still several buildings away, I hollered. "Hey, buddy. Back off."

He spun on the spot, immediately letting go of Isabelle's arm. "Who the hell are you?" With contorted face and wild eyes, he stuck out his chin and stretched even taller, focusing on nothing but me—a fool who likely challenged his manhood. His huge chest swaggered back and forth as he stalked toward me like an overgrown rottweiler.

Somehow, I hadn't lost my nerve. "I can't stand by and watch bullies hurt people." Button barked and pranced around, neither backing away nor pulling toward the unwelcome intruder. This hulk eyed up my dog, probably deciding whether or not to take him seriously. Button's barks only slowed down this guy's long strides as I pulled a cell phone from my pocket. "I just called 911. We're three streets from the police department. If you don't leave, I'll tell them you've hurt a woman and that now you're threatening me."

He sneered. "Piss off, you little shit," now closing in at a swifter pace as if hungry to tear apart his easy prey.

I put the phone to my cheek. "I have an emergency. I'm at Oak and Fourth street."

He put up his hands in surrender and started backing away. "Okay. Okay. I don't want any trouble." Then he strutted off while repeatedly looking over his shoulder and scowling.

I told the police that the man left and no longer posed a threat. As soon as I put the phone in my pocket, zillions of zaps exploded throughout my body. My mind went blank, and I forgot about Isabelle until she approached. Gaping at me, she shook her head. "Are you my guardian angel or what? That's the second time you've had my back. Thanks."

"I don't feel much like a guardian angel." Barely able to speak, things started swirling. "I feel dizzy. My, my past again." Isabelle's mouth and eyes widened. "You sounded cool calling the cops, but now you're a mess. Let me help you to that bench over there." She pointed at the spot about one building away.

She grabbed my arm and walked me down the sidewalk while brushing off chili with her other hand. Still hazy, I tried to focus. "Are you okay? Are you burned?"

"Nah. Only hurt at first. I yanked my shirt away from my skin when it happened. So it didn't burn much. And there's not much on my pants." Furrows showed in her eyebrows. "You said something about your past. I didn't get it."

Button nuzzled Isabelle's hand as we sat down. "Hey, boy," she said in a high voice, petting him on the head.

I had always marveled at how nothing appeared to penetrate Isabelle's tough shell. I started to regain clarity. "I never told you before, but as a kid I got bullied about being small. And poor. I lived with stomach aches, afraid to get on the school bus every day."

"I never knew."

"This Dean brought all of that back." I scolded Button for licking stains on her pants. "You have some chili on your hair, too."

"Oh, shit. Now I'm going to need a shower. Gross."

I held out my handkerchief. She ignored it. "I freakin' knew you for over two years and never knew about your past. That sucks, getting bullied. Dean's such a jerk."

"Yeah, it was an ongoing nightmare. There's a lot about my life you don't know because I never talked about my personal stuff. I'm learning to be more transparent."

She shook her head. "Oh, that. Talking about my baggage feels out of control. I hate it. It's like pouring out your guts and waiting for some animal to tear 'em apart." Her last statement probably related to how her mom treated her. She finally wiped her hair and shirt with my handkerchief, then gave me a puzzled look. "I still can't get over how matter-of-fact you were, calling the cops."

"I think adrenaline helped at first, but it definitely shook me up. How are you doing? You were the one being hurt by this, Dean. Who is he, anyway?"

She sighed. "It's a long story. I'm used to it, and I really don't want to get into it."

GUS said, *She's afraid to dredge up what she sees as failure.*

I studied her. "I know it's difficult to talk about, but you're covering up what you're going through. You get no support that way."

She shrugged her left shoulder. "It's too messy to get into." Then she switched focus. "I can't believe I dragged you into this."

"You didn't. I just reacted to what I witnessed. Don't think I didn't notice you side-stepping the topic."

She rolled her eyes. "You always gotta bust on me? Sounds like you avoided your shit until recently. Cut me a break!"

I grinned. "Just trying to keep it real." Then I got serious. "You didn't do anything to deserve that. Nobody has a right to treat you disrespectfully, even if you did do something wrong. When he acts that way, his own pain drives it."

Isabelle tilted her head. "You talk like people in my social work program."

I reacted. "Holy eye-opener! I thought you only worked at B & F Warehouse. I didn't know that you go to college, too."

"B & F lets me back off to part-time during the fall and spring when I carry a full course-load."

I shook my head, happy for her. "It's great that they're flexible. Your excellent grades in high school paid off."

She waved a hand, her whole body and face showing dismissal of my compliment. "I got an assistantship that covers the courses. They give those to anyone with a pulse these days."

"Don't make light of it. Assistantships are competitive. For where, here?"

Isabelle perked up. "Yeah, Landsburg University. LU's social work program rocks."

"That's wonderful. You seem passionate about it."

Her face relaxed, as if starting to let her guard down. "The gen ed courses are bogus, but the program's about helping people. That's what I want."

Referring to myself, I teased. "You must have been influenced by some incredible role model."

She picked up where we left off in the past, joking with her trademark sarcasm. "Yeah, like Einstein looking up to Homer Simpson." We both chuckled. Warmth radiated through me as our familiar jesting continued from earlier days.

Her tone became serious again. "What did you mean by Dean's pain driving things? You don't even know him."

"People typically hurt themselves and others because of the baggage they carry. If I hadn't faced my past about being bullied, I'd still despise myself and I'd let bullies hurt me as well as others."

She frowned. "What caused you to freak out with Dean if you supposedly faced it?"

I sat up straighter on the bench because my back hurt. "You didn't ask things like this in the past. You've changed."

Her tough exterior resurfaced again. "What do you expect? I'm training to be a therapist now. I want to understand how the hell things work."

Shrinking at her callous, flippant tone, I inched forward anyway because I wanted this new way of relating with her. "Okay. I'm good with being real. As long as you are."

She pressed her lips together and flattened her eyes at me.

Hesitating for a moment, I felt strange and vulnerable about sharing my deep well of pain with Isabelle. We hadn't talked that way previously. *Maybe that's part of her dilemma, too.*

I took a breath and started slowly so I could be clear and succinct. "Dean triggered my feelings about being violated and unprotected. Today touched the kid in me again, being bullied and alone with no support. But not completely. I've grown. I thought to call 911. We needed help."

The distant look in her eyes as she nodded gave the impression she had worked something out in her mind. "My grandma said that you taught about new moves. So, you did a new move when you called 911?"

"Yeah, I reached out for help. I didn't in the past. Wait, you mean you remember a saying that your grandma got from me over two years ago? I thought you saw me as crazy."

"Yep, still do. Wandering in the woods and blazing your own trail." She let it linger awhile and then smiled.

She pressed ahead. "I don't understand how you thought to call 911. I feel paralyzed and almost black out when I have panic attacks. I don't get it."

"I didn't know you had panic attacks. I imagine you feel alone during them, like I did about bullying. As if no help's available."

Her grimace told me that she knew exactly what I meant, so I expanded. "I keep gaining awareness that I'm not alone every time I touch the trauma and talk about it with support—what we're doing now. I don't just cover up or ignore it when someone triggers that spot."

Isabelle let out a long breath. "Cool." Then she slapped her hand on the bench. "Getting bullied sucks. In high school, my friend Val went through hell. Three jerks never cut her a break. Always on her case. I finally got in their faces about it. They acted as if they'd fight me. But they backed down. People didn't mess with me, even though I was small. The bullying stopped after that." Button whimpered. Isabelle reached down and rubbed his ear.

"From experience, I'd say that changed her life. I wish someone had done that for me. Are you sure you don't want to get that chili off you?" She put a hand on her hip, indicating for me to let it go.

After we both looked around in silence, I asked, "Don't you want to talk about today so you can recognize what you think and feel about things? How else can you learn from it?"

"Give it a break, mother hen." Isabelle had already moved on. She reached for Button again as she looked at her phone. "Damn. I have a project meeting with two other students in a little over an hour. I can't go back to my place and change. Dean will be there. I'm sure he's still pissed."

My eyes bulged, my mouth dropped. "You live with him?" The quivering disbelief in my words hung in the air.

She sighed with a disgruntled, shame-filled face. "We're freakin' married."

I groaned. "Holy predicament."

"I said I'd leave him if he didn't treat me better. You already saw enough to get the 24-7. He goes ballistic over most anything I say or do. Sleeps around with no intention of stopping. He doesn't give a rip about me. The night at the hospital, they called him. But he couldn't spare time away from his newest conquest. He wouldn't have come to the hospital anyway."

I clenched my jaw. "It makes me mad that you live that way. The person that's most supposed to love you treats you like crap."

She gave a weak nod, her tone now sagging like wet clothes. "He didn't start out that way, but ever since the knock-down drag-out fight with his dad, he's been hateful. I felt proud of myself today for talking with Dean about both of us being afraid to face our pasts. I even felt care for him when I asked if he'd consider going for counseling together. Only the second time I brought it up. He lost it. Said he won't ever go down that path. And what you just witnessed on the street? That was only the tail end of his reaction."

I wagged my head and sighed. "That means there's a mountain of pain inside of him, and if he's not willing to get help, it doesn't look promising. How discouraging for you."

She chewed her lip, her eyes looking determined. "I need a new move. Him still cheating on me and not even coming to the hospital crushed any hopes I had for us. About the only thing left for me is to cut ties."

She got quiet. Then I spoke with not much more than a whisper. "So you went to Sap's Bar to escape a lot of pain?"

She moaned. "Yeah, I went to drown out Dean and the panic attacks. Maybe I just wanted to drown, period." She looked around. "Can I just go to your place and get a shower? It'd be like old times when I'd come over for days to escape mom's rage fests."

"You only needed to ask. Button and I will be glad for the company."

She looked at me with a grin. "Are you still at Maple 111?"

Compelled to Talk — Gene

I shook my head thinking about how quickly Isabelle recovered from difficult situations. *Youth.* I inched upward from the hard bench, my back feeling worse than pulling weeds for hours. *Some guardian angel.*

She grabbed the leash from my hand as I pointed. "Meet Button." He licked another stain on her pants. "I rescued him from a pound about two years ago, shortly after you and I went our separate ways. He already treats you like a long-lost friend."

She smiled at that and took off walking, as if the incident with Dean never happened. Moving fast to keep up, I encouraged her. "You initially said that you didn't want to get into your story. But you ended up telling me anyway. That's great. It's a new move."

She spoke with a detached tone. "You're ever the teacher, aren't you?"

I couldn't see her face as we walked. She had made a good point, but she still seemed to hold people, including me, at a distance. Her flat tone felt like an invisible shield. Afraid that she might continue her destructive cycles, I persisted. "In the counseling program where I taught, we focused on new moves because clients stayed stuck when they thought, felt, and did the same things repeatedly. They ended up with the same results. But new moves break old patterns. Even experiencing new feelings or talking in unfamiliar ways does that."

She stayed silent.

I probed. "You look like you're focused on something. I don't want to pressure you. If you want me to stop, say so. But airing things out with someone helps."

After hesitating, she mumbled. "I didn't want to tell you at first. At the bench, I felt compelled to talk. That sounds crazy."

She tilted her head and gave a puzzled look. "Part of me felt compelled to put things out there. But I never talk about my personal life. I'm always afraid I'll get torn to shreds."

I held back my thought about it being related to her mom and, instead, encouraged her. "Sometimes it's scary. But growth keeps happening when you open up like you did."

She backpedaled. "I'm just not sure what I want."

"You mean whether you're ready to be honest about your personal life?"

"Maybe."

She shut down again. I decided to go with my hunch. "I wondered if you might not call me, even though you said you would."

Isabelle clenched her jaw. "It's just that after Grandma and Dad," her words trailed off. "It's difficult to explain."

"You mean painful to talk about?"

"Dammit!" A lid blew off of pent-up anger. Anger I'd caught glimpses of in the past, just before she shut everyone out. "I'm sorry. It just sucks to lose people, and it's even suckier to talk about."

I agreed. "Yeah, losing people steals life from you for a spell." Hanna came to mind as we walked in silence for several moments. "But at some point, when you're ready, talking about it's a new move. You gain support where you've never gotten it and it strengthens you in that area."

"Who gives a rip when someone close to you dies? You might as well throw a lollipop to the drowning kid left behind."

"Granted, it feels that way at first. I'm sorry for the loss of your grandma and your dad. I miss Sophia, too."

She studied me. "I don't see purpose in people dying. Nothing makes up for going through the hell of losing good people."

"Of course it feels like hell when you lose people you care about. Loss hurts. I've gone through a lot of loss and was terrified I'd lose you, too, at the hospital."

Her sudden glance at me showed that my comment startled her. She got quiet. I gave her space.

GUS said, *Be honest but gentle.* "When you didn't call, I wondered if losing your grandma and dad made you afraid of getting close to anyone again, only to risk losing them."

Isabelle's head drooped. Staring at Button as she walked, her head bobbed, barely enough for me to notice.

"No wonder you avoided calling me." I waited a minute before adding my other thought. "But you also said earlier that part of you felt compelled to talk."

She sighed. "I know. I just don't feel ready to unload personal things." She hit another wall. I stopped prodding her.

Tell her about losing Hanna, GUS whispered. "I never told you that I lost my wife Hanna a few years before we met."

Isabelle's mouth was hanging open. "How could I have been so clueless? Come to think of it, your past is a big black hole to me. When I used to stay at your place, you could've been one of those spies with a secret background, like in the movies, and I wouldn't have known it."

I looked over at her and smiled. "Just call me Bond. Gene Bond."

She rolled her eyes.

"It wasn't your doing. Most of my life, I listened to everyone else's struggles without letting people care for me. I never opened up with anyone, which, by the way, is your history, too."

Turning another corner and walking down the long street toward my house, she studied me, her face showing determination. "If you don't mind me asking, how did Hanna die? And how did you get through it?"

Asking questions like that didn't match the Isabelle I knew. Her curiosity floored me. "You want the whole story?" I still couldn't believe that she wanted to go there.

"If you're cool with it, I always felt like no one could relate to me after Grandma and Dad died. I want to hear what you went through."

I reflected for a moment, already feeling anguish rising up. "Words don't touch the reality of it. Hanna and I couldn't have children of our own, and she felt strongly about not adopting. Then in our later years, she got Lou Gehrig's disease. That crushed most of our future dreams and slammed the door shut on raising children. She suffered for six years, me along with her, having to watch helplessly." A tear trickled down my cheek.

Isabelle groaned.

"You sure you want me to continue?" I asked.

She gave a small nod.

"After a particularly bad bout, we knew the time had come for bringing in a hospice worker. I slept in a chair beside Hanna's bed during her last two weeks. Then, after brutal suffering, she died, with me at her side."

Isabelle watched my face with intensity, like she wanted to capture everything.

UNLOCKED

As we approached my small, one-story ranch, GUS whispered. *She has other reasons for her interest.* I didn't yet know those reasons, but I wanted to let Isabelle's curiosity lead the way.

About to reach in my pocket for the keys, I heard, "I'll be discreet." Isabelle glanced around and grabbed the key under the flower pot and opened the door. "Same old, same old." She gave another look around as she placed the key back under the planter. "Just a change of faces. Now I'm here 'cause of Dean instead of Mom."

As soon as I closed the door, she asked, "Can we just sit and talk for a few minutes in the kitchen before I shower? I know I'm gross. I'll try not to get it on anything."

After we sat down, she leaned forward, showing intense interest. "Are you cool with telling me what you actually experienced, near the end and right when Hanna died?"

"What a question!" I'm sure my eyes were two sizes bigger. "It seems like you have some reason for asking."

She snorted. "Does the wind always have a reason to blow? I'm just curious."

GUS nudged me to continue.

"I still get anxious when I talk about losing her. But I always feel more whole after I do, especially when someone accepts me without trying to fix me." Right after I spoke, I realized that I wanted to make sure she'd just listen. I needed to feel safe to tell my story.

She nodded, so I continued.

"Lou Gehrig's disease is just debilitating. It's awful." The sickening agony rose up inside me and crept through all the empty spaces like a poisonous bog. "I felt helpless over the years, seeing her struggle. Watching her life wither away, with her choking more on her saliva every day."

I took a deep breath. "After years of horrendous torment, she lost her beautiful smile. No more joy in her eyes. No more uplifting presence that felt like sunshine to me. And then, on that last morning, I felt the heaviness of it all. I just sat with her, holding her hand and saying our goodbyes." I stopped for a bigger breath, tears now dripping from my chin. "Then I braced myself and watched. I saw the light in her eyes completely disappear. Just blankness. Nothing behind her pupils anymore. Her soul had departed from her body."

Isabelle hadn't retreated one step. Some kind of recognition registered on her face, which now relaxed. A stress on it that I hadn't put my finger on had now dissipated. It made me think that she had found a connection with my experience.

I thought she'd be ready to move on from my story. But her forward lean told me that she wanted to learn something more.

"My heart tore in two," I said, "and I wailed so hard that I could hardly catch my breath. The power of it confused me because I had already accepted that she would die."

I sighed. "But the reality of her death and the horrendous burden I had been carrying never took hold of me until that moment. I knew I had to go forward on my own, and I couldn't imagine ever finding comfort. Caring for her had become my whole life. Years of gut-wrenching sacrifice, which had left a tremendous hole. It felt like something as big as the universe itself had been torn open."

Isabelle sat motionless. Then a shadow swept across her face.

She shook her head. "That sucks. Just what I said before. There's nothing good about losing people."

"Yeah, the grief smothered me for a time." After I collected myself, I let out a long breath. "But each time I share and feel known, I feel less empty. And less alone. If anything, all of it made me who I am today. I feel more whole now than ever."

Million-Dollar Questions — Isabelle

G's story burned away some misconceptions. I wasn't the only one. He had faced gut-wrenching tragedies, too. And he wasn't damaged goods because of it. He had lived it and survived—both abuse and devastating loss. Same as me. Somehow, knowing this made me feel lighter. Less angry. Like I had worn this invisible cloak of lead and the weight of it had vanished into the air.

Still sitting in the kitchen, I wanted to get his thoughts about what whirled inside me ever since my unforgettable experience in the hospital. "Tell me to back off if you want, but you said that Hanna's soul departed. Do you think people's souls continue after leaving their body?"

His eyes widened. "That's a million-dollar question. I do. It seems like you might already think that our souls go on."

I hesitated. Then my sarcasm shot forth. "How the hell can anyone really know without sailing through that opening in the clouds? Even your ozone experiences don't guarantee anything."

He pressed his lips together. "That's true. That's why some people call it faith."

"I've never been religious. But Grandma believed in God, and that our souls keep living."

About as close to mind-reading as a person could get, G probed for more. "You seem really interested in this." His eyes bore into me.

Still not ready to show my cards, I deflected. "There's a big freakin' universe out there. Just wondering."

He studied me as I grabbed a glass from the cabinet, poured myself some orange juice, and sat back down again. He tilted his head, still watching my every move.

I frowned. "What's up with you?"

"You look like the thing with Dean never happened. Your clothes are a mess. I can't believe you're not heading to the shower yet. And you look like you still want to talk, like you forgot all about your meeting."

"The mother hen again. Today's nothing new—Dean's always Dean. I'm cool. I still have about an hour 'til the meeting. I just want to check on a few things."

With his eyes almost closed, he shifted his jaw to the side. Probably trying to figure me out. "I'm just surprised at how different you are from the past. Maybe it's because of your program. But you're fascinated with topics you never showed any interest in before."

I didn't want to tell him yet about my uncanny night at the hospital. "Yeah, it's probably the program. That's a whole new wonderland." I changed the subject. "So, what are the voices you hear?"

"Leaping ladybugs, that came out of left field! We only talked about this on a street corner once. I don't think of them as voices. I pay attention to my thoughts, mainly when my gut's trying to tell me something."

His remark jogged a memory. "That's right. I saw it as intuition."

"Exactly. Some people call it intuition or just an inner knowing that's beyond what they think in their head."

More thoughts started coming to mind. "Didn't you say something back then about everything being connected, too?"

"I view everything, including people, as connected. And my inner sense tunes into that connection. Don't get me wrong. I don't see it as just me. I think everyone's inner sense, when it comes from a place of peace, taps into that greater connection."

"Hmm, connection." *That's what my high-definition experience showed!*

He tilted his head. "I'm surprised you didn't call this the voodoo shit again."

I didn't have time to harass him, so I pressed forward. "People said you talked with these voices, or I guess, I should say thoughts."

"Here we go. Time to accuse me of the voodoo shit."

I bantered back. "Get off it, would you, Mr. Defensive? I just want to understand those kinds of experiences now that I'm learning about people. You used to get your jollies from someone showing interest in that eccentric world of yours."

He gave a huff and continued with an irritable tone. "Anytime I want direction about life, I pay attention to my gut sense. I call that GUS, which you already know. But it stands for Gut Understanding and Sensitivity. And, yes, when I get direction or thoughts from GUS, I talk to him like a friend. He's my inner teacher."

"You learn from your gut?" I asked, more serious.

"Lots. About all kinds of things. Especially about being true to who I am. GUS keeps me centered in what I value."

I'm sure my whole face lit up. "That's what I want. I want to be true to me. Remember in the hospital when I said I want to get free? That's what I meant—free to be me. I'm sick of being some puppet with everyone else pullin' the damn strings."

His head bobbed a few times. "Great. Listening to your intuition or inner teacher, whatever makes sense for you, does that. It keeps you from getting lost. It centers you."

I repeated his words so they could sink in. "Listening to my intuition or inner teacher."

"Your inner teacher is like a GPS that helps you not to lose what you value. GUS is my GPS. My Gut Positioning System."

I shook my head. "Only you would spend hours thinking of this stuff!" We both laughed.

Then he crossed his arms. "You're the one showing a ton of interest in this right now. What's that say about you?"

I took on a dismissive tone. "I'm supposed to be learning about what makes people tick and I want to know what that inner sense is. That out-in-the-ozone part that's aware of connection. What is that?"

"Beyond calling it intuition?" He paused. "Some people would say that it's the spirit part of me and describe me as spiritual. But a close friend of mine would say that my conscience speaks to me. He thinks everyone's conscience is meant to teach and lead them into greater unity." Then he shrugged. "Other people that don't get it just think I'm strange."

Getting down from my chair to pet Button, I got on his case. "I vote for the last one." I rubbed Button's ears, trying to appear like I had moved on. But I couldn't stop thinking about these beyond-normal experiences. They fascinated me ever since the unreal night at the hospital. I couldn't explain it, but somehow it hardwired me to see everything as connected.

Out of the blue, G's accusatory voice surprised me. "You don't fool me." Mr. Mind-Reader again.

"Fool you about what?"

"Your energy about the meaning of life topics. You're not finished with it. Say what's on your mind."

I shook my head; he nailed it. For an over-the-hill guy, he was still sharp—probably more perceptive than any of my professors. I had one last question I couldn't let go of.

Naked — GENE

I sensed a wholeness beginning in Isabelle I hadn't seen before. She still hadn't processed losing her grandma and dad, but she no longer seemed totally detached from everything.

She had changed. I always felt privileged to be part of people's lives when they embraced authenticity and its power—that raw transformative power from living in the simplicity of who you are rather than hiding or altering yourself. I chuckled to myself about Isabelle's intentional march down that path.

Her face turned serious as she spoke while petting Button. "My grandma said you followed God and heard God's voice. So, are you religious?"

It warmed my heart to experience Isabelle's newfound curiosity. I had never seen her like this, although I hadn't been part of her life for over two years. "Some people see me as religious, but I see myself as broader or more open than how people often apply religion."

She rolled her eyes. "That's an understatement. You're out of norm, that's for sure."

"Religious words carry a lot of baggage. Painful history, too. That's why I talk about my gut sense. But sometimes I feel a higher presence or inspiration guiding me from inside—whether that's in my gut, mind, or conscience, who knows?"

Isabelle's eyes lit up. Rather than talking, she just nodded, left Button's side, and headed toward the bathroom. He, too, jumped up with a wagging tail, not leaving her side for a moment.

After she went in and closed the bathroom door, she yelled. "Can you get a pair or two of your sweats for me to check out? Something that doesn't look like it's from the last century? We're about the same size. I just want to see if something might work." Button's ears tilted toward the voice coming from the other side of the door. He stared intently at it, probably anticipating more attention from his new friend.

Ever since I brought Button home from the pound, he seemed starved for attention wherever he could get it. What a friendly, cute, mellow ball of fur. People adored him.

"Sure. I'll be back in a moment. You probably remember; towels are in the upper part of the cabinet on your left."

Coming back a minute later, I noticed that Button had remained at the door, still intent on his now-trapped friend who could not come out without bumping into him. I spoke through the door. "Here are the sweats." I bent down to lay them on the hallway floor when, to my surprise, the door opened enough for a bare arm to reach out and grab them. I shook my head. *Gosh...the younger generation.*

In a matter-of-fact tone, she said, "Gracias," and started closing the door. Button had other ideas, suddenly lunging through the opening to be with her. The door slipped from her fingers and swung wide open.

She screamed, fortunately having a towel in her hand. In a flash, she yanked up the towel in one fluid motion. Appearing shocked, she looked down and saw the culprit, now at her side begging for attention. "Well that was freakin' embarrassing." With a flushed face, she paused, looking expectantly at me for a response.

I struggled for words, my eyes still about two sizes bigger. "No problem, as far as I'm concerned."

She flattened her eyes at me and closed the door as I stood there for a moment taking in the experience of having a naked woman in my home. *That hasn't happened for a while,* a memory of Hanna coming to mind.

Then I heard Isabelle through the door, apparently not blown away by the experience. "Button's lying down and looks like he wants to stay." I heard her talking to him in a high, sweet voice. She obviously loved Button already.

"That's fine. Let me know if you need anything."

After she showered, she yelled through the door. "Do you have a plastic bag to put my nasty clothes into?"

I returned with a bag as she came out. She stuffed her clothes in it and washed her hands again. Button pranced around her as she moved.

I thought she looked cute in my sweats, but an attitude hovered in her words. "These make me look like some old granny. I guess they're better than looking gross or bumping into Dean right now."

Button gave Isabelle little room to walk as she entered the living room. I motioned to him with my hand. "Butt, give her some space."

"Did you just call him Butt?" she asked, staring at me with a dismayed how-could-you look.

"I call him Butt when I'm serious. Then he knows it's time to listen."

She gave me a stern look. "You're demented, you know that?"

I ignored her comment, already used to her razzing me like the old days. "Earlier, you sounded like you had a reason for asking about whether I'm religious or not."

She reacted. "I just wondered how you see things. I want to know what to think about all of that."

"I avoid labeling myself and others. Labels hinder people from learning directly about their experiences."

She snorted. "What the hell does that mean?"

"Haven't you ever experienced a heightened state, with a higher presence or clarity?"

She almost spoke but then hesitated. Eventually, she answered. "One time, I guess, when Grandma said she wanted to follow her conscience. I figured she got that from you 'cause she didn't normally talk like that. But her words hit me like a lightning bolt, like they came directly from the universe. It happened again earlier when you said you sometimes experience a higher presence when GUS speaks to you and that maybe it comes through your conscience."

"Great. Those are examples of a higher presence, a higher state, alerting you to something important."

Her eyes lit up. "Higher presence. Cool, the lightning bolt felt that way."

"People use various labels for similar experiences. A minute ago, you said that the words hit you like they came from the universe. Some people, like your grandma, describe it as from God. Others see it as from Allah, Jesus, or some higher power."

Nodding, she smiled. "Got it. Yoda would say, 'The Force, strong it is.'"

I chuckled. "And others think of those experiences as coming from a part of themselves. Like their gut or conscience."

"How do you know which one's right?" she asked, glancing at her watch.

I got passionate. "That's exactly what the world fights about—which religion, which beliefs, or which labels are right. The fighting's endless. Let your experiences teach you directly. That's how you awaken. Labels can cut off learning."

She reacted with a flippant tone as she opened the front door. "And I still think you're crazy."

"Just so you know, you're welcome to move in here rather than some random place. If you want—if you're still planning on leaving Dean. No pressure. Just offering."

Isabelle shrugged, appearing ready to say no. Then she paused, followed by a faraway gaze, as if to herself. "I almost said no, but that's only me wanting to do everything on my own again. I need a new move." Facing me squarely now, she added, "I just don't want to be a third wheel."

"A third wheel?" I asked.

"You know—you, Button, and me? I don't want to cramp your style."

"Isabelle, you're like a granddaughter to me. You know better than anyone; I love talking with people about what matters in life. You seem drawn to that now. It's a great fit."

She grinned. "Yeah, that voodoo shit. I still hate talking about personal baggage. It's like being naked." She gasped, widening her eyes and putting her hand to her head. Her word choice must have suddenly dawned on her.

We both burst out laughing. Full belly laughs.

Then I got serious. "You already talked more about personal things today than you ever did in the past. Maybe today symbolized a new purpose for you—being naked and not covering up or hiding what's real anymore."

Her head retracted, but her lips showed a slight curl. "Now you're plain scaring me with that weird stuff. I might have to rethink this moving in thing." She turned and took off down the sidewalk.

I yelled after her. "Alright. I'll try not to be too weird." But I had seen a familiar look on her face—a look of discovery that clients usually showed when my point had registered.

GUS pressed upon me, *Her journey begins.* I wondered what that really meant.

Secret Agents — Gene

Three weeks after my offer for Isabelle to move into my place, I parked my car in front of her and Dean's small, ranch house. I glanced around like a teenager headed for trouble. The drab, gray, one-level place didn't fit my impression of Isabelle. In need of power-washing, a green film covered parts of the siding. The unkempt lawn around it also didn't match my experience of her. I wondered if Dean dominated her life.

I sat in my car, my stomach whirling as I stared at the front door. My heart pounded about the possibility of encountering big John again, the bully from my past, in the form of Dean who probably wanted to beat the snot out of me ever since I yelled at him to let go of Isabelle. I jumped as the front door opened, similar to watching a movie where the murderer leaps out from behind a door.

"Hey, G." Her high-pitched voice sounded full of energy. My tension melted a little when she called me G again. Her face glowed, probably showing how much she needed this move. "What a rush. Secret agents on a mission!"

I crawled out of my car. "I feel more like a mouse about to get pounced on by a big ol' tomcat."

"Relax. Have some backbone. I've never seen you stressed like this. Dean never comes home in the mornings."

Still glancing around as if I were doing something illegal, I handed her a stack of boxes. I grabbed several more from my trunk. "Do you think, with both our cars, we can get all your belongings in one trip?"

Her face wrinkled in frustration. "Get a grip. I only need my books, clothes, and art supplies. The furniture stays with the apartment, and the rest is Dean's."

Not feeling like some heroic secret agent at the moment, I let out a big breath. "Great. That'll make our getaway quicker. Are you sure that Dean wouldn't have noticed clothes missing, ones you already brought to my place?"

"No way. He never looks through my things. He has nothing to be suspicious of. Where the hell are your voices? Don't they help?"

My words sounded mechanical. "They're thoughts. I don't hear as much when I'm afraid."

"What good are they if they don't help when you need them most?"

Not thinking clearly enough to explain, I cut things off. "I'll tell you some other time. Let's just get this done."

Mockery dripped from her words. "Someone went without coffee today." I bit my tongue, not in the mood for callous jesting.

Carrying empty boxes, I followed her inside—me sneaking in stealth mode and her strolling carefree like Minnie Mouse in Disneyland. I gazed at two holes in the living room wall, each the size of a big fist. A chair and coffee table lay in shambles on the stained carpet. Some powerful force must have crushed them. Red in the face when she noticed me gaping, she said, "Excuse the mess."

"Do you always protect him?" Fear made me blunter and more agitated than usual.

She ignored me and changed the topic, strategizing an order for collecting her belongings. I dropped it, thinking it best to stay focused and pack sooner than later.

In less than an hour, we filled eight boxes and loaded them into our cars. With only one more trip into the apartment to go, we each grabbed another box from my old blue Ford. The sun glistened. The neighborhood, quiet. No classes for Isabelle. Dean at work. We couldn't have asked for a more beautiful morning. Now 11AM, I wanted to move quickly since Dean had occasionally come home for lunch at noon.

I paused before we got to the door, faintly hearing words in my mind. *Leave. Now.*

Isabelle saw me hesitate. "What's up?"

"I heard the words, 'Leave now.' It could have been GUS, or maybe my fear speaking."

She frowned. "Had to be the fear. You've been jumpy as hell all morning. Dean rarely eats lunch at home. If he does, it's at noon. Not 11:00. We only have two armfuls left. Then we can make that quick getaway you wanted."

"Yeah, probably the fear. Let's get the rest and make it fast."

We went to the bedroom and gathered the art materials into one box, and two small paintings into the other. "I'll get the supplies sitting on the floor by the doorway," I said. Settling the box in my arms, I stood up and turned to head out. Isabelle screamed as a big fist closed in on my face. Then, a crushing blow and darkness.

Big John pummeled me repeatedly near the school's outdoor basketball court while his tagalongs cheered him on. Other students stood, crowding around and watching as I fell to the ground. Then John's henchmen took turns kicking me in the side while I lay groaning in the dirt. But my side felt nothing compared to my face, which felt like it had been kicked by a horse. The dirt felt safer than getting up. I lay there a long time, wondering why nobody helped. How could everyone just stand there and watch a group of bullies terrorize and abuse me?

Not yet opening my eyes, I realized I had been dreaming about my past again. *Wow, this one felt real.*

Starting to gain consciousness, horrendous pain overwhelmed me. My whole face hurt. My head throbbed, as if it was about to explode from the pressure. Finally, opening my eyes—well, one more than the other—I saw Isabelle crying and holding a bloody towel. She sat on the floor beside me, with me lying on an air mattress. Only then did I remember what we were doing, and what most likely happened.

She sobbed, struggling to speak. "I'm sorry. What a nightmare. Are you okay?"

Still groggy, I tried to answer and could only manage a do-you-need-to-even-ask look on my face, although it hurt to make any kind of face at all.

"After he left, I froze. I didn't know what to do. You were breathing okay, so I pulled the air mattress out from under the bed and dragged you onto it. I tried to stop the bleeding." She sighed. "It's all my fault."

Slurring my words, I asked, "What do you mean your fault?"

"He never goes through my things. There's no reason to. I asked how he knew I was leaving him but he wouldn't say. After he left, I checked my drawers to see if anything was missing. An Applebee's gift card that Val got me was gone. He must have scarfed it yesterday—had to be to go eat with the tramp he's hooking up with. That's probably when he saw clothes missing from the drawer and figured I'd finish moving out this morning. He knew that I didn't have classes and must have taken an early lunch to check."

After some silence, she started again. "You knew, too. GUS warned you. But I talked you out of it."

I groaned. "Yeah, should've listened to him."

Slowly gaining coherence, I tried to lighten the moment. "Some guardian angel, huh?"

She half-laughed and cried. Then she moaned. "I'm such a jerk."

I concentrated, trying to speak without slurring. "It's one thing to say you did something bad. But don't define yourself by it."

"That's just how we talked in my family. My mom called me a jerk, a piece of shit, and who knows what else. So what?" I let out a groan as she put the cold towel against my swollen face and dabbed more blood from under my nose.

Not letting go of punishing herself, she continued. "I'm such an idiot. I should've listened to you."

I pressed my lips together about her words. She shook her head. "I'm a lost cause." Then, a few seconds later, "Damn. No one pays attention to this stuff. Well, besides you."

Straining, I managed to focus. "You treat yourself like your mom did."

She reacted. "How do you do that?"

"Do what?"

"You're half conscious and look like a freakin' bloody pumpkin with your face swelled up like that, and you still pay attention to that crazy stuff."

I let out a breath and changed the topic. "Thanks for getting me onto this air mattress."

Still down on herself, she mumbled. "The least I could do after all the hell I've caused you."

I ignored her self-berating comment. "Did you call the police?"

"I told Dean I'd call them if he didn't leave. He knew I meant it. So he left."

I sighed. "Good, but we should still call them."

"I can't do that to him, even though he's a jerk. He could go to jail." She gave a pleading look.

A surge of anger pulsated through me in spite of the throbbing pain. "You're still protecting him." Then GUS whispered, *New move*. I reflected for a moment. Not reporting Dean would have been my old move, the same as Isabelle's right now. *No more.* I needed a new move on behalf of both of us.

My words finally came out without slurring them. "Maybe you can't, but I need to report this."

"I don't know why. I just can't report him. I don't want you to, either. This is between Dean and me."

Not wavering, I said, "Not after he hit me. That made it between him and me. Besides, he hit me hard enough that I want to make sure I'm okay. The doctor will want to know how it happened. I plan to be honest."

Isabelle helped me to the passenger seat in my car and drove me to the clinic. I told her to go back to my house and unload while I waited to see a doctor. She needed to retrieve her car as well, and with a line-up of patients ahead of me, it made no sense for both of us to wait.

New Move – Gene

Doctor Lavinski studied the pictures on the computer screen. "The x-rays show a mild, right-side facial fracture and a broken nose, with a deviated septum on the same side. Fortunately, you don't have a sunken cheekbone. It could've been much worse."

He handed me a mirror. I sported an almost-closed black eye, swollen nose, and distorted right side of my face—like it was injected with steroids and turning deeper shades of purple by the moment. Dean's big fist covered a large area.

After making sure that the Percocet had reduced the pain, the doctor asked, "How did it happen?"

I told him.

He shook his head. "I'm required to report the incident."

"I'm glad," I said. "I plan to report, too."

"I prescribed more Percocet. You'll need it. I want you to get your sight checked after the swelling goes down."

I thanked him and then called Isabelle to pick me up in half an hour. That gave me time to report the incident to the police.

Isabelle pulled into the parking lot thirty minutes later, looking dejected and unchanged from earlier. Her face soured, like she was expecting the worst. "Anything extra serious? What's the deal?"

"Doc said I have a facial fracture, broken nose, and deviated septum. But there's no sunken cheekbone. He gave me Percocet. Said it could have been worse."

She started driving without speaking. Her appearance told me that she was still beating herself up.

"Isabelle, I chose to go back inside. That's on me. Dean punching my face—that's on him alone, which is why I reported him."

I looked over at her, surprised at her tears again. My heart hurt, seeing her cry. At the same time, her newfound sensitivity touched me.

She kept glancing over at me now. "No matter who's at fault, I feel sick about what Dean did to you. It replayed what happened to you as a kid."

"Thanks for caring." I took a breath. "I need to say more. GUS knew. He wanted to protect me today. But now that it's after the fact, I want to learn from it. My old move would have been to overlook it. To excuse it. But I heard the words, 'new move,' and I had to make the call. It might surprise you, but after I did, I felt more whole about my past abuse."

Isabelle huffed. "That's like getting hit with a sledgehammer and saying it magically helped."

"Even though Dean punched me, reporting him felt like I finally took action about big John, the guy from my past. This time I went to people who won't look the other way—the police. Dean won't get away with it like big John did. I feel safer now, more than ever."

She shook her head. "You're unreal."

"It's not about me being unreal. It's about me listening to GUS. That keeps me healthy."

She looked miserable and stayed quiet.

Trying to lighten things up, I said, "I left myself wide open for a crack when I said GUS keeps me healthy. You must really be down to not take that opportunity."

Nothing. She simply turned at the intersection toward my place.

GUS prodded me to tell Isabelle a little more about my past. "I never said. But one day when I got home from big John and his buddies totally abusing me, I told my parents. They saw black and blue marks on my face and arms. They never saw all the bruises on my sides. My mom asked if I needed some Tylenol. Other than that, they never said a word. Or did anything."

She grimaced. "That's messed up."

"Only a year ago did I admit that my parents betrayed me by doing nothing. By not protecting me from more abuse. As a kid, it conveyed to me that 'love' won't help. That it won't protect me. GUS showed me that."

Isabelle nodded. I saw recognition of something in her eyes. *Maybe she believes love tears you down because of her mom repeatedly tearing her down.*

Isabelle parked and shut off the car. I got the impression she had something to say because she sat without moving. "After Dean left and

I dragged you onto the air mattress, I couldn't move. I kept replaying what happened."

She paused. Her eyes looked into the distance, as if picturing everything again. "Then everything got extra clear. It was that higher presence you talk about. I knew GUS warned you not to go back inside. You had stopped, as if something caught you off-guard. Your face showed surprise about what you heard, like it happened to you."

"That's a good way of putting it. I felt that way—like it happened to me. I should've known."

Isabelle's head nodded slightly. Then her eyes lit up, perhaps fascinated about the possibility of something beyond us, or at least beyond logic, helping us. I again marveled at her observational skills. *If she ever applies that to her own life, she'll blossom like a flower.*

As we stepped inside my place, I said, "Welcome home." I half-smiled, although my face ached and felt like it cracked in spite of the Percocet.

Isabelle gave a weak grin. "Something feels right about being here."

I held a cold washcloth against my face and reclined in my La-Z-Boy with Button curled up against it. He acted like he sensed my pain, probably the only reason he laid closer to me than the couch where Isabelle sat.

Isabelle's face got serious. "I didn't want to admit this, but it felt like a punch in the gut today, not just about Dean hitting you. I know it's pitiful, but I felt sick about you calling the cops on him."

I teased her. "At least you said 'It's pitiful' and not 'I'm pitiful.'"

"I'm freakin' serious," she said. "Reporting him—it's like shoving him in front of a train. Where does love fit in?"

"Hold on, can we go slow here?" I waited until her face relaxed. "I relate to the difficulty of holding people accountable. That's my history too. I saw it as if boundaries protected and loved me at the expense of the other person."

"Exactly!" Her emphatic tone conveyed that I finally understood her reluctance.

"Has Dean become less violent since you've been with him?"

The answer showed when she hesitated. "Well, he's knocked me around but he's never hit me in the face. I told him I'd pack my bags if that ever happened. He knew I meant it."

"That adds to my point. You set a healthy boundary, which helped Dean gain a measure of self-control. You didn't push him in front of a train with that boundary. He knew you'd take action if he crossed the line too far. It helped him have more self-discipline."

She scowled. Her words pushed forward at a fast pace. "Okay. I get that. What's your bigger point? I can tell you have one."

"I doubt he would have made any progress without boundaries." Her eyes looked into the air for a moment. Then I asked, "What came to mind when I said that?"

"He beat up two other women since we've been married. Part of me didn't give a damn because they had been with a married man. Mine. But, yeah, I see what you're getting at."

"I've worked with a lot of people. Self-hatred grows when someone treats others like crap and gets away with it. Their conscience works on them, unless it's buried too deeply."

Isabelle's shoulders shrunk as she sighed. "I know."

"The worst part is that people sometimes need bigger consequences when they've not gotten smaller ones. Dean needed to hit a wall to have a chance at changing. Healthy boundaries help everyone."

Isabelle tried to hold back the pain, but her red face showed the mounting pressure.

Button left my side and snuggled up against Isabelle's feet, which is all it took for grief to find its way out. She reached down and petted him. Her voice wavered with pain. "I've tried so hard to make it work with Dean. Trying to hold everything together. I can't do it anymore. The panic feels like it's from the hell of living with him. I never know when he's gonna snap. I'm always on edge."

"I'm sorry," I said. "That's scary, living that way. You could never let down and just be you."

Isabelle cried all the more, the pain rising up from a deep pit. From a long history with Dean and her mom. After the sobs died down, some of her raw experiences poured out a sentence at a time. "I feel stupid for getting hitched so fast. I wanted a strong husband who'd protect me. I thought I had that. At first. I never told anyone, except my friend Val from high school, but his dad got physical with him when he found out we eloped. Dean erupted and almost killed him. Nothing was ever good enough for Dean after that. Like it left a gaping hole in him."

She remained silent for a minute, then nodded almost imperceptibly, as if to herself. "That's how I felt with my mom, too—nothing was ever good enough."

I stayed quiet and smiled inside so as not to stretch my painful face. Consistent with past experiences, silence with Isabelle at key points helped more than words for her to admit ugly truths. My throbbing head told me to remain in the recliner. But, moving slowly, I worked my way to the couch and sat down beside her. I put my arm over her shoulder as she leaned against me and sobbed.

Isabelle had softened about not doing everything on her own. I still wondered what she was hiding from me about the night at the hospital.

Progress, Hopefully — Isabelle

Early in the morning I jumped out of bed full of energy. *Who is this person—where did the aliens put Isabelle? You never get up early unless you have to.*

I felt alive, as if some epic event was happening. Unloading with G two days ago lit a fuse in me—like that talk with him had reignited my supernatural experience in the hospital again.

I was exploding. Freer, too, thanks to leaving Dean. Living with him meant waiting for the next load of wet cement to crush the life out of me, and I didn't have to experience that anymore.

Pumped about the day, the possibilities seemed endless. The universe had expanded.

I couldn't see it at first, but I wanted something *greater* ever since the hospital, something I couldn't put words to. That experience opened me up. An invisible roof had come off, even though I still kept a lid on my personal issues with everyone but G.

When G told me his story, even calling it abuse, something clicked. I had always seen him as some nice, old guy who couldn't have related to what I lived through with my mom. But now I realized that he knew. I started paying attention. I *wanted* to talk with him about unresolved experiences. Really talk, even about other heavy baggage as long as I could just touch it here and there to feel some sense of control.

I didn't want to do life solo anymore. I had been fighting with it, as if life itself was against me, just like my mom. But after airing things with G, especially with his arm around me while I did, the opening in me from the night at the hospital got bigger. I felt adventurous—ready to live dangerously, in search of who knows what. Well, more dangerous than before.

I felt lighter, too. *Hmm...lighter? That's how you felt when you crossed over, or whatever really happened above the ICU.*

I went to the kitchen, said hey to G, and poured a cup of coffee. He looked as peaceful as a puppy that just got its treat, in spite of his purple pumpkin face. He didn't appear to feel pain today. Maybe the meds or the night of sleep helped.

"You cool, G? You still look like hell."

"Thanks for the compliment. Much better today. And contemplation earlier got me centered too. You seem to have more pizazz in you than usual."

I nodded. "Enough to take on whatever LU throws my way. I feel lighter ever since spewing that garbage out of me. I noticed it yesterday but wanted to process it. Today I feel like I could walk on air."

He studied me.

I got defensive. "What?"

"Nothing, just taking it in."

"It grates me when you do that, looking like you know something but won't say it." He gave me a *pleading-the-fifth* look, so I shrugged it off and continued. "Gotta do counseling role-plays for my Interviewing Skills class with Sailhammer this morning. My second formal one this fall, for a grade. She always picks one pair of students to watch and then gives feedback right after class. Today it's me under the microscope along with another frog getting dissected."

His eyes widened. "Holy surprise. I could be wrong, but don't practical classes for clinicians usually happen around the middle of their programs? Are you that far along?"

"Yeah, over half-way, where reality slaps you in the face."

"You nervous?"

"Nah, I feel freer after talking the other night. I'm sure holding all that in was hindering my counseling."

"Trust your gut," he said with an assuring nod.

"Don't you need to talk about what Dean did to you? I have time this morning. Might even give me practice." I thought he'd chuckle, then consider my offer.

"No, I'm good to go." The shrug on his face deflected my help with no hesitation.

"Wait a minute. You got on my case about needing to open up and talk through things, and you just had a traumatic incident less than 48 hours ago. But you come across like you don't need anyone there for you."

"Well, I don't right now. I'm doing well." His tone shut a door on talking, which didn't sit right with me.

"You always tell me not to hide things. To let others support me. When I think about it, you rarely ask for help. You're always the one giving, as if you never need anything. At all."

His face got red; something I had never seen. His jaw tightened, then hollow, defensive words followed. "I need help like everyone else."

I didn't budge. "Look at you right now, two days after a serious incident that replayed your past trauma. And yet you act like a sweet fluffy donut with no freakin' hole in you, as if you have nothing more to talk about." As soon as I paused, it made me mad, and I mocked him using his previous words. "Just like you said to me, don't you need to talk through what happened so you can learn what you think and feel about it?"

He just sat there, tight-lipped, and crossed his arms.

"I'm going to school and working some assistantship hours before class."

Three hours later, I let out a few big breaths as I anticipated a counseling role-play. Late fall now, this was my last formal one for the semester. My partner was Haley Bailey. No joke. That was her name. She always rolled with it when people got on her case. Tall, with short brown, curly hair, she acted matter-of-fact about this experience, too. Nothing much appeared to get under her skin. I didn't know her well, but I liked her. During class, Haley talked more comfortably about pain and emotions than other students. I thought that might make the role-play more realistic. I'd rather her play the role than most other classmates.

Her assigned scenario portrayed her as lesbian experiencing relationship difficulties. After we sat down and faced one another, she set her watch alarm for fifteen minutes. I wondered what direction she'd take about the topic. A lump formed in my throat as Sailhammer sat down beside us, her laptop laid open for taking notes. Being in the spotlight made me shudder, reminding me of Mom scrutinizing me when she was looking for a fight.

Tense and jittery, I knew now that I'd been way too cocky about today. I told myself, *Stay cool. Trust your training. You know more now than you did last time.*

Haley started as the client. "Sally and I have been together for four months now. We both felt right about it in the beginning. It's still good overall. I know she cares, but it doesn't feel that way as much lately. Something's changing."

Stay genuinely interested in her story, I reminded myself. I imagined being in her shoes and what she might feel like. "That's probably scary, when you feel things slipping away."

"Yeah, it is. I thought things were solid. You know what I mean?"

Keep understanding her perspective. "As if love would be enough to keep anything from tearing you apart."

"Exactly. We both thought that initially."

I felt in tune with Haley's experience. But I reminded myself to sound really tentative so she could decide for herself if what I stated was actually true for her. "And that's what's confusing? Your love felt so strong, and it's difficult to put a finger on anything that could've unraveled your unity."

"That's just it. I'm not sure what changed, but the connection's not there like at first."

"Like you don't feel as cared for or understood by her," I said with a curious tone so she could clarify if needed.

She nodded, her eyes becoming more intent. "She brushes off what I say. It's gotten worse lately."

"That hurts, when the person closest to you treats you like what you say isn't worth hearing." She started crying.

I knew I killed it, but thought, *Damn, this is real.* Not only could I feel the connection with her, but her lip quivered. Two tears trickled down her left cheek.

I sat silent, letting her experience what she needed to. *So this is what it feels like not having to fix things, and being comfortable with silence. Talking with G really helped.*

Haley put her head down. "I've told her that she dismisses me. But she just shakes her head as if it's not true, and it never changes. Except for getting worse."

"So even when you tell her that she dismisses you, she does it again, right at that point, by shaking her head?"

Her face wrinkled, her body wilted. "Yeah, she keeps doing it."

I hadn't planned my next response, it's just what came to me. "And you keep letting her repeatedly dismiss you—like you're a willing partner in continuing it?"

She halted, her head dropping all the more. Inwardly, I gaped at what I just said. It dawned on me that I let Dean do the same thing with me. Repeatedly. I never tried a new move with him. My focus suddenly returning to the client in front of me, I got mad at myself for drifting. *Come on Isabelle, don't blow it.*

Haley finally answered, her tone pleading for understanding. "I guess I don't stop because she keeps telling me I'm too sensitive."

"It's okay to feel what you feel. What do you do when she tells you that? Have you told her that she's not accepting you?"

She shifted back and forth with quicker, abrupt movements. Her face wrinkled about my questions. "No, I haven't. She wouldn't hear me anyway at those times. She acts self-righteous, like she's completely justified and I'm the one who's warped."

I didn't know what to say or do. Dean acted the same with me—self-righteous, calling me oversensitive, and telling me to get a grip. I shut down after Haley's explanation. The rest of the role-play was nothing but a blur.

Sailhammer hammered like a woodpecker on her laptop and showed no reaction. I cringed. Even though I knew I killed the beginning, I dreaded her comments about the last half.

After being the counselor, I regrouped as best I could for role-playing Haley's client. I related to the scenario—a student who constantly procrastinated. Haley did a decent job counseling. At least I felt heard and understood as the client.

Impossible Expectations — Isabelle

After class, Haley and I followed Sailhammer to the observation room for feedback. Haley received good, although not stellar, input with several suggestions for improvement.

Then Sailhammer turned her penetrating eyes toward me. "What did you think of your session, Isabelle?"

I tried to sound positive, yet honest with my thoughts. "I felt in tune with her experiences for the first half, but I could have done better in the second."

She asked, "What did you experience as the client, Haley?"

Haley glanced to the side for a moment. "I agree with Isabelle. She nailed it the first while and could have responded more like that for the last part. I actually related to some of the relationship difficulties and definitely learned from the session even though we were only role-playing."

I let out a breath, trying to be quiet about it. *You knew it was more than a role. Sailhammer might rip you apart for the second half, but Haley found the session useful. That ought to count for something.*

Sailhammer tilted her head. "Isabelle, your ability to tune into and verbalize your client's experiences was exceptional in the first half. As explained in class, stating those experiences tentatively, like you're not certain of what's happening, allows clients to decide for themselves what's actually true. That's how you evoke what's real in them."

Haley spoke. "Isabelle also seemed extremely interested, like she was just trying to understand my experience. And she did. That's what helped me go further into it."

"That means that you, Haley, did a realistic job being the client for Isabelle to connect with you like that." Sailhammer turned again toward me. "You showed genuine curiosity about Haley's story, intuitively entered into her world and validated what she felt."

She liked the first half. Great, I thought. *Now let's get the inevitable* but over with.

"You also broached further into what her experience was like when you checked if she might not feel cared for or understood. That caused her to clarify and expand on how her partner brushed off her words repeatedly."

Feeling numb, I nodded, astonished at her better-than-expected feedback.

I braced as my prof leaned forward. "One of your best responses hit the center of Haley's experience—when you went into her pain, saying that it hurts when the person closest to you treats you like what you say isn't worth hearing. That's new for you. A breakthrough. You haven't gone deeper into pain previously. Then you let the silence continue at that critical point. Excellent, and also new. You're clearly making progress."

Here comes the bad news.

But her eyes appeared soft, not stern, as she continued. "The other perceptive response occurred when you conveyed back to her what you observed—that she essentially participated willingly in her partner repeatedly dismissing her. That observation started making the point, though you didn't finish it, that trying to communicate when her partner kept disrespecting her was unhealthy. In other words, a healthier response would be for her to say that she'd continue talking as long as her partner didn't dismiss her. As long as both got heard and understood."

Sailhammer hadn't come down on me yet. I didn't tell her that I hadn't recognized a new move in place of Haley being a doormat. Even the first part popping into my head during the session surprised me because I was blind to Dean treating me that same way.

Then her face hardened as she spoke. "But what caused you to tell her that her feelings were acceptable and to ask what she did when she felt dismissed?"

There's the but. I knew it was coming. Her piercing brown eyes intimidated me. I answered with a question. "When Haley said that her partner called her oversensitive?"

"Bingo. That's when the whole session turned. That's when your energy got bigger than hers, and it instantly changed the direction of the session. It tells me that you may have strong emotions there, ones coming from your own life. You lost connection with her experience at that moment."

The air went out of me. I mumbled. "I knew something changed at that point."

"Can you see how unresolved personal pain prevents connection, not just in counseling but in life?"

The wave hit me. "Yeah, couldn't miss this one," my tone flat. "Someone's always calling me oversensitive. I hate that."

Sailhammer set her jaw, her face stern. "What you do with your personal issues is always your choice. But connection is everything." She appeared to get bigger. My eyes had to be playing tricks on me.

My head went down. "G says that, too." I had told her about G before, whom she already knew.

She frowned, making a distinction. "Gene's spiritual. I'm practical. Let's keep this grounded in reality."

Sitting there, speechless, I couldn't make sense of her last series of statements. At a practical level, both of them emphasized making connections, and both were known as exceptional therapists. They just had different ways of talking about connection. But she completely dismissed G as my valued mentor—just like Haley's partner did with her. But there was no way in hell I was going to call her on it. The stakes were too high.

Sailhammer told Haley she could leave and wanted to talk further with me. I tensed.

"Isabelle, people who dislike feelings call you oversensitive. At the same time, you reacted strongly about it, which means you may need to deal with some unfinished business."

"Unfinished business?" I asked.

Her eyes locked onto mine, and her voice boomed. "Yes. Unresolved wounds that you carry."

Sailhammer filled the room. I shrunk like a tiny insect trying not to be seen. Or swatted. I gave a blank nod.

She got up and walked back and forth, her face churning about something. She moved like a symphony conductor and waved her arms as she talked. "Your comments in class show that you're unusually perceptive, and today you were highly effective when you were on as the counselor. Your intuitive ability to verbalize your client's experience from her perspective was striking. But you also need to work through your pain if you don't want it yanking you around during sessions. That's been a pattern in both of the formal role-plays, as well as in the earlier informal ones. Did you hear both points? I don't want you to miss my encouragement—your inclinations are exceptional, and you need to face your issues if you want to be that outstanding counselor that I know is in there."

I gave a nod.

"If so, you can go." She turned toward her laptop and began pecking away.

Fortunately, she had finished "encouraging" me. I doubted that I could have held things together any longer.

Maybe she hadn't intended to pressure me. But all the air seemed to go out of the room during her discourse. It wasn't what she said, but how. The powerful energy behind her words ambushed me with a humongous ball of jumbled expectations. Not able to handle the weight of it, I teetered like a rickety seesaw from one foot to the other. A wave of fear grew, fast and furious, as soon as I closed the door behind me. Panic attacks always freaked me out.

Lightheaded, I wobbled my way down the hall. Only two people stood at the far end of it. Everything started whirling. I didn't want anyone, especially Sailhammer, to see me. She'd come out of the observation room after finishing her notes. *Hide!*

I saw an empty classroom on my left and ducked in there, hoping students wouldn't file in anytime soon. I plopped onto a chair against the wall out of view. My heart began racing as fast as a snare drum pounded by some wild, out-of-control drummer. I cringed and held my breath in terror, waiting for it to explode into thousands of pieces. Then things went dark.

The cool wall against my right arm felt good as I came to. I raised my head. Then I tilted it back and made small circles with it, trying to rid myself of any lingering brain fog. Opening my eyes, the two-foot square ceiling panels came into view. The haze kept clearing. Memory of the incident started coming back, and I looked at my watch.

I didn't know how long I was out. I guessed several minutes. As far as I knew, the attacks usually only lasted a minute or two. This one felt worse. I wondered if other people experienced onslaughts similarly to me—waiting in horror, for what felt like an eternity, for my heart to burst. I feared, too, that one day a major attack would happen in front of others. That they'd write me off as some weirdo who couldn't get her act together. But the episodes in front of people, so far, hadn't been strong ones, and I faked my way through them.

As I sat longer, my breathing relaxed and my head cleared. I reflected about what freaked me out. *Sailhammer's bigger-than-life energy felt familiar somehow. How? Oh, who!* Many parallels started emerging between how Sailhammer talked and how Mom and Dean always acted—powerful direct exchanges with immovable, unforgivable expectations embedded in them. Their vibes embodied the same message. *Anything less than my perfect picture means failure!*

I looked at the time again. Another class in an hour. Then work at B & F. Ugh. *I don't know if I can get through the day faking being okay around people. I don't even want to try.*

I usually did my school work between classes so I'd have less to take home. But I was fried. I set the alarm on my watch so I'd have enough time to be coherent for class. Then I put my head down on the desk and crashed.

Opening my car door after work at B & F, I fist-pumped with a sarcastic "yes" about getting through the rest of the day with no other major mishap. On the way home, I tried to regroup about Sailhammer's input. *It's cool. She told you you're exceptional when you're on, and that you just suck when you're not! No, that's not her point. I just need to face my unresolved issues. But...who knows what I'll find lurking underneath?* My mind kept replaying the day, sometimes interrupted by me pullin' back curtain number thirteen to peer into the dark about Mom. I couldn't see anything yet except darkness.

Coasting into G's gravel lot, I shook my head. *So much for regrouping.* I let out a long breath, feeling glad to be home. I noticed the stars and Milky Way when I got out of the car and headed inside. *What a gorgeous night! Somehow I missed it when I left B & F.*

G sat in his recliner, reading, when I walked in and threw my backpack onto the couch. He looked up from his book. "Before we get into anything, I want to apologize about earlier. You were right."

After seeing the awesome night sky, the only other thing that could make my day brighter was harassing G. I widened my eyes as much as I could. "What were those words again?"

He smiled. "You were right when you said that I haven't let others see my need. And I rarely ask for help. There's a lot more to say, but it can wait. I'm sure you've had a long day."

"Well, thank you for saying that, and before I change my mind about putting things out there, I sucked today in my counseling debut."

His head retracted as he flattened his eyes. "You think maybe that's you just being hard on yourself?"

"Well, Sailhammer mentioned that I nailed the first part, but kept emphasizing that my pain took over the second half."

"That's way different than saying you sucked."

I shrugged. "But she said a pattern shows that my past experiences hinder counseling. She had ginormous expectations for me to get personal therapy. Came down on me like a jackhammer." Mumbling, I put my head down. "Probably ought to call her that, instead of Sailhammer. Plus, I had a panic attack afterward."

"That's a bummer." After waiting, he asked, "What did you experience when she told you to face your issues?"

"I froze. Same thing happens when Dean or my mom wants something impossible."

"Like you're not acceptable if you don't meet their expectations?"

"Yeah, and that I'll get ripped apart if I don't do what they want."

G grimaced. "Just don't overlook the power tied up with believing that you're unacceptable if you don't do what someone expects. That pretty much disowns yourself."

Now I cringed. "Disown myself? I need to sit with that."

Revelations – Isabelle

I awakened with a smile this morning. I felt freer again. Lighter. It didn't make sense. *You're not even bent out of shape about the panic attack yesterday. Maybe,* I wondered, *because falling asleep last night you vowed to face your past, and to tell G about what happened at the hospital, too. You'll keep second-guessing yourself if you don't.*

Button scurried to my feet as I strolled into the kitchen. G sat in the recliner looking at the wall clock. An old one, with a pendulum swinging from it. Probably antique. He sat there with his favorite coffee cup—an off-white mug that stated "School for the Gifted" along with a cartoon guy pushing on a door that said "Pull." I chuckled to myself. *That's him.*

Before mentioning that I wanted to talk, G spoke. "I see that you're upbeat. I'd like to tell you what I've been learning since you mentioned about me never needing anything. I wouldn't want to pull you down, but I'm doing a new move by asking." Button moved beside the recliner and laid down.

I tilted my head. *That's interesting. Button usually hovers around me when we're both here.* "I'm cool with hearing you for a change. Let me get some fuel first. Then, as you say, I'm all ears."

Pouring coffee and taking a sip, I gave a sigh of pure pleasure. "It's amazing how my mood affects the flavor. It tastes awesome today."

Button never moved when I went to the sofa. G's face turned serious, his voice somber. "I took in what you said and saw a whole world I've been blind to." The long break after his statement startled me and left me wondering what direction this conversation might take. I began rocking. I had never seen him this…I wasn't even sure what to call it. Introspective? He contemplated all the time, but never this deadpanned. His blank face told me that he was peering into some great void.

He shifted forward to the edge of his recliner, but sat hunched. He started pouring out his story, a slow pour, like heavy, wet cement oozing down a chute little by little. "Without knowing it, I've lived my entire life as if I wasn't supposed to have any need."

I related to that but waited for him to continue.

"My parents treated me like I was an inconvenience. I learned not to ask them for anything."

I felt my eyes widen. "I get that. Me, too."

Unhurried, he closed his eyes while giving a long nod. "There's a good many parallels between us."

Another minute went by with nothing said. This unnerved me as badly as waiting through silences with a client.

His lips pressed together. "Bringing up any difficulties I faced—the bullies, a harsh teacher, the dreadful bus trip every day—my parents would never do anything. They'd scarcely say anything apart from, 'You'll work things out.' I had to do life on my own. That's also why it irritated me when you wouldn't allow help."

"Yeah, I felt the vibes." Then I let out a sigh, as much for me as for him. "But, as kids, it's scary when nobody's in your corner, having to figure out life all by yourself."

He stared at the floor. "In my early years, we went to church. Looking back, the church's overt emphasis was clear. 'Help everyone out there. They have lots of needs.' But their implicit, constant, message overpowered everything: 'Give, give, give, but you shouldn't need anything.' It made relationships a one-way street."

I made a pained face.

"It carved my childhood into rock." After a few long breaths, he began again. "Then came the counseling profession. The training accentuated setting aside personal needs to tune into clients' worlds. Do you hear how my whole life pushed me to overlook my needs and to prioritize everyone else's?" Hesitating, he clenched his jaw. "No, not just prioritize. Only other people's needs mattered! Mine didn't."

Wagging my head, I slapped the arm of the couch. "That's insane that our profession added to ignoring personal needs!"

G's head drooped even lower now, if that was possible. A tear trickled down his left cheek.

I waited, as if inside of some fragile bubble with him. I had previously witnessed raw honesty when he described his past, especially about

Hanna dying. But I had never experienced him facing the unknown—his unknown—and not having all the answers. In this strange and unfamiliar territory, my heart ached and reached out to him with an invisible embrace, seeing him so vulnerable…and naked! Nothing covered!

He started unloading more, his voice trembling. "Every now and then Hanna used to say that she couldn't see me. I never got what she meant until now. If I wasn't allowed to have any needs, how could I truly be present? In a way, she had no partner at times. If she wanted things in our marriage that were reasonable, I always rolled with it. I handled my personal life like I had been shaped. Care for everyone else's needs and don't have any of my own. The real me couldn't exist."

His strained face appeared to keep searching for previously unspoken realities. "Doing counseling was different. Being healthy with clients required tuning into inner experiences, mine and theirs. Can you see how my own frustration or boredom about counseling not working at times would have exposed what wasn't working for my client? Being aware helped. It made me more present and effective."

I just nodded so that he'd continue.

"But in my marriage, a good husband was supposed to be selfless. Needless. I see now that Hanna felt more burdened when I'd always defer to her desires and have none of my own. Things fell on her when I had nothing available except, 'Whatever you want.' She carried more. You know how some wives call their husbands another kid to take care of? Just more responsibility. That was Hanna and me. Why? Because she intuitively carried my needs, knowing that I wasn't in touch with my own. Despite all of my learning professionally, I had been clueless about this area personally."

He gave a long pause, his face wrought with anguish. "Childhood, church, my profession, and my marriage—all of it put a bigger-than-life stamp of approval on that way of living. It's humbling to discover how blind I've been. As much as I'd previously faced the demons inside, a big hole existed." Still hunched over, he looked up. "You remember your comment about me being ever the teacher?"

"I'm sorry. That came out of frustration."

He shook his head. "No, that little train car took me into Grand Central Station. It contributed to these revelations and showed part of the big picture. My continual teaching kept my pattern going—me always the giver, never the receiver." He took a breath, then mumbled. "GUS showed me that."

G glanced down at his watch. "Holy caboose! I really appreciate you listening. It means a lot to me. Thank you." Then he jumped to his feet. "Didn't realize the time. I need to get going."

"Oh, I guess I'll wait then. I was hoping to tell you something about when I flatlined."

His eyes twinkled. "At the hospital, GUS told me that more had happened but to give you space about it. I'm glad you're ready. I want to hear it, but it'll need to wait until after my meeting with a friend. I'm doing another new move. I'm paying attention to my needs rather than squeezing more out of myself and then racing to meet my friend."

Most mornings, G took time to chat with me. I had assumed he'd be available to hear my story this morning. I couldn't hide my disappointment. "Okay, the new move makes sense."

"I know it's really important to you. It is to me, too. That's why I'd like to give it my full attention. How about we make sandwiches when I return? We can head to Landsburg Park for a picnic under the pavilion. It's Saturday. Cloudy, but a nice day to be out."

I imagined it for a moment. "Cool. It'll be like the old days after one of your talks at the Friends of Family Community Center. You, Grandma, Camila, and me."

After G grabbed his keys and closed the door behind him, I moseyed to the couch. I started reminiscing, fond memories floating through my mind about Grandma, Camila, G, and me under that old pavilion. I pictured the huge wooden beams and the occasional wasps that would zoom around the nests above us as we chatted—always at the same table. Everyone else acted like it was ours. We'd ride each other about stupid things and laugh, but we also talked about what mattered. I felt less alone after what I called "our table talks." I finally belonged somewhere. Good memories. Until Grandma died.

As I noticed the silence of G's house, I wondered if I was trying to be like him—contemplating and all that. No way I'd tell him. He'd bust on me. But I wanted to veg and see what came up.

While scratching Button's ears, I found my whole body sinking into the couch with a smile about living here with G. In this place where I could just relax and be me. My safe haven from Mom in the old days. Simple, not cluttered. A few old knick-knacks here and there, a typical grandparent's house. Peaceful, with the added bonus of Button's never-ending TLC.

My mind shifted to the night at the hospital. When I imagined telling G about what happened, my heartbeat sped up, now sounding louder than Button's breathing. The experience still felt too raw to tell anyone but him. And too epic to have anyone trash it or to put it in some box with a label.

I petted and talked with Button. He lifted his head and watched with tilted ears as I spoke. "G's like you and Grandma. He's all-in when he listens. Doesn't judge. He cuts to the chase like Sailhammer but doesn't pressure me like her."

Then out of nowhere, I had to listen to some tunes, like some magic spell had settled upon me and could now move me at will. Looking around, I remembered I didn't have my stereo. Dean had treated it as his and would have hunted me down with a vengeance had I taken it.

I wished I had it now, only seeing G's excuse for a radio sitting on a small round table. I shuffled across the living room and turned it on, wondering if it would work. The speakers startled me as a DJ's deep voice echoed off the walls. He came across like some old guy trying to sound cool. "Oldies but goodies, nowhere but here on 94.4 FM."

"Holy oldies!" I said, imitating G. Then I chuckled. *Yeah, sounds like his station.*

About to turn the knob, the DJ's words pierced me. "This one is meant for you: *Saturday in the Park,* by Chicago." Stunned, I stood motionless.

Meant for you? His words gave me goosebumps, like he said them just for me. Then things exploded in my mind. *It's Saturday, and we're going to the park!* Coincidence?

Blown away, I listened to the lyrics. I didn't know why but I expected to hear more relating to me personally. And I did. Certain lines jumped out, as if a spotlight shined on them—words about reaching and touching each other and about changing the world.

Isn't my clinical work about impacting people's lives? Isn't that what G and I are meant to do?

The phrases and their symbolism vibrated through my whole body. *This is totally insane. I'm getting as crazy as G.*

The lyrics about waiting, nailed it, too. I had longed to escape from what felt like a cruel existence. I wanted to be free. I wanted to make peace with losing Grandma and Dad and with having been cheated out of a real mom. I wanted the panic attacks to stop sucking the life out of me. That's what I was waiting for.

Hopefully, talking through my baggage with G would do that. I hated the thought of going there. I got stoked about helping others, but facing my own pit of despair still freaked me out. I didn't know how deep it would go. And to get through my program, I needed to face it head-on.

Reflecting on the song made me think about my purpose: making a difference in people's lives. That felt bigger ever since the night at the hospital. But the lyrics about wanting it badly, made me tense, because I wasn't all-in, not yet. I still pulled back when life got messy.

After the song ended, I shut off the radio and wrote down what stood out. I stared at the words. I made a face, skeptical about some big plan behind everything. But the uncanny timing of the song raised questions. My body tingled for much of the morning as I sat in silence.

The universe sure seemed to be pointing to G and me talking in the park. *Saturday In The Park.*

Folding up the paper and putting it in my pocket, I considered talking with G about the panic before telling him what happened at the hospital. I wanted the painful things behind me.

The door opened. Still lost in thought, I tried to let go of one reality to come back to another. Button jumped up and ran to greet G. He stood at the doorway with a crazy smirk plastered on that still-swelled-up face of his—although it looked only half as much like a purple pumpkin today. He turned toward me and declared, with what sounded like a secret confidence, "You've started your journey!"

I'm sure I looked at him with a question showing on my face. "You sound like GUS told you that, but you already knew I might give you the scoop today about the hospital."

"That's true. But GUS told me that you're launching into a whole new way of life."

I stared at him as if he had just announced a future catastrophic event.

He quickly clarified. "I'm sorry if that scared you. I wanted to encourage you."

Still reeling from his remark, I managed to calm down. "Whatever. I just feel out of control."

"Hopefully, you'll keep allowing your genuine experiences and voicing them. Just as you're doing."

I didn't tell him, but I was having second thoughts now. I felt like I was standing on a precipice, with major change coming. Even more than what had happened since the hospital. G somehow knew that. That kind of knowing made my stomach queasy and it intrigued me. I bit my lip, wrestling with what I really wanted. For now, I decided to stretch with one new move—telling him about that night and, if I could just find the courage, maybe about the panic attacks, too.

Uncovering a Land Mine — Isabelle

At 11:30 in the morning I grabbed the chicken, cheese, and mayonnaise from the fridge. Feeling like I'd bounce off the walls if I didn't stay busy, I powered through some snacks and water while G and I sat at the table making sandwiches. I hoped to get to the park by noon. I wanted a long day out.

He asked, "Do you want to tell me about your hospital experience?"

I shrugged. "I will at the park. Did you notice that I brought up Grandma this morning without being bent out of shape?" The anger wasn't completely gone, but it didn't ruin my whole day like it always had before.

"I noticed. You seem more okay with it. And maybe ready to get into it?"

I back-peddled. "I like listening to other people's stories, but everything feels messy when I bump up against my own. Maybe I'm just dense or something. And whining doesn't change the fact that she's gone. Does nothing for my panic attacks. They're never going to end. I just feel mad and out of control with things like that." My knee-jerk response made me wonder if I was preparing to launch into the unknown—what G had pronounced like some prophet when he got home today.

He kept putting chicken chunks on his bread while he spoke. "I used to question if talking helped, too, especially when nothing could be done about bad situations. But getting it off my chest with friends made a difference." He studied me. "You said you felt mad and out of control?"

I scowled and changed focus. "A professor just lectured about not turning friendships into counseling. It made me question how we talk."

G hesitated, tilting his head. "There's some truth to that. Friendships get messy when one always gives while the other takes, and, as you know, I've slanted one way too much. But I'm planning to allow my needs into the mix now. Balance keeps things healthy."

"Yeah, that nails it for me. When I listened to your raw experiences earlier, it showed me that I contributed to our friendship, too."

"Balance means having fun, too. By the way, how much do I owe you for the session this morning?"

I grinned. "Not as much as I owe you. I'd say that we're just starting to get balance. I want honesty both ways. The day that you told me about the bullies abusing you, it opened my eyes to Mom's B.S. Like it wasn't my fault. You weren't even saying it for my benefit. It was just honesty about you, and it helped me chill about Mom."

The faraway look on his face made me think that GUS might be telling him something. "We heal not just from counseling but through reaching and touching each other in safe, honest relationships."

I was speechless. I looked at him like he had just slapped me in the face.

G asked, "Is everything okay?"

Words finally came. "Just mind-blown. I heard the same freakin' words in a Chicago song this morning. Words about reaching and touching one another."

"That's just how we talked about it in our counseling program. But keep tuned into that," he said. "If you don't have rigid conclusions about coincidences, you can learn from them."

"Tune into and learn what? You lost me."

"Open up about possible connections. Keep watching and listening for whatever relates to the song."

I shook my head about this wonderland of his as I walked over to the fridge and pulled out two Gala apples. After putting them in the cooler, I sat back down and replayed the lyrics in my mind. Nothing happened. I put up my hands in surrender.

"What were you doing?" he asked.

I gave him a frown. "Opening up, like you said. About the lyrics."

"The hidden things of life don't just happen at the snap of a finger. You touch them and let them percolate a little. That's when you get revelations. Issues are the same way. You reach and touch people not by commanding it to happen but by helping them to open up little by little to whatever is real, emotional, or painful in them. Just like you're doing in your program. You don't have to do that here."

"Give me a few minutes. I'm going to my room to jot down some thoughts before we go. I don't want to lose them." I took off. Button leapt to his feet and followed.

After getting my thoughts on paper, I sat for a minute on the edge of my bed. As soon as I paused, the song's words about reaching and touching one another went through my mind again. They got me stoked. *I need to go with it, touching this deep place in me. I don't want to look back a year from now with regret about never facing it.*

Returning to the kitchen, I sat down across from G again. "Can we just touch on this topic and then give it time like you said?" After he nodded, I asked, "What would it look like, getting to what's real or emotional in my situation?"

"Before you told me about the song, you said you keep getting mad about the loss and panic not changing. More is beneath the anger."

"You could say that's within the realm of possibility."

My sarcastic side-step didn't deter him from putting things out there. "Something makes you angry, like feeling out of control, as if you're supposed to handle everything perfectly and then get angry when you can't. That's how you sound to me."

I grimaced at his words. My voice got louder. "But I should at least be able to stop the panic attacks. For two years I've tried everything, from exercise to shutting off what I'm thinking or feeling. But the attacks keep coming."

G's hand motioned toward me. "Look at all your energy about it. That's what I'm talking about—you're trying to control or stop the attacks and then get mad when you can't."

I reacted as if he had just told me to let a hammer hit my finger. "Wouldn't you want to stop them?"

He put his hands up. "Let's slow down. Of course I'd want them over with. But that doesn't mean that it works that way." After putting the lid on his sandwich, he looked up at me with wet eyes, his face blotchy. "I was stuck in my pain about abuse for years because I was trying to control or change that issue without learning about it. That's how most people stay stuck. They do the same things repeatedly instead of learning key lessons."

The tears and passion in his voice told me he cared, but, for some reason, he was getting under my skin. I had the feeling we were uncovering a land mine. Hoping that G's insights would help, I tried to regroup and continue. "It cuts off learning?"

"When people can't control things that they think they should, they turn against themselves or others instead of learning."

Ignoring his point, I shook my head. My voice erupted from somewhere deep inside. "But everybody acts like life should be under control. I'm the only defect who can't do it!"

My heart raced. Panic and whirling suddenly overwhelmed me. G leaned forward, his hand reaching for me. I blanked out after that.

When I came to, my head lay on my arm, somehow not on my sandwich. At first, I heard echoey, calming words. "I'm with you. Let yourself be where you are." G had been holding and massaging my hand but let go as I lifted my head to look at him.

"Are you okay?" he asked.

"What happened?" I managed. Then everything started coming back. "Damn! That freakin' blindsided me." Button snuggled tighter against my leg. Glad to have him there for comfort, I reached down to pet him.

We sat quietly for several minutes. G finally spoke. "That's scary when you get caught off guard like that."

I made a pained face. "See, they'll never stop. Can't even hold a damn conversation." Before G could say anything, I clenched my fists at my sides. "This is too much. I can't do this! I'm calling Val. I need time to just veg."

G gave a slight nod. "Do what you need, and be kind to yourself."

Lightheaded, I wobbled to my room. Clicking on Val's number, I hoped she'd answer. I hadn't talked with her since the morning I told her about Dean almost killing his dad, and how it started a downhill slide in our marriage. Even if I hadn't selected her number, her speed dial way of talking made her immediately identifiable.

"Hey, Izz. Been a while. What's up?"

"I wanted to connect. Just needed to get away. You doing okay?"

"Yeah, been dawdling around the gardens a lot. That time of the year. It's my chill place." Val still lived with her dad but had a separate apartment above the garage. He let her make several gardens on the property as long as she shared what she grew.

"Do you mind if I swing by? I've never seen your gardens. I can help weed or pick veggies. I just need some time using my hands instead of my head. You know, too much LU stuff."

"Awesome. I'll be here. See you when you show." She ended the call before I could say bye.

Fifteen minutes later, Val and I gave each other a hug. I scanned the grounds. "This place is amazing! You did all this?"

"Took two years to make the grounds how I wanted! But hell yeah." With no breath, she rattled off the list while pointing. "Beans, carrots, corn, cauliflower, asparagus, beets, spinach, tomatoes, kohlrabies. All the cucumbers, squash, and melons are in that section."

"What are kohlrabies?"

"Taste like mild radishes."

Breathing in the air and taking notice of the sprawling green paradise refreshed me. I turned toward her flower garden. "You don't see ones like those every day. They're so colorful."

She reeled off another list before I could blink. "Dahlias, strawflowers, lilies, dianthus, poppies, asters, azalea."

"Those rocks are striking. They complement all of the beautiful colors."

She studied me. "See, you need hands-on stuff like this instead of the heady mind games at LU."

"Don't tempt me today. I might agree with you after the way my mind's been whirling around. I needed a break."

"Izz, I'm telling you. Can't beat veggie therapy. Am I right?"

"At the moment, it's those rocks I can't take my eyes off of. I don't know why. Maybe 'cause they're so unique." Just then, a tiger swallowtail landed on one. It made me think of Grandma. "What were you working on before I got here?"

"Hoeing the veggie gardens."

"I'll help if you have another hoe and tell me what to do."

We hoed for an hour as she updated me about the old gang. The work helped me chill about what happened earlier at G's, but info about the gang didn't thrill me. Almost nothing had changed. Between my old life and the new, I'd take my current existence any day.

Back at G's by 1:30, I hadn't eaten lunch. He looked up from his book when I opened the door. He just watched as I went to the cooler to check on the sandwiches, then said, "I ate mine and put yours in the fridge when I didn't know how long you'd be. Or, if you'd still want to go."

"Thanks. I'll eat mine now." I grabbed it and sat down at the table while he watched from his recliner. "Working in the garden at Val's did the trick. I'm calmer now."

"Glad to hear that."

After swallowing a bite, I gave a sigh. "I know the attacks will keep happening if I don't get to the bottom of them and I need to pull out that root to make it through my program. You probably saw what triggered it, didn't you?"

G's face tightened. "I'm torn. Key reasons for the panic got exposed, but I'm not sure that you're ready to face more."

His words about the reasons showing piqued my interest. "I'm too wasted to have another attack. So as long as I can focus and we can tap into a few key nuts and bolts about it, let's do this."

He tilted his head. "Just tell me what you need as you go forward. And speaking of needs, it will help me, really, both of us, if you go slow."

I nodded, so, in a soft voice, he started. "You might remember that when you left, I told you to be kind to yourself. Why? The pressure and harsh judgment toward yourself are fierce. No one could hold up under that intensity."

"Harsh judgment? What intensity?"

He repeated my words. "Can't even hold a damn conversation."

"Okay. Maybe."

"And right before the panic, what did you call yourself when you couldn't handle life like other people seem to do?"

It took me a minute because that's when everything had started fading. I mumbled. "A defect."

G let that sit a minute, then shook his head and looked at me as if I had condemned myself to a hopeless life. "That's what precipitated the panic—harshness toward yourself about not measuring up. Like you're a throw-away or unforgivable for screwing up, just like you treated yourself after Dean punched me."

The harshness was undeniable. I had no choice but to admit it. "Got it."

He kept giving space before he'd start with more. "And your shoulds are like a loaded gun—pressuring you to either live up to some lofty standard or get shot."

I bobbed my head in agreement. I saw his point, but I couldn't imagine living life any other way. It was all I knew. But I was too exhausted to argue. "I hate this."

"What's that?"

"Being exposed. I've never had a big attack in front of someone. Nobody's ever seen me losing it. What a pitiful blob. It's like being naked."

He tilted his head and grinned. Then my mind went back to the day he told me that being naked symbolized my new journey. "Damn," I said under my breath as I shook my head.

He waited a little. "You also said that everyone acts like you're supposed to have life under control. To me, 'everyone' meant a particular someone."

My whole face cringed as I let out a breath. "Mom."

"When she came down on you that way, I guarantee that it was more about her own life than yours. Wasn't her entire existence dramatically not under control?"

Maybe from being around G a lot, only one word oozed out when everything registered. "Holy." I sunk in my chair.

He asked, "What's happening in you?"

"Just letting it sink in. I never saw it before. So the trauma has been most connected to pressure from mom to live under control?"

He gave a slow nod. "What happens if someone sees you not having life together, like I just did?"

"Oh, that's easy. I'll be written off as a loser. Shit. I see. That's how Mom treated me."

After giving some time, he spoke just above a whisper. "I guess I didn't get the memo."

I gave a weak smile. Then his eyes looked down as he said, "That's a lonely place—having to live with no cracks in your armor or else be branded a loser."

I hung my head. "I feel overloaded."

His lips tightened. "Sorry. Maybe I pressed a bit much."

"No. I'm glad we pushed through. But it's time for the brakes. My head's spinning. You still want to go to the park?"

Two o'clock now, neither of us spoke as we loaded his old blue Ford with our supplies, minus the sandwiches. In the silence, everything cleared. G had pegged it. My go-to was to trash myself when I didn't have my act together, and to think others should too. I hated being cornered, and I didn't know if I could change. I needed a breather and looked forward to going to the park, probably about as much as Button, based on how he was panting.

The Trap — Gene

I couldn't read Isabelle's face as I drove to the park. She had wanted to deal with her issues, but maybe I pushed too hard. I decided to give her time and to check later. In the back seat, Button kept glancing around, watching every movement along the way.

Cloudy and breezy, the day bubbled with activity. Landsburg Park, on the outskirts of town, sat at the edge of a pine forest. Nature usually cleared my mind. I hoped it would do the same for Isabelle.

As the park came into view, I saw half a dozen kites flying in the open area near the pavilions. I smiled at the colorful artwork in the sky and at people's bright faces. Kite flying always lifted my spirits, as much from watching as flying them. Perhaps they symbolized freedom to me. Only one little string holding them to the Earth.

The lake, too, welcomed us—cattails waving at us in the breeze, flowers blooming along its banks, ducks feeding and swimming in it. Isabelle's face relaxed as she finally looked up.

Glad to see no one sitting at the small pavilion, I pulled the wheeled cooler toward it while Isabelle walked Button. Her face brightened as she watched him sniff and explore with occasional short bursts of speed. I kept studying the kites flying off to our left. As we approached a picnic table, I saw a young man observing Isabelle. He instructed a little girl on how to fly her bright, yellow SpongeBob SquarePants kite. Isabelle hadn't noticed the guy who could barely take his eyes off her as she walked past.

After Isabelle tied Button's leash to the end of the picnic table, we unloaded the cooler and sat down to eat our snacks. The end of the table toward the lake angled slightly away from the kite-flying area—behind Isabelle's left shoulder but in view for me.

"Don't look now, but there's a guy in the kite area behind you who keeps watching you. Maybe he knows you, but it comes across as more than that."

Isabelle frowned. "You know the first thing people do when they're told not to look."

"Got it. But you did good." I gave a smug look.

She flattened her eyes at me, the meaning clear. *Cool it if you know what's good for you.*

I couldn't stop my playful mood. As she took another bite of her apple, I said, "Button's watching the action. Call him. Then you can pet him and casually see who the guy is."

"Get a grip, would you?"

Although she frowned, it must have gotten the best of her. She called Button and started petting him. Then I saw her glancing over at the kite area as she wrestled with Button. She sat back down and shrugged her shoulders. "Nope. Don't know the guy."

I razzed her, pouring on the honey. "He sure is handsome. Dark hair, well-built."

"G! Drop it! I'm not telling you again."

After we ate several bites, she made eyes and shook her head. "Yeah, he's hot, but I'm not going down that road again. Not after Dean."

"Yeah, that leaves a burn."

She stayed quiet at first. "And when it happens repeatedly, trust is blown all to hell." Her face tightened again. "Plus, I can't believe you're playing matchmaker. I'm still married. He's probably hitched, too. You saw the little girl with him."

"I would've thought that, too. But not after I saw how much he watched you." I paused to create the right effect. "And he's wonderful with kids."

"Enough already!" She jumped to her feet. "A mother hen's got nothing on you. I'm doing a new move, taking action instead of just words. Button and I are giving you a timeout. You can torment yourself for a while." She untied the leash, and off they went toward the path that circled the lake.

I chuckled to myself and took another bite of apple. At sixty-eight years of age, I had finally slowed down enough to enjoy life. And to take time for the important things, like razzing Isabelle. Turning again toward the kite area, I saw the same guy studying her intently as she strolled toward the lake. Although forty or more yards from me, the lost gaze in his eyes was undeniable—smitten at first sight. He acted as if the world had stopped except for her. Even the little girl holding the kite string tapped his side several times before he realized she wanted his attention.

The quiet refreshed me. I sat munching on some crackers, thinking about how much better food tasted outdoors. After half an hour, Isabelle marched around the other end of the lake and back to our picnic table. She tied up Button and let out a big breath as she sat. "Something's still eating at me, if you're okay with talking for a few minutes."

"No problem. Just take your time. More awareness happens that way."

"I don't get it. It's not just my mom. Everyone acts as if life should be controllable. Sailhammer even acts that way."

My focus shifted because of distant but distinct words in my head. *YES, AND IT'S A TRAP!*

"Your eyes looked off into the distance." She chewed her cheek a moment, then asked in a mechanical tone, "What did GUS say?"

"Good observation. He agreed with you about that being the norm. But he insisted that it's a trap."

Isabelle fidgeted. She bounced around as if trying to contain a wild animal inside.

"Your constant movements tell me that you're likely to race through our conversation. Then you can't learn. I'll keep talking with you as long as you're paying attention to going slow. That's my need for when we talk."

She pressed her lips together. "Okay. I'll try."

"Even if many people act like life should be under control, let's examine the evidence. Look at the parallel between how strongly you think you should always have control and how harshly you treat yourself."

"I don't know. Maybe. So you're basically telling me to be passive and to let life go all to hell without even trying. Mom would've ripped me apart for that."

Passionate now, I reminded myself to keep a peaceful rhythm. "Most people, the same as you just did, look at actions on one end or the other, as if we should control everything or become totally passive. That's rigid thinking."

Her head flinched back slightly. "What the hell's left if it's neither of those?"

I motioned with my hands like I had just pulled a rabbit out of a hat. "Ta-da. Learning! Take time to pause and learn. Let your inner teacher lead you instead of reacting or repeating unhealthy behaviors."

With no hesitation, she asked, "Meaning?"

I shifted back on the bench and waited.

She rolled her eyes but gave a slight nod.

As if on cue, a flock of geese honked and flew overhead. We took several minutes to watch them circle and sail down to the lake. One after another they swished into the water with exquisite beauty. No territorial fighting. No collisions. Just an orderly group flowing with grace. *Makes me think of Hanna and the peace we felt on our many trips to the mountains.*

"Nothing like nature to help us become present and aware." I closed my eyes for a few seconds, which made Button's panting sound louder. "Difficulties provide opportunities to slow down, learn, and escape rigid thinking."

Her short, choppy phrases and turmoil in her face showed a battle to forge ahead at a slower pace. "How? No freakin' way. I couldn't learn a damn thing when panic hits! The attacks blindside me, and my heart thumps like it's going to explode. Then I just freeze. The only thing that comes to mind is to hide!"

Staying calm, I said, "Difficulties cause fight, flight, or learning in people. We both took flight during our overpowering situations. Once they hit, we were too overwhelmed to learn. But in a safe space like we have here, you can learn how to alleviate them."

"Alleviate? How?" she asked, her face blank.

"Learn that you're acceptable even when you don't meet expectations or have life under your thumb, instead of turning against yourself."

The fidgeting stopped and her head tilted. "How does that get rid of the panic?"

"Imagine not having those overpowering shoulds. Like the ones you pounded yourself with just before you had the attack in the kitchen."

She stopped and took a minute to reflect. Her body relaxed and her head bobbed several times. "I always freaked out the most when I didn't feel able to do what was expected of me. Failure wasn't an option. Because I wouldn't be accepted—I'd get blown away! By Mom, and by Dean."

I almost responded, but stayed quiet.

Her eyes studied something invisible. "That's the catastrophe. That is the panic! Trying to control something or do something to arrive at some picture-perfect place. And I'm afraid I'll be torn apart if I can't. Or thrown away."

Feeling like a proud parent, I gave time for that to sink in before I spoke. "And I saw you falling apart and didn't toss you aside. You saw me unraveling about my abuse, too. You didn't reject me. Well, for the most part." I had to get a jab in. Then I smiled. "We don't deserve being thrown away for failure or weakness."

She sat quietly shaking her head, but much calmer now. "The pressure's been enormous, and I couldn't see it. I never thought about learning something new. I only saw two options—striving for control or being some pathetic doormat."

I looked up, spotting the guy and little girl with the kite walking toward us. Up close, he looked like a linebacker. Bigger than I'd thought. Despite looking as solid as rock, softness showed in his eyes. Kindness. He greeted us, or maybe I should say, Isabelle, with a warm grin. "I'm Carlos. I wanted to say hi; and this is Emily. Great day to be out, isn't it?"

Warmth radiated throughout me when his little girl spoke in a high sweet voice. "Hello." Her eyes twinkled as she peeked out from behind him and gave a cheerful wave.

Isabelle blushed and sounded tongue-tied. "Yeah, hi. Uhm, awesome day. I'm Isabelle."

I gave a slight shake of the head. *Now there's two under that dazed, lalaland spell.* "Hi, I'm Gene. Glad to meet you." I shook his hand, then leaned down and shook Emily's, whose face brightened and cheeks colored.

Carlos hesitated, then repeated his earlier greeting. "Just wanted to say hi." Then he started slowly backing away down the path, but his eyes seemed unable to unlock from Isabelle's. "I suppose Emily and I will be going. Enjoy the rest of your day." As he ambled away, I raised my eyebrows at Isabelle.

She frowned and scolded me under her breath. "G, you're walking home if you don't put a lid on it!"

"I didn't say anything! And, hey, I'm the one with the keys." I jingled them to make my point.

Before I could react, she snatched them out of my hand and smirked.

UNLOCKED

"You snooze, you lose. Like I said, cool it, or you'll have a long stroll home."

Conditional Love – Gene

Over the past week, I wondered how Isabelle might be doing since the day in the park. I had apologized to her on the drive home and told her not to take me seriously about jumping into some romantic relationship while being married. I admitted to overdoing it with teasing occasionally, to which she answered with sarcasm, "You think?" We had also lost sight of talking about her hospital experience due to focusing on the panic attacks. But we both knew a breakthrough had happened.

Today, she came into the kitchen a little after 8 AM. Earlier than usual on a Saturday. I asked, "How'd things go at B & F Warehouse? Those hours add a lot to your week." She simply said "Fine," while her intense gaze showed something on her mind. Then I noticed a book in her hand. No title evident. The end of a pen jutted from it.

"Is that, by chance, a journal?" I asked.

She poured some coffee. "For Dr. Ledbetter's course. We're supposed to keep track of our experiences that relate to class topics. This past one focused on shame and conditional love."

"Interesting."

She sat down with her cup and started writing in the journal. After several minutes, she stopped. "Other lessons from the program are starting to click since we talked last Saturday. The more I learn, the more things seem connected." Words trailed off as her pen ramped up. Several minutes later, she closed her journal, took it to the end table by the sofa, and laid it down.

Returning to the side of the kitchen table, she stood, letting out a sigh, her face serious. "The pressure must have been off the charts for how mad I got at myself when I couldn't meet expectations. I see now that I carried a humongous load and lots of shame and it resulted from conditional love." She didn't explain, but her textbook comments told me that they were coming from class.

She's tuned in. Give her space. "Yep."

"I only felt safe with Grandma and you. Well, and my dad his last few months before dying. But Grandpa, Mom, and Dean acted as if they hated me unless I did what they wanted." She crossed her arms. "I couldn't see that it was conditional love until this week!"

"That's run of the mill for people—measure up or else expect repercussions when you don't. Like a tongue-lashing's justified when you fall short."

Isabelle shrugged and half-shook her whole body, maybe trying to shake off that old way of thinking. "I need to get out of here." I thought she meant out of her body, but then she asked, "Do you want to go to the park again today? Something seems right about being there."

"Sure. How about we take discs along, one for Button and one for us to throw?"

"Awesome. Does Button just chew on it, or does he play catch?"

"He gets more excited about playing catch than any treat I give him. Watch. Even with you here, he'll leave your feet when he sees his red disc."

I went to my bedroom and came out with a backpack of discs, pulling out Button's red one. He darted through the room and sat down, ready and waiting at my side as soon as it came into view. His eyes focused on the disc like his life depended on it. I gave it a small, wobbly toss across the living room. With the speed of a cheetah, Button took after it and leapt into the air, catching it in his teeth and returning it to me.

Isabelle sucked in a quick breath, her eyes scarcely blinking. "Did he come that way, or did you train him?"

I tried to appear nonchalant but probably sounded like a proud parent. "I trained him, but it didn't take much. He catches on quicker than a straight-A grad student."

I threw it a second time, Button leaping and catching it with ease again. Then I put the bite-riddled disc back into the pack. He never took his eyes off me as he walked by my side to the counter. "Do you want to swing by Subway instead of making sandwiches? I'm buying."

Isabelle's face lit up. "Let me get my sneakers."

After hurriedly throwing supplies into the cooler, Isabelle returned to her room a second time. I wondered for what. Then, just before going out the door, she stopped. "How about I drive today." She stated it more as a directive than a question.

Her sudden change reminded me of when GUS tried to redirect me at Dean's and her place—when I should have listened. *Hmm.* I said, "Go big or go home."

She rolled her eyes and headed out the door with Button and me following. I didn't know what the eye-roll pertained to, but I figured we were used to each other by now.

After we got in her car, she spoke in a distant voice. "I felt like I could never be me. I had to be different for everybody else. You know what I mean?"

"You can't be your true self when you feel unsafe like you did with your mom and Dean."

She started the car and eased onto the street, her head tilted. "I never heard anyone talk about true self. Not even in my program. Cool. That nails it for me."

I got passionate. "Your true self becomes more present as you gain awareness of what's you and not you. And being open and honest reveals what's inside. It sheds light so you can learn and grow into who you're meant to be. That's what you said you wanted. Don't you feel more alive talking like this? Living in your true self changes the world."

Isabelle stared at me, the car swerving across the line and back. "That's freaky that you just used other words from the Chicago song."

She struggled to reach something in her pocket, not swerving as much this time. "I grabbed this at the last minute. They're *Saturday in the Park* lines—words about waiting, reaching and touching each other, and now you just added the other ones about changing the world. It feels uncanny that today is Saturday, we're going to the park again, and the song makes me feel free and alive! All of it's unreal." She shook her head, probably trying to take in this often-undervalued invisible world.

My heart sped up when I saw the lines she had written. "Can't you see that the universe is waving a flag for your attention?"

Her voice came from a faraway place. "It feels weird looking at life this way—like an old TV show my mom watched called *The Twilight Zone*. Different realities happened at the same time. I don't know if I trust any of this, but something epic is happening. I just don't know what the hell that is."

I stayed quiet in case she had more to say.

Using a previous line of mine, she asked, "How much do I owe you?"

I teased back. "Ozone talks are free."

"I'm ready to let loose and enjoy the day. Maybe later I'll tell you what happened at the hospital."

After picking up subs and drinks, we both seemed to disappear into some inner world. Silence felt right.

Reflecting on last week, I pictured less turmoil on Isabelle's face than when she had first moved into my place. More carefree. Like she had been locked up for most of her life and was now emerging from prison.

GUS spoke: *She's awakening.* That warmed me and caused me to see beauty everywhere on the way to the park. Life felt rich to me, as if a cloud of peace enveloped me. I watched a young child help his mother push a baby in a stroller. His high chin and satisfied smile made me chuckle. Not far in front of them, a couple, arm in arm, walked down the sidewalk captivated by one another. Across the other side of the street, a man with a sweat-soaked T-shirt talked with a shop owner while remodeling the front of her shop. His frown told me that he had been trying to straighten the warped window frame he held in his hands. Perhaps he realized he simply needed to replace the old frame.

Isn't that how life is sometimes? Some things in us are usable, but other things need to be replaced. We generally try our best, but more inside us is warped than we know. Hmm. Hanna would have told me to speak for myself. And Isabelle would, too.

Smiling at the thought of relaxing outside on this beautiful day, I wanted to take it all in. I wanted to notice it. Fully. Especially Isabelle's hospital experience, if she still felt inclined to tell me. Something told me her story would be profound.

Jumping in with clarity beyond my regular thinking, GUS said, *It's real. Learn from the details.*

Connection – Isabelle

My body tingled on the way to the park as I absorbed the world around me. I felt alert and alive. But, somehow, calm, too. The smell of cut grass, the sound of the car engine, the touch of the steering wheel against my hands, and the sight of people and activities along the way seemed similar to my enhanced HD episode at the hospital. Just not as sensational or life-altering. Then my intense desire to drive today struck me. *That's never happened before. Hmm. It's crazy how relaxed I am. Rusty car and all, I don't care what people think. Maybe I'm ready to be in the driver's seat instead of others always taking me for a ride. Oh... give me a freakin' break, I'm getting more like G every day.*

Seconds later, I forgot about driving and started reminiscing about the past. I gave a soft shake of my head about various directions my life had taken, marrying Dean being one of them. But the head-shake had no judgment, just the naked reality of what happened. *The messed-up choices I've made...at least I'm learning not to hate myself.*

My mind drifted to how self-conscious I had always been about my car. Or should I say how ashamed? I remember counting my money and realizing that I had enough to get the one I had spotted at Jenson's Used Cars. Giddy after driving it home from the lot, I couldn't stop smiling. Or staring at it—a 12-year-old, rusted-out Chevy. Red, my favorite color! Well, other than the rust over the wheel wells. My parents came out to see it sitting in the driveway. Dad gave a thumbs up. Mom just stood there with a sour face and hands on her hips, then turned without saying a word and went back into the house. I didn't care because I had paid for it, which meant it was one thing she couldn't control.

I heard the exhaust getting louder on the way to school the day after buying it. Probably a hole, I had thought. On a high about owning my own car and getting freer from mom, I shrugged it off and felt ready to take on the world.

UNLOCKED

A large group of students stood under the huge tree near the school's back entrance, smoking cigarettes, and watching everyone come into the parking area. Barely able to sit still in the seat, I pulled up to the curb. Grinning and waving at them, I assumed that they'd be happy for me. But they burst out laughing—bent over with hands on their knees and all that. I shrunk right in front of them as their obnoxious and degrading tone penetrated me like invisible tentacles latching onto my heart and mind. "What a bomb. You're lucky that junk heap doesn't collapse!"

I laughed with them to cover up how, inside, I curled up into a fetal position. I couldn't shake off their piercing insults, and it continued an ever-mounting inward retreat after that. That debilitating event, in hindsight, forged an unbreakable vow—a promise to myself that kept expanding well beyond being protected from Mom: *Never let my guard down. Stay hidden.* After that day, I always parked at the side lot and entered school from that entrance to avoid being seen in my car.

It's been right in front of my face the whole time! Only acceptable if... I wonder how much of my fear and pain really comes from that freakin' demon. From conditional love.

As my mind came back to the present, driving with G beside me, a picture started showing. Things were connecting: hearing about G's life, facing my past, listening to the Chicago song and to Dr. Ledbetter's recent lecture, and being jolted by G's larger-than-life words about true self. Each of these was playing a part, pushing me forward on the path I saw that night in the sky. Or wherever I had gone when they jump-started my heart. In spite of feeling oblivious at points since starting over, somehow that high-definition glimpse of a path meant for me is taking place. Life…maybe God or the universe…or whatever…seems to be showing me that. And I don't even know how I feel about any of that voodoo shit yet.

I just know that I know, like the night at the hospital. And that's enough for now.

Windows rolled down and feeling the breeze as we coasted into Landsburg Park, I felt no shame about my car. Still mystified by how connected everything seemed, I looked around before getting out. *What an awesome day!* Ducks searching for food in the grass. Sun shining.

White, puffy clouds against the deep blue sky. Flowers showing off. And G sitting beside me not saying a word. *Maybe some inner world's taking him for a ride, too.*

Making our way to the picnic area without talking, we unloaded the cooler and sat down under the pavilion. Sub in hand, I noticed the birds chirping and the sun glistening through the waving leaves. Button sat upright on the grass with his back to us, like a king watching over his kingdom. I guess he realized that no suffering souls needed care today.

Taking our time and eating quietly, we finished our subs and chilled a bit. I asked, "You want to hear my epic tale?"

"You said you wanted to let loose for a while."

"Thought we did. I just get these energy surges when my mind goes to what happened in the ICU."

"Anytime you're ready, I'd love to hear it." G leaned forward, his words faster than usual and his face intent. Alert.

"How do you do that?"

"What?" he asked.

"I know you're dying to hear what happened. But you kept waiting instead of harassing me about it. I've never met anyone that patient."

"I want people to make their own choices without pressure. But I can't wait. GUS said to learn from the details."

I tensed. "Damn, what if you think my story's ridiculous?"

"Isabelle, be you and you'll be fine."

"But I've always seen others as crazy when they tell bizarre stories, and now it's me."

He mocked. "Yeah, now you're the one pulling the voodoo shit."

I flattened my eyes at him. "Yeah, but you hear voices."

I loved giving him grief. Connecting that way helped me to feel less guilty about cutting him off during my mad-at-the-world years.

"One other thing," G said, "GUS' words made me want to hear what you felt like. For you to describe it in detail."

"It feels imprinted in my mind. I couldn't forget anything about it, even if I tried." Already shaking my head, an electric current flowed through my body as I imagined being there again. "It felt unreal. It might have been one of those near-death experiences you hear people talking about. I don't know why they call them near-death when somebody actually dies and comes back. Like I did. I'd think they'd call them death-experiences."

G wet his lips, waiting but not taking his focus off me for a nanosecond.

"Everything stayed blurred at first, not from drinking. It was weird. I don't know how, but somehow I knew that the fuzziness had always been with me and kept me from seeing what's real. That's crazy, I know."

"It's okay," G said. "Go ahead. Tell it in your own way."

"Then everything cleared. At first, from above the ICU, I watched all the doctors and nurses running into the room and starting to work on me. Dr. Hamilton, the doc you met afterwards, wore her black-framed glasses. Not the ones she wore the next day when she talked to us. She came into the ICU and yelled orders to the others while they hooked me up to machines. Two of them called my name a few times, pleading with me to return. That made me want to go back to my body."

G's eyes got big as he listened.

"But that's when things got insanely bright and clear. Like LED lights compared to old fashioned light bulbs, except way more. Then the hospital room and staff faded into the background while a cloud of white light surrounded me. Not a tunnel like people usually describe, but more of a cocoon. The light engulfed everything. Permeated everything. Like everything was alive and connected."

G gave a gentle, assuring nod. "You remember, in the past, I told you that I saw everything as connected? White light connected it all."

"Cool. You hadn't said before about it being white light. But that fits. When it was happening, I knew without doubt that everything was connected there, and here, too. We just can't see those connections."

G stayed quiet. His searching eyes made me wonder where his mind went. I asked, "Do you have anything to add?"

"Yes, that triggered something. I'll tell you when you're finished. I don't want to distract you."

G remained focused and waiting, so I continued. "Even though I never believed in an afterlife, I thought this could be it, and that I had died. But I wasn't afraid. I felt light, as if I was floating. Free and peaceful, too, with no strain at all. Beyond anything I could've ever imagined."

G's eyes twinkled as he gave a subtle grin and lowered a cheek into his left hand.

"Enamored by all the beauty around me, I wanted to stay. Especially because I felt completely at rest. At one with all of it. But I knew I had to go back."

He stayed silent. The memory of school students laughing about my car came to mind. I tightened and fidgeted as Button came over and nestled against my feet. "You might think I was dreaming or hallucinating because of the alcohol. But you have to believe me. It felt more real than anything I had ever experienced. More real than anything here."

He assured me. "I believe you. I don't think you hallucinated or imagined it. You know that I've had unusual experiences like you're describing, although not to that degree. But I want to hear exactly what happened."

Relaxing again, knowing that he believed me, I got back in touch with that eventful night. "After I adjusted more to being there, the love and safety I felt, inside and out, overwhelmed me. It felt tangible, like soaking in a tub of perfectly heated hot chocolate on a cold, winter night. I know you could ask how I knew it was love and safety. I just did. I never experienced security and love that saturated my whole body. No fears or weight of the world on me. I could let down and just be me. It's what I always wanted. Words can't explain it."

"Fascinating," G said, his elbows leaning on his side of the picnic table and studying me.

"Then I saw pictures similar to a fast-paced high-definition movie whirling by. I watched endless glimpses of my life, even bad memories, but I didn't feel ashamed. Just love. When everything registered, I couldn't deny how I had thrown away the real me." I took a breath. "That changed me. It made me want to be true to myself no matter what. I didn't know where all that clarity came from, but I knew that I knew. I get that it'd be easy to write it off as some insane dream."

He wagged his head. "Not at all. It makes sense to me. Sometimes, not all the time, I experience a more distinct knowing or clarity when GUS speaks to me."

I studied him for a moment, taking that in before going on. "When those clear pictures of my past sunk in, I saw that I had lived in fear—

fear of messing up, fear of being judged, fear of being alone, and even fear of being me—that my decisions came mostly from fear. I hid. And after our talks and the timely lecture from school, I realized my biggest one: that I'd be rejected if I didn't meet expectations. I was afraid of conditional love."

G shook his head. "It's amazing that our earlier talk tied into your spiritual experience. That's what I'd call it."

I joked. "Yeah, these coincidences are freaking me out. But I saw with every ounce of my being that I'm supposed to be true to me. That we all are, and I'm meant to help others do that." After a lengthy pause, I sighed. "Then, after all of that settled, I heard one of the doctors or nurses cry out. 'Isabelle, come back to us!' I knew I had to return, but I didn't want to. That's all I remember. Nothing at all after I floated down and rejoined my body on the table. Does that last whole part make sense?"

"Very much." G's whole body nodded, reminding me of Button wagging his entire rear end when he was happy. "It fits with what GUS has taught me during times of extra clarity. Keep watching your life for how things connect to that experience."

I breathed out a few long breaths, having had one person hear my story and not write me off as some lunatic.

True Self — Isabelle

Lost in my story about getting a second chance at life, I had zoned out about where I was. Glancing at the pavilion and Button resting against my feet reminded me that G and I were at Landsburg Park. We planned to throw discs after talking. As soon as we got up from our benches, Button rose to attention. I wouldn't have been surprised if his paw had saluted us. I unhitched his leash while his eyes remained fixed on us, probably watching for the red disc.

G pointed at the backpack sitting on the other end of the table. "Do you want to do the honors?" Button stood motionless, waiting like a saint for the glorious coming.

After I grabbed the unmistakable one with tooth-marks, Button rushed to my feet. Casually moving into the open area with him darting around at my side, I came to a halt. He sat as still as a statue. I gave the disc a hard snap and gasped, thinking I threw it too far for him to reach. He chased it down with lightning speed, then bounded into the air with the grace of an antelope. Snatching the airborne streak as if he had done it a thousand times, he landed and spun all in one motion, carrying it back, not to me, but to G. Before he got to him, G pointed at me, saying, "Button!"

Like an arrow, G's energetic companion shot across the grass until he reached me. Then he sat, holding the disc loosely in his mouth. I took it and waited a moment. Wanting to see how fast he'd catch on, I threw it another direction. Just as beautifully as before, Button overtook his hovering red treasure and leapt into the air, seizing it and returning to me. Taking the disc, this time I faked one direction while turning the other and throwing it to G, who caught it. Button adjusted in an instant, ran full tilt, then stopped at G's feet and sat.

G looked over at me. I swear that his smug face oozed, *Wait until you see this.* He threw at such a high angle that the disc almost sailed back to where he stood. Button caught on immediately. After running about ten yards, he pivoted and returned to within a few steps of G, snagging the diving red saucer from the air before it landed. Button, G, and I had a blast for the next half hour.

"This'll be it," G said, wagging the bite-marked prize in the air. "I like stopping when he shows that he still wants to play. That way he's eager for the next time."

After launching the last one and waiting for Button to retrieve it, he sat back down at the picnic table and asked, "Anything more to your story?"

I reflected for a moment. "Even before it ended, I knew I'd have help. That stayed in my mind even when I came to. Seeing you in front of me when I opened my eyes blew me away. It all made sense. You were the perfect person to help me learn to be me. It couldn't have been just a coincidence. Then, only weeks later, the Chicago song floored me, how it tied into my new path, about living with purpose and changing the world."

I couldn't help harassing him. "Don't let it go to your head. The part about helping a guy wasn't about you specifically."

His gaze distant, G barely acknowledged my dig. So I went with it, staring out at the lake without saying anything for a few minutes. The gentle breeze soothed me, the quiet of the park lulling me into a mellow state of mind. Only then did I hear birds chirping in the distance, and faint voices of children laughing and playing. Those sounds, too, gradually began to fade into the background.

In the stillness, something dawned on me, my mind ramping up from a zen-like space to buzzing with energy. "This all ties into what you said about true self, doesn't it?"

G's focus finally shifting, he turned toward me. "Go ahead. Say what you're thinking. All the details."

"Changing the world happens through changing people's lives. But that starts with ourselves, when we learn to be who we are. Who we're meant to be." I paused, my thoughts still bubbling up. "You said that living in my true self means learning what's me and not me."

He waited.

Scarcely able to contain myself, I fumbled with what I wanted to say, pouring out my words in choppy phrases. "Remember, in the past, that I asked about GUS, about what inside you is in touch with that higher presence you talked about?"

"Yup," he said as he tilted his head and studied me.

"After being saturated in that brilliant cocoon, I wanted to say that people are connected to the light. That I'm connected to that light and higher presence! But I didn't say it because I knew it wasn't all of me. Knowing everything I do now, I'd say it's the really true me—what you call true self—who's connected to that higher presence. When the intense connection happened, I knew that the true me wasn't just in touch with the light, but part of it!"

G's eyes got big. "Holy stars. That gives me a nugget to chew on."

"In that higher clarity, I saw that living in fear caused me to feel disconnected. And alone. Now I know it was because I wasn't really being me. I had separated from my true self. That's why I came back wanting to change my life and be the real me."

G's face got serious as he cautioned me. "That's great, but don't lose sight of how. You keep growing into your true self not by trying to change yourself, but by having the courage and integrity to be authentic."

His clarity jolted me. After what I had experienced, that nailed it. But it scared me, too. "And what if I'm not brave enough?"

"Get support. Find safe people who want authenticity, emotions and all. Support helps you to be brave."

Taking a breather to let that sink in, I looked over at the kite area. It struck me that I had been hoping to see Carlos, the guy from last week. Two people were flying kites, but not him.

"You looking for the hunk you saw last time?"

G caught me. I tried to play it off, but I'm sure I turned red. "Give me a break. You're still harassing me about that guy? Don't you have better things to do than rag on me?"

Smirking and bobbing his head, he made big eyes. "Just thought you might be looking for him."

I shook my head. *Lighten up. Time to start practicing not giving a rip what people think, even if he's just busting on me.* I said nothing.

After reflecting more, I sighed. "I came back knowing that we're all connected by light. We're just blind to that here."

G's eyes roamed for a moment. "That's one of the things your experience taught me. You said that only your true self was part of the light. Which means being authentic or transparent connects us, and hiding or putting on false fronts disconnects us."

A burst of clarity exploded in my mind. "Looking back over my life when I was above the ICU, my mistakes seemed exaggerated to make them easier to see. After Grandma and Dad died, I tried to keep a lid on all the pain. I hid, cuttin' off everyone and livin' as a freakin' zombie."

G nodded. "Everything good came to a halt. I'm sure you felt alone."

"I did. I even stopped painting, which was my one lifeline beyond Grandma. Well, and you. I floated like a dead leaf in the wind. Pullin' back sucked the life out of me."

G tilted his head. "I had forgotten that you painted." He sat up straighter, his face brightening. "Holy coming-to-life party, you're awakening! At blazing speed. That means that the voodoo shit's overtaking you."

I got up and punched his shoulder.

He yelled, his eyes widening. "Ow, that hurt!"

I mocked his voice. "Ow, that hurt!" Then I grabbed Button's leash. "I'm ready to pack it up if you are. I gotta add more to my journal."

Or Else — Isabelle

The holiday season and semester break flew by. I had aced everything in the fall except *Interviewing Skills I*. Sailhammer had given me a B, which made me mad. Her syllabus had weighted the clinical component the heaviest. That told me that my skills in the role-play with Haley last semester still hadn't satisfied her.

Fortunately, my regular talks with G seemed to be helping me feel more secure. At least panic attacks hadn't been occurring. But, midweek, I found myself biting my lip and hesitating at Dr. Sailhammer's doorway when I saw her typing. She had emailed me to set up a meeting, giving no clues about why. My mind wouldn't stop racing since then, imagining the worst.

Glancing up, she told me to take a seat while she typed the last of her unfinished thoughts. Finally, she turned her chair toward me and leaned forward. My heart skipped a beat when I saw her serious face. "Isabelle, I consulted with my colleagues about your situation."

My situation? What situation? I'm sure that my rapid blinking gave me away. I thought I had made progress. I waited for her to explain.

"The department recognizes your excellent academic work."

Her voice made me think of a train on its tracks that hadn't gotten to its destination. I braced.

"I provided them with an overview of your clinical skills. I emphasized how you've shown glimpses of exceptional ability, but that it's noticeably hindered by countertransference issues. That's why you received a B. Obviously, you will continue in my Interviewing Skills II course that you are currently taking. But after their input, we decided to require personal counseling if you want to continue in the clinical track."

My mouth opened. I felt hot.

She pursed her lips and crossed her arms. "You're welcome to choose another track and not go for therapy. But if you want to continue in the clinical specialization, that means going for personal counseling."

I told myself to keep cool and not sound defensive. Or angry. "I thought I had made progress clinically, and I already took steps to face my issues."

Undeterred in the slightest, she persisted. "You made a little progress clinically. The faculty want what's best for you, and our profession requires us to be gatekeepers of clinicians entering the field. We take pride in our clinical program and want our students at the top of their game when they graduate. And those steps you've taken? Where did you go for counseling?"

Her eyebrows went up about an inch when I hesitated. "As I thought. You told me that you know Gene Singleton. From what I know of him, I'm sure you've touched on issues at times. But formal counseling makes a difference. It sharpens your skills and clarity for working with clients."

Still reeling from the unexpected blow, I asked, "So you're saying that, if I don't get formal counseling somewhere, I'm booted from the clinical track?"

"I had hoped that you wouldn't respond negatively to the news. We don't want to lose you from the clinical program. I personally think it's where you belong. That's if you want it badly enough. If you're not willing to use this as a growing opportunity, you need to choose another specialization or not continue. It's your choice. Faculty members conferred as a group to determine what will help you the most, and this is the consensus."

I gritted my teeth at her lingering words. *If you want it badly enough.* Sailhammer sounded so calloused about it. Feeling numb, I tried to stay afloat as she explained the rest of the requirements. Always acting with purpose, she pressed ahead as I sank deeper into some ocean of no return. By the time she finished, I had been listening from underwater, her voice barely audible.

I hoped I didn't miss anything irretrievable. She said she'd put it in writing. Still staggered by this turn of events, I stood slowly, hoping my legs would work. Then, grabbing my backpack and slinking out the door, I mumbled to myself. "At least I escaped this 'life sentence' without the added humiliation of a panic attack."

Glancing once at G in his recliner when I opened the door, I mostly avoided eye contact. I tried to sound upbeat. "Something smells good." I reached down and petted Button, hoping G wouldn't suspect I was struggling.

"Meatloaf. You're hauling a ball-and-chain behind you. What's up?"

"Nothing. Just got some busy work to do."

"You're hiding. If you don't want to talk now, fine. But if you want to keep being your true self, you'll want to voice what's bothering you at some point. Remember about being authentic?"

I scowled at him. "Damn, G, lighten up."

He gave me space and got up to set the table. I took my backpack to my room. Button pranced around me the whole way. Then we hugged and loved on each other for several minutes. I called out to G. "The warm fuzzies from Button are unreal. Talk about unconditional love."

I heard him respond. "Yep, he's a walking blankey. Supper's on, if you're up for it."

After washing my hands, I returned to the kitchen, and sat down to eat with him. As usual, Button rested against my feet. I forked some meatloaf and broccoli onto my plate, wondering where to begin. "Had a meeting with my advisor today. I would've had a panic attack if I hadn't learned from you about unhooking from pressure to meet expectations. At least I'm trying not to rip into myself." I took several bites.

"The meeting didn't go well?"

"Sailhammer's so anal."

"What happened?" he asked.

"She said I haven't made enough clinical progress and that I need to deal with my countertransference issues or I won't be able to continue in my specialization. The only other option would be to choose another track. But I want clinical. I practically begged her to change her mind and told her that I've already taken steps to deal with my baggage. She didn't give a rip. She suspected I hadn't gone for formal counseling and said I won't reach my best without it."

He winced. "That's a bummer, especially when you've been facing some issues."

"Yeah, the timing sucks." I let out a sigh of frustration. "I was pumped about my progress. Thought I was in the clear, but it's never enough. That's the story of my life."

"Like you need to be more than you are."

I huffed. "That's how she treated me! She told me I need a letter from a counselor verifying my progress or else I get the boot."

"That would be scary. It flies in the face of you trying to unhook from pressure."

I stayed quiet as we ate. Then I went to the fridge, poured another glass of water from the pitcher, and plopped back down onto my chair. "This is conditional love—the 'or else.' Isn't it?"

"It'd be normal to feel trapped and pressured in your situation."

I jumped in. "And what's your but?"

G went slow. "But conditional love gives you no choice. You have to do well, or you get treated like you're unacceptable. But your advisor is giving you a choice, even if it's difficult. You can get counseling and continue, or you can decide not to and switch tracks. That doesn't make you unacceptable."

I gave another huff. "This is messed up. I thought you'd side with me."

After waiting a minute, he spoke with a soft voice. "Isabelle, it's scary when you feel pressure to face the demons inside."

My tone mechanical, I asked, "What's your bigger point? I know you have one."

"You remember in your ICU story, how light connected everything—there and here?"

I hesitated. "Yeah."

"The 'or else' choice is an example of what seems bad to you at the moment."

I gasped. "What do you mean, seems bad? It's bogus. Sailhammer's throwing her weight around, even though she claimed the department made the decision. It's not fair."

"Give yourself time to feel what you need to feel. But when we were eating in silence, GUS told me it's good timing. It's connected. And it's for a bigger purpose. So I'd encourage you to learn what you can through it."

About to let out another flurry of words, I closed my mouth and stopped, then spoke with a somber tone. "I know enough to take it seriously when GUS tells you something, like when he warned you right before Dean hit you. But I still think the timing sucks. How can it be good timing when I was already learning?"

"I want to tell you about my two friends. That okay?"

I let out more air. "Pfff, yeah. What do I have to lose?"

"They're perfect for helping you learn to be authentic. They're twins—the brother is an existential counselor and the sister, like me, mentors people about living in their true self."

I rolled my eyes. "Well, don't expect a high-five. I just need time to think."

"I can see that the pressure to do what your advisor wants touches old wounds. I agree, space will help. Are you okay if I add one or two more thoughts, not as pressure, just as input for your decision-making?"

I waited awhile to answer, then couldn't help being sarcastic. "Might as well throw me a big freakin' lifeline."

G burst out laughing, which caused me to laugh. After the chuckling died down, he shook his head and continued.

"Even if your advisor hadn't required counseling, I had been meaning to mention my friends. They're just what you need."

I gave my best skeptical look.

"Both of them show more compassion than anyone I know. At some point, just say the word if you want me to check with them. The brother would formally fulfill your advisor's requirement. His sister wouldn't, but she would be another mentor about true self. She'd be a great role-model for you. What do you think?"

"Don't press it," I sighed, with a weak smile. "Sailhammer got pushy and I dug in my heels."

A Dream – Gene

The next week flew by without any follow-up from Isabelle. Pressing her wouldn't help, so I kept telling myself to let it go.

Saturday morning, she came to the kitchen brighter than a rainbow after a storm. "Hey, G. Smells awesome out here. I could breathe in this cloud of bliss all day long." She poured some coffee, sat down, and looked at me. "Sorry about taking it out on you after my meeting with Sailhammer. Didn't know it at the time, but I felt a lot of shame about not measuring up again. Plus, I didn't want to get sacked from clinical."

"Thanks. It's understandable, though. You were up against a wall."

"Yeah, you were right. Old wounds again."

Baiting her, I asked, "What were those words again?"

Her puzzled face told me that she didn't catch my drift about "me being right." At first. Then she frowned but seemed to take the jesting in stride.

Still bubbling with energy, she went to the cabinet and grabbed the quick oats, something I got her started on. After pouring almond milk on a hefty bowl of oats, she sprinkled blueberries on top. Sitting down, she took a bite, and sounded like a commercial. "Great way to start the day!"

"I like them better than cooked oats."

"Me, too. You want to hear my dream?"

"Sure," I said. "I love to see what stands out in dreams."

"I used to be afraid of what you'd zero in on. But I want to know what you see in it—a vivid one, kind of HD again."

"All the better. Glad to say what I notice."

She took the plunge without even taking a breath. "You know how things were with my mom—it happened the same way in the dream. Blasting away, screaming her head off that I'd always be a failure. She said my art was shit, and that thinking I could counsel people was a joke. She fired like an automatic weapon, shrieking over and over that my professors would only let me through the program because they felt sorry for me."

I made a pained face and wagged my head. "I'd call that a nightmare, being torn down like that. I imagine it left you with a bad taste when you woke up."

"That's just it. It didn't," she said. "Something clicked in the dream."

"Interesting. Like what?"

"I didn't argue with her at all. I didn't say anything until she finished ranting. It's as if her attack had no effect on me."

I sat quietly, taking that in.

"Then, when the onslaught ended, I said I didn't need to prove anything to her anymore, or to anyone else. I told her I'd only stop by if she treated me with respect. And that anytime she ripped into me, I'd be outta there—that I wouldn't let her treat me like garbage anymore. I told her I had drug-free people in my life, healthy ones who'd support me. Then I split."

My mouth fell open. "Holy new move! Talk about breaking old patterns."

"Mom looked like it sunk in when I said, 'healthy people.' What's crazy is the healthy people were you and the twins you mentioned. Just don't get a big head."

I waited for her to finish.

"What I didn't tell you is that before hitting the sack last night, I made the decision to meet with your two friends."

I couldn't stop smiling. "You'll never regret that decision. Isn't it interesting? Last night you merely chose to add support, and the dream shows that you already felt more of it."

"That is weird how that happened!" She shook her head as she mumbled something about coincidences again.

"That's a new decision compared to your past."

She tilted her head. "You mean not allowing support from people in the past caused me not to feel support inside me, too?"

"Exactly. That's my own experience with my friends. And after opening up with you, too, about not believing I should have any needs, I felt as if I mattered more. I felt less alone and more solid than I ever have. More secure inside."

Shaking her head again, she went on. "The security felt tangible in the dream, like the three of you made me stronger. My mom's poison didn't have power over me. I didn't need her approval."

I nodded. "I bet that felt really good." I couldn't help myself. "Look what the bad-advisor thing sparked: the 'or else' that you first saw as destructive to being your true self."

She grimaced, acknowledging my point. "I couldn't see it at the time. It felt like the opposite of what I needed."

Recognizing a teachable moment, I said, "Life brings everything you need for growth when you work with it to learn instead of fighting it."

She wrinkled her face. "Yeah, what a tall task, living that way." She paused, then refocused. "After I woke up, the dream still felt real. It still does, like it pertains to my life right now. It got me pumped about meeting your friends. I feel afraid to talk to a counselor about the mom issues, though—putting myself in a stranger's hands and being interrogated with a spotlight on me. I'm exaggerating, but it feels that way to me."

I encouraged her. "It's scary taking that first step with someone you don't know. But the dream may be playing out the security you'll experience as you gain their support. I'll let my friends know that you'll be in touch."

Freud's Penetrating Eyes — Isabelle

Two weeks after my dream I walked down the hallway from the receptionist's desk at Landsburg's *Holistic Health*. Composed of four wings that focused on nutritional, physical, psychological, and medical health, the modern-looking clinic treated people holistically through professionals communicating across disciplines for better outcomes.

Fidgety, I glanced at the pictures of people hanging on the yellow walls. I paused to study one, not able to stop chewing my lip or tapping the glistening, hard-tiled floor with my foot.

That's freaky! Freud, I assumed, the bearded, intellectual-looking man in the picture. I vaguely remembered seeing him in one of my textbooks. His penetrating eyes appeared to follow me as I started walking again. *What am I getting myself into?*

I saw the number eight above the open office door that the receptionist had indicated. She told me the counselor's name: Mr. Matar. *What nationality is that?* I felt more naked now than the day Button flung open G's bathroom door. And, more frazzled, like pulling one loose end would unravel everything.

I dreaded talking about heavy issues with some guy I didn't know. *Bet he has a big beard and looks intellectual. Probably eccentric, too… well, like G.* I managed a slight chuckle, trying to keep things light. But my nerves tingled like little soldiers running around inside my body on high alert.

I poked my head around the doorway. A dark-haired, dark-skinned man stood at a desk, searching through some papers. He appeared to be in his mid-thirties and was missing part of his left arm.

I swallowed the lump in my throat. The added unknown variables on top of the unpredictability of counseling made me shudder.

I knocked on the door frame, feeling wobbly—like Jell-O—and afraid that unknown parts of me might squish out in places as we talked.

He looked up and smiled. Immediately, I noticed his eyes. They looked kind and gentle beyond words. As if he'd have no other thought during a crisis than to get others to safety. *There's only one place I've ever felt that safe. Button...That's right; G said he's compassionate.*

"You must be Isabelle." His tone showed no pretense. Warmth radiated across the room. "So, you know Gene. He told me you'd be calling for an appointment."

"Yeah, I call him G. We've known each other for a few years." I glanced away, my feet shuffling in place—part of that Jell-O squishing out. I disliked new situations. Especially being in the spotlight from years of being under Mom's scrutiny. *Bet it won't take long for that topic to come up.*

"I'm Abdul Hakeem Matar. Everyone calls me Abdul Hakeem. I look forward to knowing you," he said as he came out from behind his desk and shook my right hand. I tried not to gape at his partial arm. I wondered why he didn't have a prosthetic.

He asked me to sit down in one of the two chairs angled toward a third, which I assumed was his. A rich golden and rouge-colored rug lay between them and a small round table with a lamp stood on one side. With, of course, a tissue box on it. The office appeared welcoming. Interesting pictures, a number of plants, and an artificial ficus tree in the corner. The diverse people in the pictures, some of them children, showed various expressions...as contrasted with the sterile-looking pictures in the hallway. That eased my heart rate a few beats after being creeped out by Freud's eyes following me.

I took a big breath and sat down as he put a few papers in a desk drawer. I thought that practicing counseling with peers at LU, from both the counselor and client perspective, would have prepared me for this. But the thought of confessing my life's garbage with a stranger made me lightheaded. Even nauseated. I expected that what I'd say would get shot down. As I settled and waited for him to join me, the thought struck me. *Oh, my mom again.*

Calm and soft-spoken, he sat down and told me I'd receive counseling at a quarter of the cost after this first session. Probably after seeing my blank face, he offered a fuller explanation. "I don't know if Gene told you, but he initiated a possible arrangement: LU provides clinical interns for the center in exchange for counseling LU social work students at a reduced cost. I liked that idea, so I approached LU and the center's director about it. They both approved it, for all sessions after the initial one."

That thrilled me. I almost had to pry my fingers off the credit card when I had handed it to the receptionist—the equivalent of a day and a half of part-time work at B & F.

Abdul Hakeem reviewed confidentiality and other logistics, which I had already practiced in my interviewing class at LU. As he talked, his eyes and tone of voice conveyed deep sensitivity. Beyond-normal care. I couldn't have imagined anyone humbler and safer than him.

Finally, he prodded me. "I'd like you to start with what matters to you. What motivated you to come for counseling?"

Still tense, I started. "Well, my advisor told me I needed to face my countertransference issues if I want to continue in the clinical program." I handed him my department's verification form. He glanced at it, nodded, and laid it aside.

"Thank you for your honesty. You don't look upset about it, but some people could feel rejected after hearing that from their advisor." His tone, soft, showed no judgment.

"I guess I did at first. I didn't think of it as rejection. But I'm cool with it now."

"Your advisor's requirement tells me you likely carry pain that prevents you from being present with clients. But it still doesn't tell me what you want. Your advisor got you here. That's not the same as what interests you most."

I chewed my lip. "Don't I need to talk about loss and other past issues to get through my program?"

"While that may be true, counseling works best when you start with what you care about—when you begin with your energy and areas of importance. Dealing with loss and other pain will likely tie into that along the way. If you didn't have to do what your advisor wants, what's most important to you?"

Not yet buying I could simply talk about what I wanted to, I hesitated. Then, like water seeping through a crack, I said, "Maybe the new path I'm on?"

"Wonderful! That's what I'd like to hear about. Everything about that path—what started you on that journey and what interests you about it."

I sat there stunned. I hadn't previously seen counseling as constantly hooking into people's energy. Into what matters most to them. But he wanted me to talk about what mattered to me: my hospital experience and about learning to be my true self!

After twenty minutes of talking about that epic night, my new path, and briefly about my background, Dean, and Mom, I felt relaxed. Unusually calm. Halfway through, I told him what I thought about counseling. "This feels a lot like talking with a good friend about things you can't tell most people. Except you listen a lot better and you get it, like G."

His tone sounded matter-of-fact. "Effective relationships ought to do that."

"You also mention what you notice about how I say things. G's the only other person that does that. I learn more when he does."

"Yes, that increases awareness. Gene told me you're observant. That's going to make you a great counselor."

"He told me that, too. But my advisor said that personal pain hinders my effectiveness."

He tilted his head. "You sound as if you question that."

"I guess I do. I'm probably just afraid to uncover that mess. It's crazy, I'm in social work and I still don't trust that talking about issues always works like it should. I keep thinking I'm an exception. That I'm unreachable. But I'll give it a go if it helps me be my true self."

He studied me. "You come alive every time you mention your true self—several times when you talked about your experience in the hospital, and just now again. Your passion to understand it might be the motivation you need for facing those 'unreachable' areas." He made quotation marks with his fingers.

"And not facing those areas hinders my true self?" I knew the answer but still wanted to hear what he said about it.

"Yes. You prevent fulfillment anytime you cut off a part of you—through hiding or ignoring those parts or simply through living inauthentically. You cut off awareness and learning." He paused and then probed. "What does true self mean to you?"

"Me being me." I said it as if it was as simple as clipping on a nametag. "Nobody's ever asked me that before. But I want to be true to myself, instead of putting on a different face to fit whatever the next person wants."

"Good. That's central," he said. "Would you like to learn more about it and apply it to your life?"

Grabbing a Ghost – Isabelle

Half way through the session with Abdul Hakeem, I was all in. Talking with him got me pumped. Existential therapists, like him, focused on meaning-of-life issues. I had just studied that in my theories course, and I couldn't get enough. Touching those topics piqued my curiosity about, and kept jogging the memory of, my ICU experience. I dug my fingernails into my arm just to make sure this was real.

When conversation slowed down at one point, Sailhammer came to mind again. "I'm stoked to learn more about my true self, but what about my issues? I still have to do what my advisor wants or I can't go forward."

He tilted his head and pressed his lips together. "As I said earlier, we will do both. Learning more about you causes recognition of not-you. And vice-versa. I typically start with what's at the forefront for people, which usually means whatever most bothers them. Or what motivates them. At the moment, nothing appears to bother you that you want to address. So let's keep going with your bigger energy—your passion— which centers on being your true self."

My heart quickened. "I'm all in if you are. So, what happens now?"

He asked, "Did you notice all of your excitement about it? How eager you sounded?"

"Yeah, I caught that." I liked his in-the-moment responses.

"That's your true self showing, full of life, far more than the stilted demands of meeting some standard. You only needed permission from some authority—me, in this case—to honor your passion over the requirements. And, hopefully, before too long you won't need some authority's permission."

I wrinkled my face, my tone flat. "Yep, authority issues."

He continued. "Then, like breathing fresh air after being locked in a small, stuffy closet, you came to life by hooking into what you value.

Your desire to learn about being you overshadowed the requirement. Well, for the most part, because you showed some energy about that, too."

"But, in the end, don't I still need to meet the requirements?" I asked.

His eyes twinkled as he smiled. "You will keep shutting down your true self when your main focus is on pleasing someone, in this case, your advisor. When it's your central goal. It's not authentic; those decisions aren't moved by you."

He gave me time for that to sink in. Then he got practical. "Do you have to meet requirements? No. You could choose not to meet them and accept the respective consequences. Do you see? Even with standards you always have a choice. Be moved by your own choice."

I nodded as he continued explaining. "When you act like you don't have a choice, you react to the world, to authorities, expectations, and rules as if you're a victim. You give away your power. Then those people and standards essentially make decisions for you, rather than you truly choosing your own life path."

During the silence that followed, my mouth hung open. He had said it so simply and it clicked. I saw the distinction between reacting to Sailhammer or deciding I really wanted this counseling experience. *Working on stuff just to please her would have sucked the life out of me, and it wouldn't have helped.*

His soft tone pulled me back to the moment. "The longer we've talked, the more your motivation has kept shifting to what matters to you. That's living in your true self rather than reacting to expectations."

"Okay. I do want to learn to be the real me, but nailing it down and living it out is like grabbing a ghost."

He chuckled. "I like your honest, direct communication." Then he leaned forward. "Your true self is the continuously developing better version of yourself that makes life-oriented choices. Decisions like that make you feel more alive, fulfilled, connected—able to love and learn and be at peace with who you are. Those choices expand you rather than keep you trapped. Your choice to gain what you can through counseling here is doing that."

"Whoa, I never thought about it as keeping peace with myself. I've been mad at myself ever since I can remember. So, being at peace with myself shows I'm living in my true self?"

"Yes, it's key. Who doesn't want that in life—peace with yourself, with your conscience? Then you're not divided. You're not fragmented or at odds with yourself."

I wondered aloud. "Peace with my conscience. I imagine living like that cuts down on anxiety." My thoughts traveled miles in a matter of seconds.

He asked, "What comes to mind when you think about living life that way?"

"That I've rarely lived like that, until recently. I reacted to what others wanted—mommy issues again," I said as I rolled my eyes. "Always had to do what she wanted."

He studied me. "Life must have felt empty when you weren't paying attention to what made you feel alive, fulfilled, or at peace."

"That nails it. Lost, too. I had no clue about what got me pumped. I rarely thought about it. Even with my advisor's requirement, only after talking with G did I think about what I wanted."

"And what gives you life now?"

"In the past, art made me feel alive. I used it to escape, where I could let down and just be me. But, now, anything that relates to my new path after flatlining gets me stoked. Learning to be me without hiding. And talking with people who get that. Like you and G. That's why I thought you'd describe true self as 'the authentic self.'" I did air quotes. "That's what two of my professors talk about."

"That's part of it. Authenticity—being you without putting on a front for anyone, including yourself—allows connection inside and outside of you."

As giddy as a kid with a new toy, my fascination with this unexplored frontier consumed me. "You keep mentioning connection. I know it's important after the night at the hospital. But getting hold of it practically feels like holding onto a ghost again."

"Difficult experiences, especially ones beyond our control, require us to reach beyond ourselves for something greater: for further understanding, for higher-level abilities, for support from others, or for a higher presence. We reach for other connections, just as children do when learning new developmental tasks." He put his hand to his chin. "I picture it like an acorn bursting through its self-contained shell to expand and put roots into new places."

"Cool. Apart from my grandma's help, that puts words to what I felt like as a kid. Trapped in a hard shell. Looking back, I tried to get everyone to like the shell. No wonder I didn't feel loved."

"Which leaves you feeling empty and unknown. Unable to grow into who you're meant to be." His eyes roamed for a moment. "And the pressure of circumstances beyond your abilities cracked that shell, causing you to need more connection. Ones you may not have reached for otherwise?"

I gave a sober nod as that reality struck me. "But it took a ton of pressure before I finally cracked. And reached."

He let that sit for a minute. "Earlier, you mentioned briefly that you're married but separated. I'm guessing that caused some of the pressure?"

Lost about what to say, I tightened up, aware that we had shifted to the painful areas. Professors called it, 'Doing the work.' But, unlike them, Abdul Hakeem's purpose centered on me learning to be me, so I told myself to go with it.

About to speak, I waited as he looked at me with those soft, gentle eyes and said, "If you're ready, share one or two of those experiences. Possibly one when you made a true-self choice, and another when you hid behind some shell of not-you."

As I paused, his tentative suggestion of paying attention to what's me and not-me resonated throughout my whole body. It took a minute, but my mind went back to some of his words about true self. "I'd say that I made a life-oriented choice when I applied to the social work program. Dean tried to slam that door shut. Usually, that would have stopped me from applying and caused me to hide behind the same old people-pleasing shell. I always gave in to what Dean wanted, just like with my mom. But I couldn't let go of the program. It felt bigger than me. I couldn't find peace until I went with it."

"That's excellent," he said. "You're already learning to contrast your true self with the superficial shell that's not you. That's the lesser version of yourself that some people refer to as the false self. Others, the disconnected self."

Hearing new ways of thinking about my true self and what it's not made me jump forward in my seat. "Disconnected! That fits with how I feel whenever I stop being me. Detached and lifeless. So, feeling connected versus disconnected helps me know the difference, when I'm me or not?"

Abdul Hakeem's eyebrows rose. "Yes. Wonderful insight! You've heard the quote, 'Life finds a way.' I would add, only with connections. Think about it. A child's birth and growth require connections—first the umbilical cord, then close, supportive relationships for ongoing growth. Your true self expands and grows stronger the same way: through connections and support, particularly during difficulties."

"I always pulled back when things got tough. I did that when I lost Grandma and Dad. I got mad at the world and shut everyone out. Then I got depressed and wandered around in some dark cloud."

I thought I saw his eyes water as he spoke. "I'm sorry for your losses. Losing people close to you tears you apart. I'm sure that devastated you."

The depth of his gentle tone reached into my heart and evoked a well of hidden pain. I started crying but tried to stop it. "I'm sorry. I don't normally get so freakin' emotional."

With tears in his eyes, now unmistakable, he urged me, saying, "Please don't resist your true self. Genuine tears need connection like this. Not shame."

I began sobbing uncontrollably after his soothing, almost pleading, words. Feeling emotionally naked, I covered my face with my hands. I grabbed several tissues from the box on the little table. After the upheaval all but stopped, I wiped my eyes and nose and looked up.

Staring into space, I said, "After Grandma died, some deep hole got opened up. I never lost it like this about her passing." I turned to him and asked, "How did you do that?"

His eyes and voice conveyed nothing but sincerity. "Do what?"

"Our first session, and you got to the pain I've had buried since high school."

"True self wanted to come out," he said, as if no one would ever think otherwise. "Tears are part of that. Hiding them, during the safety of counseling, keeps repressing and fragmenting you. You increase awareness and learn what's you and not you through expressing the pain."

"I get nauseated at the thought of showing pain to anyone. My mom had no patience for it and could turn on me in seconds. But I feel more whole after letting go like I did. I needed that."

"Because, until you did," he said, "hiding the pain kept you disconnected. It's like disowning part of you and wondering why you lost yourself."

That hit home. "I did that most of my life: hiding what I felt and then losing myself. The more I shut off the pain, an empty bottomless pit opened up. Nothing, and I mean nothing, could fill it after that!"

He got emphatic. "That, Isabelle, contributes powerfully to most people's mental health issues. You create a gap or hole inside when you hide your genuine experiences—because you also hide you when you do that. Then nothing fills that emptiness except learning to be you again, emotions and all. Until you do, you feel anxious, alone, and depressed, or you chase addictions to try to fill that hole."

"Damn, I never thought about it that way. But living life as an open book seems impossible. You mean I need to show my scars all the time not to lose myself?"

"That's a great question." He paused. "Not all the time. Find a few caring friends, like Gene, where you can be fully you. Then your true self will feel safe enough to be present, to come out of hiding and make more connections."

I sat there shaking my head. "I'm just a rookie at this. But I get how counseling will help me sort through what's me and not-me."

"And that's a tremendous foundation for going forward," he said. "We only have two minutes left. Do you want to see how this relates to social work? It should give you more to process personally, too."

With limited time, I couldn't have picked anything better than applying all of this to being a clinician. "Awesome."

"What do therapists focus on overall with clients? What have you learned so far at LU about that?"

I shrugged and went with my gut reaction. "Professors always talk about self-awareness and insight. They focus on authenticity, too."

"Excellent. Yes, authenticity means genuinely describing your experiences as they are. That way you can sort through what's you and not you. And self-awareness and insight reconnect you with your experiences, often ones you hide from yourself and others. You become more whole through that. Integrated. Also, you gain security because you're no longer rejecting parts of yourself."

"Secure." I nodded, other thoughts now hitting me. "I feel steadier and more whole since my talks with G, although I didn't feel like that coming here today. I got scared, but at least the panic attacks have started going away—probably thanks to facing more of my baggage instead of hiding it. I'm getting more comfortable in my own skin."

He studied me as my mind wandered. "You have more thoughts about this?"

"I never saw the bigger picture. Making connections. Inside and out."

He grinned. "You catch on quickly. One last thought before you go. Better connections increase security. Your personal stability. That's why some people describe the true self as the secure, connected self. And the false self as the insecure, disconnected self."

I shook my head in wonder and wanted to continue processing that later. The delight on his face told me that he couldn't be happier for me.

The session had flown by. I marveled at what all had happened. Even though the painful part should have drained me, I walked out of the room half giddy and wanted to skip down the hallway like a seven-year-old. I not only learned a lot personally, but things came together professionally. *Hmm...life-oriented versus hiding. What the hell.* I skipped down the hallway with a big smile and waved as I passed the receptionist.

Ballou's Bagels — Gene

I couldn't wait to find out how Isabelle's session went with Abdul Hakeem. I didn't expect him to discuss it with me because of client confidentiality, so I'd need to find out from her. He worked miracles with anyone who had the slightest motivation. She'd be enlightened at the least.

I whistled as I drove to Ballou's Bagels, anticipating meaningful, personal talk with Abdul Hakeem and Saanvi. It always enriched me and gave me clearer sight about my life.

Pulling into the parking lot, I grinned at the sight of them. Each sat at a table with a tall cup and pastry. I hopped out of the car and yelled. "I'll join you as soon as I get a coffee and donut!" I could've eaten donuts every day but tried to limit them to once a week when the three of us talked.

Cherished prizes in hand, I sat down with two of my favorite people. "What a day! Great to be outside. Especially when it's with you two."

Saanvi greeted me. "We feel the same." Abdul Hakeem smiled and lifted his cup in my direction as if toasting me.

Pointing at the trees off to her left, Saanvi said, "We've just been enjoying watching those birds. A pair of them keeps grabbing those small berries and feeding one another."

I watched them for a few moments. "I love seeing them this close. Their markings and unique colors. I wish I had trees like that on my property to attract birds. I don't know if I'm just made this way or not, but it fascinates me to see things up close. All the details. People, birds and animals. Flowers."

After sitting in silence for several minutes, I asked, "How are you two doing?"

Abdul Hakeem gave a slight shrug. "Very well, other than the nerve pain acting up more than usual today."

I grimaced. "I thought you seemed more quiet than usual. I know we've talked about it before, but I wish something more could be done for your arm. Something ongoing like that has to be exhausting and even scary at times."

Abdul Hakeem pressed his lips together and nodded, as if not worth rehashing it again.

With difficulty, I let go of following up and slowly turned to his twin sister. "How about you, Saanvi? Work ironing itself out? Getting time for any hikes? What's on your mind?"

She hesitated. "I'm doing well, but as for hiking, I need to get out. Work has been consuming me lately. A close friend encouraged me to check other job options, which I've done. So I'm ready to set a boundary about work and to do that right in the moment if my boss treats me poorly again. That feels right."

Abdul Hakeem looked her in the eyes. "I'm happy to hear that. When you treat yourself with respect, others tend to do likewise."

After Saanvi finished talking about her work situation, I leaned toward Abdul Hakeem. "I'm so glad Isabelle made an appointment with you. I know you can't say anything because of confidentiality, but she's ripe for counseling. And she's a gem."

He nodded and smiled.

I shifted my attention back to Saanvi. "She'll call you sometime soon. It's in your court, but I think you'll enjoy spending time with her. She's thirsty for the inner life."

She beamed. "Anyone interested in learning about that world makes it more real for me. I'm looking forward to meeting her." She picked up her pastry, about to take another bite. "I've been thinking lately about how each of us are single. What's that about for each of you?"

Having already thought about it, I jumped in. "I'm tickled with my life and wouldn't change a thing. I liked being married, but after losing Hanna I wanted to explore. The mysteries of life. Travel. Culture."

After taking a sip, Abdul Hakeem asked, "How can you be sure that you aren't just avoiding future loss?"

I reflected. "I can't. I just don't have that desire, and I've not sidestepped any opportunities." I chuckled. "Also, I don't carry significant grief other than healthy sadness at points. But I know how easy it is to deceive ourselves. What about you?"

"I take life in seasons," he said. "It's possible that I'm afraid of more loss after losing my parents. But my friendship with you two would say otherwise. For now, places where I can be fully me, like here, fill whatever hole my parents left. I simply have no interest in dating. You're the one who brought this up, Saanvi. What about you?"

"I'm still working through my thinking on this. I don't feel obligated in friendships, whereas with a partner that often changes for people. At least for me, I'd feel more responsibility to do what a partner would want."

"Interesting," I said. "I never thought about it that way. As if partners can have ownership over each other, and even if they don't they might still act like they're obligated to please each other."

Saanvi's hand slapped the table. "That's it! That says it for me. Friendships, like here and with my other close friends, have no ownership. No responsibility to make each other happy. I know it doesn't have to be that way for couples, but it usually seems to go that way."

After a bite of donut and sipping some coffee, I asked Abdul Hakeem, "You remember what I talked about last time? About me acting like I shouldn't have needs?" After he nodded, I said, "That seemed similar for you: over-giving and not letting others give back to you. Have you thought more about it?"

He wagged his head. "That will be an ongoing issue, partly because I don't want to slow down using my newfound counseling gift." His eyes widened. "I've counseled for three years now, but it still feels new. It's rewarding to make a difference in people's lives. I lived my whole life without purpose until finding counseling. It awakened me."

Saanvi and I waited as he put his fingers to his chin, his eyes searching for something. "I'm aware of letting others give to me so that I maintain a healthy balance. I'll keep watching that as I go forward. But motivation is everything, and right now I don't have it about slowing down my work." He groaned, more noticeably than usual.

I pointed to his arm. "It seems severe today."

His jaw set, he nodded. "Focusing on counseling takes my attention off of the nerve spikes, unless it flares up stronger like today. I could take meds more regularly, but I want to stay mentally sharp for counseling. But if making a change becomes necessary, I will."

I shook my head. "It's difficult for me to watch you deal with ongoing pain."

Saanvi chimed in. "Me, too."

"Watching you taps into my pain from seeing Hanna suffer. It never ended. I always felt helpless, like something more should have been done."

"I relate to that, Gene," Saanvi said. Turning to her brother, her voice broke. "It breaks my heart, watching you suffer year after year. I'd have taken it from you if I could, but I didn't realize the toll it takes on me until Gene said it."

Abdul Hakeem's face softened. "Thank you for caring. I'm sorry that you're impacted by it, too." Before continuing, the warmth in his eyes seemed to reach out and hold Saanvi a moment, then me. "I'm managing, even if I have to pour myself into counseling others for now. And our friendship provides the balance I need. With you two, different from counseling, I get to talk and learn about my own life. I always come away with fresh insights. I get to feel known, and not alone."

After hugging each other and leaving the bagel shop, I crawled into my car no longer feeling helpless about Abdul Hakeem's nerve pain. Their caring embrace must have done the trick. Relaxed and peaceful, I found myself whistling again. In my happy place. Abdul Hakeem's words about feeling known and not alone stayed with me. *Where does that happen in life? How often do people become known and accepted, struggles and all? Maybe that's why we each talk about feeling so enriched after our time together.*

I didn't see Isabelle's car in the lot when I got home. Then I remembered she'd be gone all day because she had a shift at B & F Warehouse. That meant not hearing about her counseling experience until tomorrow morning. I told myself to be patient.

After going inside and being greeted by Button, I eased back into the recliner with *The Daily Post.* Looking over the first page, an article entitled "B & F Scandal" caught my attention. A policeman had pulled over a car with a headlight out. The driver, as well as four passengers, appeared to be under the influence. The article went on to say: "A search revealed heroin in the glove compartment. The passengers claimed they were unaware. Charges pending."

Isabelle didn't do drugs. But some of her friends worked at B & F, ones who had graduated from Landsburg High School. *What if she happened to be with that group and didn't say anything to me? Not likely, but what a coincidence.*

Saanvi's Phone Call — Isabelle

I woke up early, alert and still vibrating with energy ever since meeting with Abdul Hakeem. Even the long shift at B & F yesterday couldn't cast a shadow over what had happened. I checked the forecast before going out to the kitchen and saw that the sun might break through in an hour or two.

I hadn't seen G since my session and couldn't wait to tell him about it. As usual, he sat at the table drinking his coffee and gazing into the air, his mind probably floating around in some alternate universe.

"Hey G." I poured some coffee into my cup and waited for a response. Or, more likely, for him to come back to Planet Earth.

Half a minute later, something must have registered. "Good morning, Isabelle."

"Counseling rocked yesterday. Couldn't have picked a better counselor."

"Of course," he said with a smug face, appearing ready to launch some smart-ass comment. "I recommended him."

Flattening my eyes at him, I sat down with dark roast Guatemalan pleasure-in-a-cup. I bantered back. "Don't let me get in the way of patting yourself on the back." Just smiling, he took the busting in stride. Button left G's feet and snuggled up next to mine. I reached down and rubbed behind his ears. What a rush. Flakes of pure sweetness always swirled around inside me when I petted him.

"I don't need to give details," I said, "but I got afraid of counseling beforehand. After starting, though, everything clicked. Abdul Hakeem's awesome. Compassionate, great insights, paid attention to what mattered to me, and went at my pace."

"The man's got a gift."

I leaned forward. "He focused on true self, too. On making life-oriented choices and being at peace with myself. You know, doing things that make me feel more alive or fulfilled so I can learn to be me."

"That's a good way to think about it. And Saanvi will trigger more. What a dynamo."

I wrinkled my face. "I just don't want to inconvenience her. I don't feel worth her time."

"That's probably how you felt with your mom growing up. That might be how you approach relationships with women."

I shook my head and didn't say anything. He nailed it. Living with G sometimes felt like ODing on counseling. He always tuned into deeper dynamics. To most people, that'd be like pouring pepper on their Cheerios. I wanted new insights, but G rarely stopped pouring the pepper.

G sat back in his chair and pointed at a newspaper article lying to his left. "Didn't know if you were with your friends that night."

I shook my head. "Not my friends. My group always drank at Fitzpatrick's. This was the druggie gang from my high school days. Students called them Landsburg High. Too bad they never turned things around."

I started toward my room and noticed his face relaxing. "You look relieved. You actually thought I might have been doing drugs?"

G fidgeted. "No, I thought you might have been along that night and were trying to handle the pending charges on your own. You know, not asking for help again. It seemed too coincidental that another group of graduates also worked at B & F."

I made the best skeptical face I could. "I guess I'll overlook your lapse in judgment." Turning toward my room, my mind shifted from busting on G to having second thoughts about calling Saanvi. *Do it before you don't.* I grabbed my phone and searched for the number G had given me. I clicked on it without hesitating. She answered. When I checked if she wanted to meet, she said, "Sure. Would you like to talk while we hike this morning? We could meet at White Pine Trails in about fifteen minutes."

"You mean, like, leave now for there?" I asked, my voice jumping up several notches.

"As long as it suits you. It's my first day off work, and I want some nature time."

Still wide-eyed, I struggled to wrap my mind around this. "Okay. I'll see you in fifteen."

She said, "Look for the red Jeep."

On the way, the beauty of the day mesmerized me. Windows down, the cool breeze blew through the car. Low humidity. Sunny and clear blue sky. In the low seventies. Perfect. The last mile before turning into the parking area, the fragrance of the pines filled the air and triggered a memory about Christmas. As a young teenager with my parents, I walked by trees for sale in a car lot. Knowing that Mom would say no, I had asked Dad for a tree to decorate. "Even Grandpa lets Grandma do that," I had pleaded. But Mom's "no" came crashing down on my sliver of hope even before Dad got a chance to answer. That had been my last memory of Dad, Mom, and me out somewhere together. Mom completely lost it after that.

When I pulled into the parking lot, I saw Saanvi lacing her hikers, with her left foot propped on the back bumper of a shiny, red Jeep. Her short, black hair glistened in the sun as she finished tightening her laces. She looked fit and a little smaller than me, wearing black jeans and a burgundy-colored top.

With a bright face and big smile, Saanvi sauntered over to greet me. She glowed in a way that felt powerful as we stood face-to-face. I couldn't put my finger on what to call it, but when she spoke, the word wholesome came close. "Hi, I'm Saanvi. Really glad to meet you."

Jittery, and finding it difficult to contain the ping-ponging energy inside me, I reached out and shook her hand. "Isabelle. Thanks for getting together with me."

I tried to hold back the bounce in each step as I strode over to the trail entrance with her. Wringing my hands and rubbing them against my jeans, I didn't know what to do with myself as we started hiking.

The trail weaved up through the woods, initially wider but narrowing as it went. Side by side at this point, Saanvi looked over at me. "Gene said that you're a social work major at LU. You like it?"

"Except for the gen ed classes, yeah. I like understanding what makes people tick."

Her eyes lit up. "People are fascinating. You think you'll do that for a living?"

"Maybe, but I've always liked art, too. I want to get back into it sometime."

She glanced over as we ascended past hundreds of slender saplings standing like an army of poles on each side. "It sounds like you stopped for awhile. Why? If you like it so much?"

I chewed my lip as I thought. "I guess, 'cause of my mom's comments about it." I tensed and quickly changed the topic. "What about you? What are your interests?"

"I enjoy science and computer security. And rich conversations."

"Computer security? Is that your job?" I asked.

She nodded. "Comp Ops Corporation on Washington Street."

"You're into science and technology and you like talking with people? That usually doesn't go together, does it?"

"For me it does. I like exploring beyond the usual limits. Learning from different perspectives. Some people think science gives them clear answers. But its answers only raise other questions. More possibilities always exist. I like depth with science and with people."

"Depth?" I asked.

"As a teenager, I saw life as clear-cut. Like simple answers should always work. Then my life changed. It no longer fit into a tidy, neat package. That scared me at first. But now I wouldn't trade the unending learning and wonders for the oversimplified B.S."

She struck me as direct but sincere. No air of pretense. Nothing hidden. People have told me that once in a while in life, they came across rare individuals who exuded no walls. Open books, comfortable in their own skin. And in no time at all, they felt like they had known that person their whole life. That's what stood out about Saanvi: transparency, like my program emphasized. It made me think that I didn't need to be concerned about sneak attacks or hidden agendas. *Or retaliation, like anytime I didn't please Mom.*

She stepped between several large roots rippling across the trail. I followed. "I know what you mean. I used to want clear answers, too. Life felt simpler that way. But my clinical training opened up a whole new world. Like how culture, upbringing, and environment shape us. We don't all have the same starting line or even the same answers that work for us."

Saanvi gave a big nod. "So true. What made you go into social work?"

I tightened up again, not wanting to talk about my mom yet. So I kept it simple. "Seeing people stuck in life, and wanting to help."

"A few of my friends went through Gene's counseling program. They wanted to help people, too. Is that why you're into learning about true self? To help people?"

Breathing hard as we came up over a steep bank, the words poured out. "Yes; I could live and breathe learning about it!"

"Me, too. It's life-changing and, as I said, I like depth. Most people want lots of superficial details about someone's life before they go into personal areas. But if they start shallow they usually stay shallow. It's difficult to break our habits. I'm always ready to jump into the deep water."

"I used to stick to surface talk, but I'm ready to go past that thanks to being at LU. And talking with G."

She stopped and put her hand to her forehead. "I forgot to mention that my boss could call sometime today. I hope not. I normally don't answer calls when I'm outdoors, but it's a serious work situation. So as long as I get reception out here, I should take the call. If he does, it'll only take two or three minutes. Besides, I want it off my mind."

"No problem." We passed a swampy area off to our right with dozens of frogs serenading us. After pointing at one, I turned back toward her. "You said it's serious. How bad, if you're cool with talking about it?"

She didn't hesitate. "My boss doesn't have the best people skills. He only thinks about what the company needs and immediately pressures everyone to make it happen."

I sighed. "I'd hate that. I don't react well to pushy authorities."

"Several people quit recently, two of them from computer security. That put more demands on me. I understand deadlines and all that. I'll even do more than my share, but I can't allow him to bully me to do more than what's possible."

"I don't know how you keep your cool with a boss like that. I would've already had a panic attack." I gasped as soon as the words came out of my mouth.

She looked over at me, catching my reaction. "We all carry pain, and we grow through it when we feel safe enough to learn."

I let out a breath, relieved by her sincere face and tone. "That nails it for me. I never felt safe to learn. Well, until talking with G."

She suddenly stopped, pulling her cell phone from a pocket to look at it. "Felt it vibrating." She took a long breath and pressed her lips together. "I thought so. My boss." She turned and retreated about a dozen steps on the trail, glancing back at me one more time.

I pointed at a large rock. "I'm cool. I'll just hang out over there and take in the landscape until you're ready."

She nodded and answered the phone. "Hello, Saanvi speaking."

Parking myself on the rock, I soaked in the lush, green woods. The peacefulness refreshed me as I took several deep whiffs of the rich forest air. A smooth rock shaped like a small hippo bordered the path on the other side. It drew my attention. *Not your everyday rock.*

My mind shifted to Saanvi's call, thinking how stressed I'd be about it. But maybe she didn't get fazed by much. I wondered if she lived like one of those connected, high-powered people who everyone wants a piece of. She appeared that whole. *That* desirable. She came across as more outgoing than Abdul Hakeem, but I hadn't seen him in social situations. *She's probably on the phone all the time. Maybe I'll be in the way... Damn; there's the life-sucking thoughts and shame again.*

I tensed when I overheard a piercing voice coming through the phone. Her chin dropped as she listened. Then the voice got even louder as she held the phone away from her ear with eyes looking at me that conveyed, "Here we go again."

After the voice finally stopped, she spoke with clarity. "Sir, I'm on my first day off in weeks and I need it for my health. The job has been stressful and I'm not able to help with the increased workload today."

She pulled the phone away from her ear as the voice erupted a second time. Then, still with respect, she persisted between the voice spikes.

"Uh, sir. Yes, I understand sir. I'm aware of the vacancies and the crisis at Comp Ops right now. Yes, but I feel disrespected when you treat me like this. I realize. Yes, sir. You have demands from higher-ups that need to be met. I get that. I'd be the first to help if you treated your employees with respect. But threats and arm-twisting your employees have caused your crisis. If you want my honest input, let me know. If not, I'm off work today."

My jaw fell as Mr. Megamouth's shrieks pierced the quiet woods. She cringed, now angling the phone away from her at arm's length. Her boss sounded the same as my mom—a screaming eagle coming in for the kill.

Then Saanvi turned toward me, rolled her eyes, and half-grinned as the murderous voice continued to cut through the air.

Until the moment that Saanvi shut off the phone and returned it to her pocket, I hadn't realized that my whole body was braced. Rigid. Just an extension of the rock under me. My mouth still hung open as I stared.

She shrugged. "About what I expected, but it's done. You ready to go?"

Carey

Saanvi's Security — Isabelle

Still sitting on my rock, I gaped at Saanvi, trying to wrap my mind around what I had witnessed. *How did she not lose it? Or shut down?* Her honest and clear communication intrigued me. Even with a boss who disrespected her. Verbally attacked her. I thought she'd be more…well, submissive, like me. Less confrontive of authorities. I marveled at her clarity in a difficult situation. She didn't sound rude or angry. And she still conveyed willingness to help her boss if he simply treated her with respect. *Who in their right mind wouldn't want an employee like that? He must be a real piece of work.*

Authority figures throwing their weight around crippled me. I couldn't move after her boss' intensity, even though I only heard him screaming over the phone. From a distance. It wasn't even directed at me. I'm sure that I appeared planted on the rock as if I had roots clinging to it.

She studied me as she made her way back up the trail, my befuddled face probably catching her attention. "This work situation has been brewing for a while. I wanted to talk to my manager personally rather than on the phone but he kept putting off the meeting. He probably knew I'd be honest."

"That call was beyond intense," I said. "He went ballistic. I heard the screams from here!"

She smiled. "Yeah, the last part he mostly cursed at me. That's part of the disrespect, so I hung up."

"I shut down when authorities tear into me. I get paralyzed. You seem unfazed."

She paused. "No, my heart's still racing about it. I dreaded the call. But talking with friends prepared me to know that I had a way out. I didn't need to take his abuse. So I felt good setting the boundary."

I blinked several times. "Aren't you afraid of getting sacked?"

She shook her head. "I have a few other options in the works. And I sensed it was time to deal with it."

"What do you mean?" I asked.

"I usually avoid conflict, and, somehow, it keeps happening lately. My health insurance company won't cover what its policy states that it will. My landlord hasn't fixed my leaky kitchen faucet or my front door that won't lock. The renter to the left of my apartment keeps blasting music at 3:00 A.M. Pictures even fell from the vibration two nights ago. The universe keeps providing opportunities for growth."

"Wow, you've been gettin' slammed. I hate when life's in your face like that." She nodded as we both started up the trail, quiet for several minutes.

I wondered how Saanvi stayed clear-minded with all of that. Especially with a supervisor harassing her that way. I had never met anyone like her. Expressive, respectful, able to be bold when she needs to. G respected people, but I didn't know you could be bold and respectful at the same time. Especially with a boss. And for a woman to be all of that meant I could possibly be like that someday. She even seemed more well-rounded and balanced than my professors. They showed certain strengths, but also major flaws.

Behind her on the narrowing path, I said, "Saanvi, I'm curious about something."

She stopped and turned as I spoke. "You said that the universe gives you opportunities, and that you sensed it was time to deal with your boss. That's how G talks. You mean intuitively, beyond reaching your limit at work?"

"I do. Circumstances and my limits sometimes point the way. But my inner senses also lead me or make me more aware in situations."

"Do you mind me asking about how you sense things? Whether it's from some higher power or just intuition?"

"Not at all. I'm good to go as long as you're ready to dive in," she said, glancing over at me frequently as we started hiking again. "I grew up following Islam's teachings on peace, like Abdul Hakeem and my parents. It's just what I knew. But I've seen people be inspired regardless of their labels, usually when they honor their inner experiences over people's expectations or rules."

"Inspired? Like what G calls higher presence?"

Saanvi grinned. "Exactly! I used to see higher presence as only from Allah, although I didn't call it that. I called it my Allah sense or being inspired. But then I experienced moments of that same inspiration coming through Gene when we first met. That same peace, clarity, and insight, and he had looked to God. At the time, I viewed God and Allah as different."

I did a double take and slowed down walking so I wouldn't miss anything. "G didn't tell me that he looks to God, or at least that he used to."

"I'm not sure if he still does the same way because we eventually stopped using labels." She had slowed down, too, and locked eyes with me. "We recognized the same peace, love, and clarity inspiring how each of us wanted to live. So we started connecting beyond religious words—ones that sometimes limit people's understanding because of all the attached baggage."

"I get that."

She kept making eye contact as she talked. "Words fall short in explaining indescribable experiences. Beautiful ones. Can you describe a sunset?"

Her question nailed it. I didn't know if it was rhetorical or if she actually wanted me to answer. But it put all of these hard-to-explain inner experiences into perspective. *How do you explain love, beauty, wholeness, or fulfillment? Or true self, for that matter?* Searching for words, I started. "No. Words never do it justice. It's like trying to explain a rainbow to a blind person."

"That's why we don't use labels as much. Gene and I grew to see the journey as about connecting within ourselves, with each other, and with life, not about insisting on certain words. I'm just glad to find people interested in making those connections."

"Me, too. I didn't have a clue until recently. But now I feel like I'm hooked on some drug and can't get enough."

She smiled. "Your fascination reminds me of me. Bouncing around with energy and scarcely able to contain it."

"I can't believe that I'm pumped to tell you about my hospital experience. It took weeks to feel ready to tell G."

"Your hospital experience?"

I poured out my story as she kept asking questions. Then I asked about her background.

"Abdul Hakeem and I are from Firozabad, India and came to America after our parents died in a glass-making furnace accident. We had worked together at that factory for years. For a year or two leading up to the tragedy, our family had dreamed about moving to America when we saved enough money. Then, after the accident, Abdul Hakeem and I wanted to honor the memory of our parents by carrying out their dream. Thirty years old, we sold all we had and flew to America."

"That must have been hell—the accident, being on your own, and leaving everything you knew."

"More than I can say," she said, nodding. "You saw my brother's severed left arm. That tragedy happened three months after my parents died. Abdul Hakeem transported large glass vases from the factory to several warehouses. The neglected company truck lost a front tire while going around a bend. Abdul Hakeem crashed, with glass shattering and flying everywhere. He almost died. It's a miracle he didn't. But losing half his arm devastated him."

I sighed. "That must have been a horrible place to work. It wiped out your family." I stopped and gasped, thinking I was too blunt.

Instead of getting angry, she spoke with sad eyes and a somber voice. "That's all we knew." Then she looked off into the distance. "Not only did Abdul Hakeem lose the lower half of his arm, shards of glass splintered into the rest of it. Thousands of pieces, causing severe nerve damage. That made it impossible to reattach his arm or a prosthetic. He suffers daily because of the pain."

I shook my head and looked down. "I don't know how you can go on after something like that."

She moved in front of me as the path narrowed again. "I felt helpless. Heartbroken, watching him in agony. Seeing him lose all hope. Grief had overwhelmed both of us when my parents died. Then his accident on top of that caused me to distrust everything I had been taught. My culture. My religion. I questioned life."

"I can't imagine what could have brought him, or you, out of that," I said, feeling inadequate. Before answering, she crouched under a head-high log crossing the trail and I followed. Spellbound, like a kid listening to ghost stories, I might have plowed into the broken, spiked limbs protruding from it, had she not ducked under it first.

"We moved to America, knowing we needed something different. We thought that carrying out our parents' dream might lift us out of despair. But living here, at first, crushed the dream. People treated us like outsiders. They looked at us with fear. As if we were terrorists."

"I'm sorry. That's disheartening. And I thought my life sucked. How did things change?"

"Gene."

I thought I didn't hear right. My voice raised several notches. "Gene?"

"I don't see it as about him, now." Her head tilted as she kept striding forward. "Back then I saw it as us sinking in quicksand with Gene throwing us a rope. In hindsight, both Abdul Hakeem and I saw him living in a way that got more out of life."

"Got more out of life?" I repeated, enthralled by her story.

"Working with life rather than fighting it, similar to how trees bend the way the wind blows. That's the inspiration that came through him that first caught my attention. It's astounding what that way of living did for him, and it confused me because he didn't look to Allah."

I reacted. "But that's too much to expect, to work with life when it rips you apart!"

"We didn't start there. Only in time did we come to live like that."

Then she told me how they met Gene. "He saw us drinking coffee one morning in Ballou's Bagel Shop on 5th Street. On his way to find a chair, he stopped at our table and said he hadn't seen us there before. He asked if we were new to the area. After telling him that we had come to America to fulfill our parents' dream, he asked if they were here, too. He saw our startled faces. We had been desperate, needing hope, and he offered to sit and listen if we wanted to share our story. His genuine interest, little by little, caused everything to come pouring out. We sat at that table for over two and a half hours talking, crying, and drinking coffee. We became close friends that day."

We had stopped at the crest of a hill, staring at each other as she said, "There's nothing he wouldn't do for us. Or us for him."

Tears came to my eyes. My voice broke. "That helps me appreciate him more. I took him for granted in high school. Maybe I still do. I just saw him as crazy G."

We both laughed as we started again and weaved our way through a crevice between boulders the size of small houses. Then the trail widened into a larger open area, with occasional towering trees standing at attention like peaceful giants. Chest-high ferns waving like oversized fans blanketed the forest floor.

"I've never seen boulders like that," I said, gazing at them with wonder. "And these humongous trees and ferns look prehistoric, as if some T-Rex might stroll through."

Butterflies and Birds — Isabelle

Saanvi and I stood in silence, wooed by the primordial scene. I absorbed refreshment from its beauty as I breathed. No litter. No sign of people's carelessness. Just the forest's tranquility that revived me. I wondered if nature's purity somehow tapped into a person's true self—into that same peace and fulfillment you get from making life-oriented choices.

Winding along the path again, Saanvi continued her story. "Our lives changed dramatically after meeting Gene. He told us that first morning about his wife dying from Lou Gehrig's disease and how it transformed him into a better person. He said a pain-free life couldn't have done that. It's not what he said that registered; it's what I saw and experienced as he talked."

"What do you mean?" I asked.

"I witnessed his unwavering acceptance of life on its terms and how he learned what he could from it. Unexplainable peace and wholeness emanated from him, even when he talked about the loss of his wife."

She stopped for a moment and gazed into my eyes. "I don't know if I have the right words for it. But he seemed to integrate those horrendous life experiences into himself. Rather than rejecting or disowning them, as if they weren't part of his lived experience. I think that's the wholeness that Abdul Hakeem and I experienced during our first talk with him."

She shrugged. "Somehow, life made more sense after hearing his struggle—how pain can reshape us for the better." She kept talking as we started once more on the trail. "You know, labor brings birth? Insurmountable obstacles and horrendous pain can awaken us into higher places, into more of who we're meant to be. My eyes opened to more of life's wonders after that, and something clicked for Abdul Hakeem, too. He found his purpose and took graduate counseling courses where Gene taught."

We walked silently for a few minutes. The tree limbs and leaves waved back and forth as the occasional breeze cooled the air.

Saanvi said, "I appreciated that Gene shared his suffering with us and showed interest in ours. What a gift. Abdul Hakeem and I felt safe to talk more about our lives after Gene told us about his. We felt less alone."

I reflected on that and shook my head. "I still don't open up enough. I've always kept a lid on everything. But I see what you mean. You can be more real with people who get real and when they show interest in what you say. They won't look at you like you're crazy. As much."

"It's a whole different world talking with psychologically-minded people. Starting with Gene, our closest friends came from that program. They're less guarded and more open to personal learning than most people. Not always, but usually."

I nodded. "You saying that makes me think about how I'm changing. Shutting down isn't my default anymore. I'm a little braver to connect with the rest of the world. I give the credit to G, but don't tell him I said that."

She gave a warm smile.

I asked, "Did Abdul Hakeem say what G was like as a professor?"

"The students had a saying about him," she said. "He lives in his own world until you tell him your story. Then he's in yours."

I couldn't stop laughing. "That pegs him. Both parts."

She laughed. "The students saw him as unique, but they loved him for it. I do, too. I admire how he's true to himself without explaining or apologizing for it."

We moved quietly for another twenty minutes, passing only three hikers. I studied Saanvi as she observed the lay of the land. I rarely, maybe never, had close friends who wanted to talk at a personal level. Ones I could count on. I wanted that with her but thought it too good to be true. Then we came to a stream with a four-foot-high waterfall. Perfectly positioned for enjoying the sight, a log on the bank became our makeshift bench as we sat side-by-side. I never had a big sister but wondered if it would have felt like this—being able to talk freely and trusting that she'll never leave you.

The sound of the waterfall intoxicated me. The water streamed across the rocks, diving and splashing into the lower level while bubbles jostled for position at its base. More than feeling the soothing presence of this peaceful paradise, telling another woman my story and hearing hers felt cleansing. Inspiring. A new experience for me. Aside from my one friend

Val from high school, I hadn't connected with women. Probably the mom issue again. Even my friendship with Val had been superficial. Not so with Saanvi. Like a magnet, she pulled deeper conversation out of me. While sitting here, I told her about Dean, the Chicago song, and about the dream where I didn't react to my mom's abuse. I felt known and no longer alone.

I started to ask, "Was? Could?" I gave up.

She said, "Don't hold back." Her genuine interest in talking personally made me want more of it. I didn't know why, given our brief time of knowing each other, but I trusted her. I felt okay about letting down my walls. And her stories told me she lived with a zest for life—the very way I wanted to live.

I went with it. "Could my dream have been a foreshadowing of support from you? I know it sounds ridiculous. But you appeared so secure and honest with your boss, and in my dream, that's exactly how I felt with my mom. I never experienced that before."

"Perhaps. My dreams always symbolize something about my life, even the future sometimes. Support makes me feel secure and unafraid to be me. You've heard the saying that individuals are only as strong as the people surrounding them? That's me."

I sat on the log, hungry to scarf up every ounce of food for thought that she might put in front of me. I knew it would make me stronger. I could feel it.

She continued, her face relaxed, her voice calm. "Like with my boss, I'm clear about it. I've talked with Abdul Hakeem, Gene, and two other women I'm close to. I don't have any question about what's healthy or not. I'm clear about not being my boss' doormat. You can be clear with others when you're clear with yourself. The harassment from my manager barely scratches the surface of the strength I get from my friends."

"So why would you need me when you already have unbelievable support?" I dragged out the words to emphasize the point.

"Isabelle," she said as she shook her head and looked me squarely in the eyes. "Thanks for your honesty, but talking like this makes me stronger. It strengthens me to tackle whatever comes along. Talking about inner experiences with you makes that world more tangible. More accessible. Especially when lots of people act like it doesn't exist."

"I do feel more okay about myself, talking like this. As if nothing's wrong with me. Probably because you get me. That first happened with G, and now you and Abdul Hakeem."

We sat for a while just being present with this special gift of nature and each other. If it weren't for looking stupid, I would have yelled into the air, "Life doesn't get any better than this!" After years of no connection with my mom, this felt like a dream—relating in meaningful ways with a woman who valued me.

After sitting in peace for another ten minutes, my clenched jaw startled me. *What's up?* I waited for a minute and then it dawned on me. *I feel pressure to live like her. To be able to live above my struggles.* I shrank back and, in my head, I started berating myself. *What a nut job. I can't even enjoy this awesome experience.*

We hopped up from the log to head back to our cars, Saanvi and I chatting about feeling refreshed by the waterfall. *Refreshing at first,* I thought. *Now I feel like a hypocrite in this messed-up mind game.* Then a thought jumped in, *No hiding!* That hadn't been on the radar. I noticed her watching me.

She flattened her eyes, as if trying to figure me out. "Isabelle, you have something on your mind. You can say whatever you want. I plan to do the same."

"Back at the waterfall I felt peace for most of it. Then I got afraid, thinking I won't measure up to how you live. You don't have any obvious hang-ups." After a pause, I said, "My mom always expected me to live like that. Without any flaws."

Saanvi grimaced. "That's a lot to live up to. I'm not perfect by any means, but I'm glad you said something."

"I'm sorry. It's just that you seem so secure."

"That's because I've had a lot of support recently and, right now, I'm with you—someone who wants to talk transparently. About personal things. That helps me feel safe to be me. But sometimes I'm shy, especially in groups. And with people who mainly want small talk."

"You, shy? I can't picture that."

She asked, "Don't you pull back more when you know that people aren't interested in talking personally or meaningfully?"

I nodded, having felt that at points with Val.

"That's me, too. I don't feel so secure and whole in those situations unless, like I said, I got extra quality time with my friends. I've also had a longer history of that than you. You'll gain security as your support system grows."

After starting the return trail's descent, we came out of a thick, brushy area that opened up into a spacious meadow with wildflowers. Even the purple blossoms on the thistles added to the array of colors. We stopped to take it in.

Saanvi said, "You and I faced major life events. Meaningless chit chat doesn't cut it after that. Don't get me wrong, I like fun as much as the next person. But I needed something more than fun after the tragedies. I see that same hunger in you."

"I tried to go on without needing anything. I just got depressed. But now that I see what's possible, I want more. I just wish I hadn't shut people out for so long."

"But, in the end, the obstacles caused you to make other connections. Superficial relationships weren't enough. Material things weren't either. Only connection to something greater than yourself started fulfilling you."

"What do you mean, something greater?" I asked. "Abdul Hakeem also mentioned that."

"Having meaningful relationships with others, serving purposes greater than yourself, or opening up to the inspiration or higher presence you carry. Those things expand you beyond your current thinking and abilities."

"Look!" I whispered, pointing at a flock of small birds. Like military jets in a tight formation running a scripted flight plan, they suddenly swooped down and to the side, staying the exact same distance from each other. "Isn't it cool when they do that?"

"I'd call it miraculous. Murmurations."

"Murmur what?" I asked.

"There's no conscious decision-making—no top-down leading that's forming their shape-shifting clouds. Just murmurs of wings when they instantly turn that way without warning. How is that possible?"

"Who knows? G would probably say, 'Holy bird, that's a million-dollar question.'"

She chuckled. Her laugh made me feel warm inside.

She explained, her scientific bent showing. "Scientists can't fully answer that question. They agree that it demonstrates some higher form of energy working collectively in relationship, or an unseen intelligence connecting everything. People's labels differ about that presence or universal life force. And about whether it's part of people or beyond them. But an invisible universal connection shows."

My heart raced as my mind returned to the night in the ICU. "Talking with Abdul Hakeem and you about my hospital experience makes me think that everyone's true self is part of that universal life force. Or one with it, whatever people might call it."

She pointed. "That's how I see it. Watch those two butterflies by the big thistle to your left. Pay attention to what you experience as you watch."

After waiting, she asked, "What came to mind?"

"Grandma. And good memories of her. She always liked butterflies."

"She must have meant a lot to you."

"She did. She was my safe place."

Saanvi smiled. "Anything else you experienced as you watched?"

"I don't know if this is what you're meaning, but,"

She interrupted. "There's nothing you need to do or say for me. Just pay attention to your inner experiences without expectations of what they should look like. You learn more that way."

Then I said what came to mind. "The butterflies danced and stayed close to each other, as if connected by an invisible string. Almost like the birds. And two words jumped out at me as I watched: dance and connected."

Saanvi gazed at the butterflies as she spoke. "I dance with life like that."

"You mean that you move freely with what life does? Like watching for its move so you know how to move?"

She nodded.

"Cool. I never thought of it as a dance. Even with that invisible string, the butterflies still looked free. Neither controlled the other, like I can't control life and it doesn't control me?"

"That's a great way to put it," she said, studying me. "Living in a dance frees me from thinking I should be able to control life."

I got chills when she said that. "That's probably why G talks about new moves—it's about reading the moment to make better choices instead of relying on old habits and hoping that life cooperates."

She smiled as she started hiking again. "You already spark more life in me than most people. Maybe it's your hunger for more that opens things up."

With Saanvi leading, we trekked most of the way back in silence. At first, my mind roamed over our conversations. Then the woods came alive. The pine trees, the moss on the ground, and the leaves on the saplings looked greener than I had ever seen. *How did I miss nature's richness all of these years?* The forest seduced me into a childlike wonder. Walking felt effortless, and it seemed as if we were moving in slow motion. Everything oozed depth and detail as I gazed at the ground with what felt like supernatural eyes. Even the dirt path with ants, beetles, holes, and grooves looked like a universe to be explored.

Almost giddy, I said, "My inner world always scared me in the past, but today I felt energized when it related to yours. It's as if I'm seeing for the first time."

Saanvi looked back at me and grinned. "I know the feeling."

I didn't want the day to end. I wanted more of this mysterious life. Saanvi aroused that in me, way more than G. Maybe because she was cool. And G was, well, eccentric. I hoped my insatiable hunger for this new wonderland wouldn't smother her.

After reaching the parking area, Saanvi and I hugged each other and planned to meet every other week. I plopped into my car, the old seat springing several times beneath me. As I drove, little Energizer bunnies hopped all around inside me. *Doing the dance.* I shook my head in wonderment.

I backed my car into the lot beside G's place when I got home, but felt no desire to get out. Talking with Abdul Hakeem had gotten me psyched, but with Saanvi my energy rocketed off the charts. I couldn't put words to it or to why I sat staring at the neighboring brick building twenty-five yards from the front of my car. After my session with Abdul Hakeem yesterday, I had kept busy. But this time I just sat, even though I felt ready to burst.

Something stirred inside. Saanvi symbolized the life I wanted during my supernatural experience—being me rather than bending like a cardboard cutout to people's expectations. She wasn't perfect, but I saw her determination to live true to herself.

UNLOCKED

Fifteen minutes later, I finally felt ready to go in, but I didn't know what to do with myself. With whatever was happening inside. Something good would probably come of it. But it needed time, maybe even help, to come out.

Painting — Isabelle

I hadn't painted since before living with Dean. I had lost interest when my marriage turned into Heartbreak Ridge. But, today, as soon as I returned from the hike and stepped into my room, my paint set drew me to it like a kid anticipating a favorite ice cream cone. Unusual. Perhaps mentioning art to Saanvi triggered the surge of energy. Or maybe an invisible wave of adrenaline inside was urging me somehow.

Not taking time to eat lunch, I opened my paint set. Unfolding my easel, I stretched a canvas onto it, primed it, and did an underlay. With an empty house except for Button against my feet, nothing distracted me from following this compelling inclination to paint.

With no clear direction in mind, I began painting a young adult surrounded by a mist. Hands on her knees, she leaned over and looked down. Without planning it, I dabbed the blue paint with the brush. *Oh, a lake; she's looking into a lake!*

In the past I always planned what I put on canvas, but this time I gave it no forethought as I started the reflection in the lake. A young face took shape. A smaller body, too. A bright-eyed girl glowed and stared back at the adult. I pondered it for a moment. The lake looked like glass. No ripples. I would have expected a mist around the girl like the grown up, but I had painted none. Curious. I asked aloud, "Is it your joy, your simplicity? Is it your childlike freedom, or lack of responsibility?" Button lifted his head from the floor, tilting his ears toward me as I talked out loud. Then his head sagged back to its place.

As I paused, I felt weightless for a moment. The word *purity* lit up in my mind. "Oh, true self!" Button lifted his head a second time, then gave a "Humph" followed by a sigh as his head flopped to the floor again.

Some of Saanvi's statements rang in my head while I worked. I couldn't put words to my feelings, but I didn't want to. I felt like a butterfly dancing with life and didn't want to hinder the free-flowing energy. Peaceful. Yet uplifting; inspiring. Maybe even intoxicating. I wanted to follow Saanvi's advice—pay attention to my inner experiences without judging them. Having no expectations of what they should look like.

Lost in the thrill of creativity, I finished touching up several places. The inner pull to paint had waned. Hunger, now, took its place.

I put my brush down and stared at the painting. *Damn, that's good.* Outside of my program requirements at LU, I had taken several art courses to develop what people had called unusual raw talent. But this painting far surpassed my previous works. Not only the features of the woman and girl jumped off the canvas, but I couldn't take my eyes off of the dynamic colors and picturesque setting. The process of painting felt rewarding, too. A deeper expression somehow manifested spontaneously. Not orchestrated. *Mysterious.*

Sitting and studying the painting, I remembered staying in the car and taking time to reflect on the talk with Saanvi. I spoke aloud. "I see why G contemplates."

Button's head remained glued to the floor this time, his body twitching as he dozed. *Probably dreaming about chasing squirrels or catching discs.* I nodded to myself. "Space allowed time for inspiration. To go beyond my regular abilities. The same as athletes putting on their game face in silence. Then they're in the zone, and the game feels effortless. That's what this felt like." *Oh...now I'm even talking to myself like G.*

The following day I still felt stoked about talking with Saanvi and about painting. That is, until Dean showed up at LU after my theories class. I had blocked his calls, and he hadn't known how else to reach me. He said he wanted to work things out. I agreed to meet him on Thursday at Potbelly Deli for sandwiches, although I had major reservations about it.

I told G when I got home. His face tightened as he asked, "Do you feel peace about the decision to go?" I shrugged and said that I always felt tense when it came to Dean. G hadn't squawked like a mother hen for a while, but he did with this. Even though he thought I shouldn't meet with him, I couldn't let go of it. I had to try. I'd carry guilt if I didn't.

Finally Thursday, my stomach jumped, almost coming out of my body when Dean swaggered down the sidewalk toward me. At LU he had poured on the sweet-talk with enough syrup that caused me to cave in to my desire for one last chance at making things work. But, as he approached, an unmistakable scowl covered his face in spite of his forced smile. *Give him the benefit of the doubt,* I prodded myself as we walked in the door. *He's trying.*

After we ordered sandwiches and sat down at a table near the door, he started in on me. "Isabelle, I'm trying to make things work here and you're being a bitch about it. If you'd just come home, you'd see what you're missing."

I sighed. *He's way more agitated than usual. There's no chance of this ending well.* I tried to be calm and logical. "Tell me what I'm missing, then. How have you changed since the day you almost killed the guy that helped me move?" I felt a surge of heat inside as I questioned him.

Dean hunched over, trying to keep his words between us, but that was like sitting on lit fireworks to stop them from exploding. "I still owe that twit for reporting me. I got sixty days of service because of that piece of shit. He better not let me see him walking alone or he'll pay for it." His threatening voice, although somewhat stifled, sizzled through the deli.

I glanced around. Five other people at tables, two young couples and… the well-built guy from the park back in the fall. *What was his name? Carlos. Oh, great, what timing.* Everyone's widened eyes told me they knew it was only a matter of time until Dean would blow.

I should have ended it then. But I leaned forward, trying to keep my voice soft. "My friend only helped me because I asked him. He didn't deserve a right cross to the face."

Dean's voice spiked through clenched teeth. "Right there you go. You caused things to go to hell. If you hadn't dragged him into it, everything would've been cool."

Hoping he'd match my lowered voice, I said, "I want to grow. I've been focusing on that. But talking can't work unless we each take responsibility for our own part. I'm willing to look at how I could communicate better, but I also need you to own how you've hurt me— coldcocking my friend and cheating on me."

All restraint blowing away, Dean stood up, leaned over me, and screamed, sticking his finger in my face. "See, you're blaming me right now." Then he slammed his fist on the table. "You're the one that's freakin' messed up!"

I stood and grabbed a ten from my purse, laying it on the table. "I can't do this. It's over."

I took a step toward the door as he reached out and grabbed my trailing wrist, yanking me back to the table like a flailing puppet on strings. I half toppled to the floor but caught the chair with my free hand to stay upright.

After regaining my balance, I looked him in the eyes with utter seriousness. "Let go or I'll call the cops."

His voice boomed through the deli. "Like hell you will."

I tried to pry open his steel-like fingers. Instead, he twisted my wrist to force me to sit back down again.

"Dean!" I winced in pain and looked over at the man behind the counter. "Can you call 911?"

The man's eyelids looked plastered to his forehead as he reached for the phone. I thought his call to 911 would stop Dean, like when G did that on Oak Street. But this time, Dean raged like a tornado hungry for whatever stood in its path.

Everything happened in a matter of seconds. His left hand still holding my wrist, he drew back the other one with a clenched fist. I waited for the blow when Carlos came up behind him and grabbed his arm.

"It's not okay to hit a woman," he said with calm authority.

I gasped, waiting for the inevitable. *Dean's going to kill him!*

Dean, several inches taller, turned like a wild lion whose prized carcass had been stolen. They stood there for a second, eyeing each other up. Without warning, Dean's fist shot through the air. Like an expert fighter, Carlos blocked the punch with his left arm and quickly delivered a blow to the gut.

Dean grunted, bent over at the waist, gasping for air. He tried to recover and lunged at the interfering stranger. With shocking speed, Carlos immediately struck the side of Dean's head, knocking him to the floor, unconscious.

It was over in an instant. I stood there gaping at this nightmare-come-to-life as I heard the sirens suddenly stop outside. I had always seen Dean as this invincible hulk that no one would mess with. Even though he was the larger of the two, he stood no chance.

My unforeseen protector turned to me, only a little out of breath. "I'm sorry, Isabelle. I don't like to fight anymore, but you shouldn't be treated like that."

Almost collapsing, my legs wobbled when I looked into his eyes. My mouth just hung open, unable to form words. Two officers charged through the door, preparing to handcuff Carlos. But the worker behind the counter quickly explained that I'd be decked out on the floor had this customer not stepped in. After they examined Dean further, the taller officer, a woman as big as a fullback, took charge. She questioned me as her partner took notes. Then they questioned the deli worker, Carlos, and the other two couples who had watched in fear. Before the officers returned to Dean, who still lay motionless on the floor, they approached me about pressing charges. I said I'd think about it. Then they gave me their information for contacting them once I made my decision or to add anything that I might have forgotten.

The police interview with the deli worker revealed that he was also the manager. He pressed charges. After Dean finally stirred, the officers helped him to his feet while handcuffing him and reading him his rights. Normally, Dean would have resisted and screamed out, blaming everyone around him that he got screwed. But his glazed eyes and unstable legs told me he was still foggy from the knockout blow.

Seeing the police head out the door with him, I noticed Carlos motioning to get my attention. "I'm heading out. I hope things get better for you."

The sensitivity in his eyes made my stomach whirl. I gave slow hazy nods, unable to say anything. I stared blankly as he turned and left.

I looked around the room one more time and widened my eyes at the manager. I mouthed the word "sorry." I grabbed my purse to leave, wagging my head about the outrageous insanity that had just transpired. Total mayhem that I should have foreseen. It still didn't feel real. My whole body started shaking. I glanced out of the large front window before leaving the deli. Carlos, moving slowly on the sidewalk, had still been watching.

We caught each other's eyes. My heartbeat quickened. After that unusually long moment, he walked away. My mind went into overdrive. *Were the weak legs and whirling stomach from the pandemonium or from…him? Could he be attracted to me? I couldn't imagine why, after witnessing my insane, humiliating ordeal. But what else did I see in those eyes? Sadness? Did he feel pity for me or was he just sad about what happened?* I felt mad. No, foolish. I wanted to hide for the next month.

The following morning, I laid awake for a while in bed before getting up. The space gave me time to reflect on yesterday's bombed reconciliation. Dean needed more serious consequences for him to change. I got up and phoned the deli manager to thank him for calling 911. He asked if I had pressed charges too. I said that it was my next call and that I should have done it previously when he hit a friend of mine. Then I called the number the police had provided. The woman officer answered. After I pressed charges and asked several questions, she said, "Dean may go to jail this time because of a prior, as well as another unresolved situation. Both of those incidents happened about the same time: punching some old man and allegedly beating up a woman."

G was the old man. The woman—she had been sleeping with Dean and he beat her up when she put a stop to their rendezvous. According to my friend Val, the woman reported him but then changed her story and withdrew the charges when the cops showed up.

I had seen the good in Dean when we first met, but I couldn't reach it anymore. He made that clear. I needed to let go—divorce him and move on. But my heart ached, my whole body sagging at the thought of him slipping into a point of no return.

Carey

Not Ready — Gene

Isabelle had gone for her lunch date with Dean. The memory of him blindsiding me wouldn't stop, and I kept imagining the worst for her. I hoped that my stomach wouldn't keep churning until tomorrow because I wouldn't cross paths with her before then. My niece's wedding and the following reception would keep me out late. With only twenty minutes until I needed to leave, I headed to the hallway to grab the vacuum, dressed in my finest. I thought that cleaning the living room might distract me.

On the way to the closet, I glanced through the gap in the doorway to Isabelle's bedroom. I couldn't help myself. The painting on the easel drew me to it as powerfully as an addict to a drug. I lost my breath as I walked into the room, unable to take my eyes off of it. "Holy DaVinci!" I said aloud, still barely able to breathe. The painting moved me—not just the colors, but the symbolism, too.

I glanced down at Button. "Well this might've done the trick, distracting me from worrying about her." Standing there and studying it, I almost forgot the time. Even after racing out of the room and grabbing my keys, I couldn't take my mind off of the painting. The whole one-hour drive and also later, it consumed me. I could scarcely focus on the wedding ceremony. Or people's conversations at the reception. The painting, a masterpiece beyond my comprehension, left a deep impression on me. I kept shaking my head about it all evening long.

The next morning, I sat at the table when Isabelle came to the kitchen. I couldn't read her. No sluggish demeanor. No bounce in her step. Somewhere in between. Her jaw set and lips pursed, she appeared to be processing something.

I waited until her face relaxed and asked, "How did it go at the deli?"

Her eyes got big as she enunciated each syllable individually, "Hor. Rend. Ous. Ly."

"That bad?"

She exaggerated her face and said each word with distinction. "Of historically epic proportions!" Then she relayed the whole story.

"That's awful," I said. "I'm surprised you're not more discouraged."

"It made everything clear. I feel peace about ending things. I would've second-guessed myself if I hadn't given it a go yesterday. But I'm absolutely certain about moving on now. I'm not okay with being a freakin' doormat anymore. He would've hit me in the face yesterday if that guy hadn't stopped him." She sighed. "I'm learning about myself, and learning's a big fat zippo for Dean. We had almost no connection as it was. Now it's an unreachable chasm."

"I'm glad that you're clear. It's still sad when relationships come to an end. There's always loss."

Her shoulders sagged. "Yeah, I'm sad it didn't pan out. I'm bummed for the lost time. And I feel sick for Dean and how his life's spinning out of control." Her voice became distant. "I knew him before he almost killed his dad. He cared. I saw his sensitive side. But that day changed him. I couldn't reach any tenderness after that."

We talked for another five minutes. Then I told her how I happened to see her painting. She wrinkled her face. "I don't like anyone else to see my work until I'm ready."

"I'm sorry."

She stayed silent. Then she asked, "What did you think?"

"It's a masterpiece. For anyone who cares about growing in their true identity, it's inspirational. The meaning will touch a person's heart whether they know it or not. I'm not an artist, but the art is stunning. I couldn't take my mind off of it after seeing it."

Isabelle blushed. "What do you see in it?"

"The portrayal of the lake without ripples shows our need to receive clear reflection for gaining awareness. For growing into our true identity."

"I saw that, too. What else?" she asked.

I pictured the painting again. "Clear reflection frees us from the suffocating pressures and fog of adulthood. It helps us embrace our childlike true self and its purity."

"It's simpler just to say that all the shoulds of adulthood cause identity theft. That's what happened to me."

"Holy nutshell! What a great way to put it. You painted it. What else stood out to you?"

She tilted her head. "When I finished painting and studied it afterwards, the word pure came to me about the girl. I knew that it showed true self."

We sat and talked for ten minutes. During a lull in the chat, Isabelle said, "I need to stay busy to take my mind off the deli incident. What do you think about going to the park and taking Button for a walk? Nature always clears the air after stress." As soon as Button heard the word walk, he came to attention.

Half an hour later, Isabelle and I strolled down a path with Button at Landsburg Park. He jutted one way and another, tugging hard on the leash.

Her face brightened. "He must be getting all kinds of good whiffs. He's pumped."

"Butt, heel!" The leash slackened, and he slowed to the same pace as Isabelle.

She praised and patted him as we rounded the pavilion. "What a rock star! You're such a good listener."

Just then we came face-to-face with Carlos and Emily. Isabelle froze. He looked down for a moment and fidgeted.

Then he appeared to recover and said to Isabelle, "I hope you're doing okay."

Flushed in the face, she struggled for words. "I, um. I'm. I should thank you, ah, for yesterday."

Oh, he's the one who saved the day. She never said.

He shrugged and spoke with a soft voice. "No need to thank me." Then he grimaced. "I don't like what happened. He just pushed things beyond reason."

They both looked away, as if at a loss for words. Emily's cute voice cut the tension. She pointed at me and asked Isabelle, "Is Gene your grandpa?"

I grinned as Isabelle said, "You remember his name! Yes, he's always been like a grandpa to me, and a good friend."

Carlos' dark hair and put-together appearance made me wonder if he might be self-centered. But the more I heard him speak, if anything, he impressed me as humble. And Emily, with similar features, looked adorable.

Her eyes bright, she pointed to Button. "Can I pet him?"

Isabelle moved to his side and petted him, then motioned for Emily to join her. "Sure. This is Button." Isabelle leaned down and asked, "Do you like dogs?" The enraptured young girl nodded with her whole body. "Do you like coming to the park with your dad, too?"

Her whole face frowned as she dragged out her unabashed reply. "Noooo, that's Uncle Carlos."

Isabelle glanced up at him and blushed. "I'm sorry. I shouldn't have assumed."

Carlos chuckled. "No problem, my sister's daughter. I like spending time with her at the park. Don't I, Emily?"

She gave a huge grin and look of adoration at Carlos as he bent down and talked to Button while rubbing behind his ears. Isabelle turned my way in time to see me giving an exaggerated nod of approval. She flattened her eyes at me, trying not to be seen by our new friends. Then Emily skipped over to the monkey bars. I followed to keep her company. I enjoyed getting to know her while I occasionally watched Carlos and Isabelle chatting. From what I could tell, their eyes never left one another.

On the way home from the park, I razzed Isabelle. "You two connected really well."

She steered the conversation away from my point. "Of course. He's a nice guy. And Emily's sweet, too."

"He spent time with Button, who doesn't warm up easily to most guys. If Button's keen on him, that tells me a lot about the man. Abdul Hakeem's the only other guy that Button takes a liking to."

Isabelle didn't respond.

"Emily's seven. Adores Carlos." I asked, "Did you two happen to talk about Dean?"

"Some. I thanked him again for jumping into the mess. I told him that yesterday cemented the end of my marriage." She shook her head. "He didn't judge me about how I could've ever hooked up with a guy like Dean. But he got it—how much Dean changed after the beginning. He mostly just listened."

She told me about the rest of their conversation. The more she said, the more I liked Carlos. Then, after some silence, I asked, "Did he get your phone number?"

She snapped back. "Don't even go there."

"You don't think it's worth considering?"

"Don't be a mother hen. I'm married until signing divorce papers. I'm not ready for some new guy to smother me. I want freedom right now. I like the idea of having no one to answer to!"

I backed off. "Sorry for bugging you about it. I'm glad you're paying attention to what you need, and trusting when you're ready or not. That's living with awareness and paying attention to your true self."

After some silence, she spoke with a soft voice. "I needed that. Thanks. I usually run ahead without paying attention to what I need. And I need time to learn about what I think and feel without bringing another person into the mix."

A week later, Button and I moseyed down Eagle Street, a different way than normal. Just ahead of us, Carlos exited a small grocery store called Mamma's and caught sight of us. He looked at his watch and then waited on the sidewalk until we reached him.

"Good to see you again, Gene. Hey, Button." He bent over, putting down his two bags of groceries to pet him.

"Glad to see you, too, Carlos. You must live near here."

"I do. On Hawk Street, 633. A place with my sister, Adelina, and Emily. You close by?"

"Not too far. We're on Maple." As soon as 'we' came out of my mouth, I knew I'd catch flack from Isabelle when she found out.

His eyes lit up. "You mean Isabelle and you?"

I nodded. "We've been like family since she was in the ninth grade."

He petted Button once more and picked up his groceries. "I'd talk more but gotta run. Could you tell her I asked about her?"

After agreeing, Button and I turned to head home. GUS spoke more distinctly than in the past several weeks, *Honest friendship.*

I didn't know what to make of it until Isabelle came to mind. *Oh, maybe she's not interested in dating, but she might be ready for an open, honest friendship with Carlos.*

Treasure — Isabelle

Ever since the deli debacle, I felt more peace in everything I did—talking to LU classmates, doing my assistantship work, engaging with professors. Abdul Hakeem noticed the change after processing my experiences related to the crisis with Dean. Half-way through my session with him, he said, "Your contentment keeps increasing. You seem more at ease." I reflected. "Deciding to divorce Dean took a load off. Until then, I second-guessed myself, maybe because Dean did that with me."

"We often treat ourselves the way we've been treated."

His statement stuck, not only about Dean, but about Mom and me. She had no patience for me. Then I didn't with myself.

His gentle eyes looked into mine. "Also, being more at peace comes from making more choices that give you peace. It tells me that you're more centered in your authentic identity—in your true self. You're less at odds with yourself because other people's expectations and values don't direct you more than your own."

Friday morning, I sat in my car at White Pine Trails waiting for Saanvi. Just seeing her red Jeep pull into the parking lot made me smile in spite of the gray, dreary day. The sound of birds singing filled the air when I closed my car door and headed around her Jeep to greet her. We hugged as soon as she finished shutting off her phone. It felt natural, like connecting with a long-time friend even though we had only known each other a short time.

Saanvi asked, "You want to take the blue trail? It's shorter than the red-marked trail that we took last time."

I joked. "Cool. I guess you don't need your phone to set your boss straight this time."

She laughed as we entered the woods under the overhanging pine branches. "No. He treats me nicer now, even though he still snaps at others. I think he knows I won't put up with it. I'll just quit. And, for now, he needs all the employees he has." After pausing, she asked, "What's the backpack for? I love the two-toned purple."

"Thanks. Grabbed it at the last minute just in case I find something I can use for art work. I painted after we hiked last time. I'd like you to see it in person before I tell you about it."

"Can't wait. I'm glad you're pursuing art again. You sound drawn to it each time you bring it up. You come to life." After several more steps, she asked, "How was your lunch with Dean?"

"What a major disaster. He had come to LU one day, sounding softer. He said he wanted to meet and talk about getting back together. I didn't want to bring up the d-word, but I told him if our meeting didn't show that we were both willing to learn, it could be the beginning of the end. I thought he might take me seriously after saying that. But not even close. At the deli, he was on the attack from the get-go." I described the whole chaotic scene as we walked.

After listening, Saanvi said, "That must have felt embarrassing, your life on display up close and personal."

"I felt totally humiliated, especially with Carlos watching."

She kept watching me as we hiked. "Anybody would've. But you don't seem angry at yourself, like you let go of it."

"I have, and of the marriage overall."

"You mean divorce?" she asked.

"Yes," I said, with a calm voice. "I'm clear about it. I just hope I keep my head about Carlos."

She probed. "Because you might already have feelings for him?"

"That obvious, huh?"

She nodded. "Isn't it amazing how many feelings we can have at once?"

The whirling mess came pouring out. "They're like a spider web, with layers all stuck together! They've been building. But I can't talk about it with G. He's a guy!" Saanvi chuckled and waited as I collected my thoughts and stepped around a branch blocking half of the path. "I didn't want to admit how I feel about Carlos because I'd feel guilty moving on. Like I'd be cheating on Dean. But my legs go weak when I'm around him. I just want to fall into his arms, even though I don't! Everything I know about him, which isn't much, I wouldn't change a thing. His tender voice and thoughtfulness. His dark, wavy hair. Dreamy eyes. Like no one else exists but me when I talk with him. And he's insanely hot!" I made eyes. Saanvi belly-laughed.

The entangled web of emotions continued spewing and sputtering out of me. "I can't get him off of my mind, and I don't want to. But the timing's not right. I don't want to lose myself again. I'm just starting to become aware of my feelings and what I need, and I'm afraid I won't be able to do that if I have to pay attention to what some guy wants. But I'm even more terrified that I could miss an opportunity of a lifetime with someone who seems perfect for me."

"Wow, did you need to talk, girl!"

"What a rush! I didn't even know all that was in there." I shook my head. The flurry of thoughts that flew out of me made me think of Val's rapid-fire way of speaking.

"That's just it," she said. "You'd be blind making decisions without self-awareness—without being aware of your needs and priorities."

My face tightened. "Yep. Blind and clueless. Still might be."

"My mother always said that the treasures are within, not outside, us. And that you need to sort through all the relics to find the gold."

"How do you sort through it?" I asked.

"Through awareness and expressing 'what is' saying your genuine experiences out loud. Undefended and unaltered, just like you did. Then that whirlwind inside comes out into the light and you can recognize the gold."

"And what's the gold in my case?" I asked, still feeling lost.

"Maybe you already spoke it. That there's more than one thing important to you. Perhaps that's what you need to tell Carlos."

I nodded. "Never considered that. I only thought of date or don't date."

We walked for several minutes enjoying the new terrain, the path becoming nothing but a blanket of rocks elevating over a knoll. Needing to watch our footing, we worked our way through the uneven landscape in silence. Then I asked, "What about you? Are you seeing anyone or even interested in that?"

"It's funny you ask. Gene, Abdul Hakeem, and I just chatted about this. I told them that I prefer the honesty in my friendships and how it often fades for couples."

"Why would it fade?" I asked.

"Ownership. People sometimes act like they have the right to expect or govern what their partner should do. If you love me, you'd do such and such."

My mouth hung open. "Dean treated me that way all the time."

"And then if you didn't do what he expected, he probably acted justified about being upset at you until you did." I stared at her; she nailed the dynamics I had never questioned.

"That's ownership," she said. "It's conditional love."

I shook my head. "I'm still trying to wrap my head around it. G and an LU professor both talked about conditional love recently."

"In my friendships, care is at the forefront. Our honesty is too, because we want that as friends. But it's a free, peaceful honesty. No condemnation. No expectations of some result. Do you see how there's no possession of each other? No selfish pressure pushing for certain outcomes, as if the other person has to do what you want?"

"You're lucky to have friends like that. In my experience, most people push for their own agendas."

We came around a bend, about a quarter mile to go to the parking area. I spotted it just off the edge of the trail—a rock shaped like a flat arrow. Well, a five-inch-thick arrow, and over a foot long. Eye-catching and unique, streaks of red, orange, and gray stretched across its surface. As soon as I saw it, I wanted to paint words on it. Something about true self.

Too big for the backpack, I strained to pick it up and held it across my arms. It felt heavier than the fifteen-pound boxes I transported around B & F Warehouse.

Saanvi said, "I can help."

I groaned. "Thanks, but I got this. It'll be good exercise."

I always tried to avoid inconveniencing people, which meant Saanvi at the moment. Lugging the hefty slab as far as I could, I tossed it down and waited to catch my breath. But hoisting up my treasure each time took its toll. I carried it about thirty or forty yards at a clip before giving it a pitch for a breather again. Then I worked it into my arms for another stretch of the trail. We both chuckled as I labored down the path, sometimes dropping the rock because of laughing hysterically.

Coming around another bend, a couple stepped to the side to make way for me and my massive stone arrow. Seeing me covered with dirt, or maybe because we were still joking about the hilariousness of it all, they burst out laughing, too.

Saanvi got her kicks from my tussle with the weighty load. She ran ahead to get her phone and snapped a picture when I came into the parking lot—sweaty, with scratched, dirt-covered arms from carrying the stupid rock!

Even though I only hauled it several hundred yards in total, I collapsed when I finally got to the car. I lay on the ground for a few minutes, panting like I had run three football fields back-to-back. Then, after brushing some leaves out of my hair, I stood up, heaved my prize into my arms again, and placed it onto the car floor in front of the passenger seat. I hoped the rusty flooring would hold.

Compelled – Isabelle

Coming home from classes on Monday, I opened the door to a brown ball of fur and wagging tail. Button never failed to smother me with his undying enthusiasm as soon as I stepped into the house. G sat in his recliner, reading. "Hello, Isabelle," he said, as he usually did when I got home—not quite the same welcome as Button's.

After asking about each other's days, G said, "I ran into Carlos when I took Button for a walk. Coming out of a grocery store on Eagle Street."

I tilted my head, wondering if I heard a hint of apprehension in his voice. "Yeah, anything up?"

He pressed his lips together. "I assumed he lived nearby and said that to him. He said yes and asked if I was close by, too. I told him we were on Maple Street and didn't catch that I said we until it came out of my mouth. He caught it, too. I'm sorry."

I wrinkled my face. "I know you didn't do it on purpose, but now he can find me. I'm not ready for anything serious."

"I know you're not. But if he does find you, you could simply be honest about how you feel, which I'm willing to bet is mixed."

I reacted. "But why talk if I'm not ready to date?"

"You act as if it's either/or, and that the only reason to talk is if you want romance. What about an honest friendship and telling him that you don't want anything more than that?"

"Hmm." I sighed. "Saanvi mentioned honest friendship, too. But I don't know if I'm ready for that with him either."

"Why? Hasn't learning to be your true self when you're with others been at the forefront? This would be a great chance for practice. Especially with a man you wouldn't be dating. That might help you the most."

I mumbled. "Maybe."

"Just so you know, the moment I left Carlos, GUS said, 'Honest friendship.' When I paused, you came to mind. That's why I'm encouraging you."

"Yeah, encouragement," I said with a sarcastic groan.

I sat in my bedroom staring at the rock I hauled home. I had cleaned it up and put it on a chair so I could begin creating. I shook my head about how I had changed, about how consumed I got with unseen things now—my inner experiences, intuition, and true self. A whole new world kept opening up. A fascinating one with unending learning and possibilities that made life richer. Treasures within, like Saanvi said. I didn't want to chase others' approval anymore. Instead, I wanted to keep learning my value; to be at peace with myself. Those inner treasures were beginning to fill me up, making me feel less empty and alone. Looking back, I hadn't known that a purer me had been trapped inside. A genuine me who didn't fold to the demands of the world. *I want this, and I can't give it up. Even for Carlos.*

Pressed against my feet like the other time I painted, Button moved twice to snuggle tighter. I waited for inspiration as he settled into place.

Dipping the brush into black, I painted words across the top third of the rock, allowing the natural colors slashing across its midsection to show. Then I formed white clouds surrounding the words, with the sun in the upper right of the arrowhead. Not knowing why, I dabbed red to begin painting below the rock's natural streaks. Two hearts slightly turned toward each other and holding hands flashed in my mind. I painted them down in the lower right and put smiles on each. Then I formed an open treasure chest filled with golden musical notes, some of them floating outward toward the hearts, others toward the sun.

Apart from faint breathing, Button lay motionless on the floor as I read the words aloud. "Seek true self in yourself and others and fill your life with treasure." *Cool. Talking about what matters to each other,* I thought as I studied the hearts holding hands. *When friends speak from the heart like Saanvi and I did, hearts connect and you find treasure.*

Near the end of the Interviewing Skills II class, professor Sailhammer ripped into Lukas, a fellow student. After over an hour of rigid movements and semi-controlled spikes in her voice, she lashed out, throwing her hands up in the air. "Don't you know by this point that it's empathy, not sympathy? We're in the second skills course now and I've pounded that home repeatedly. Get a grip!" The belittling condemnation mushroomed like a cloud across the classroom. Students' eyes widened as they sank back into their chairs. Head and eyes down, Lukas' freckled face contorted with pain. The erratic blips of destruction from the intimidating figure up front continued onward like a malfunctioning machine in an assembly line.

In the past I would have made myself invisible. Or froze and waited for the inevitable worsening onslaught to build into a second or third demoralizing assault. Like with my mom. But I felt hot at first. Then just determined. I couldn't let it go. *No one's honest with her!* I knew what I had to do.

Sailhammer finished collecting her materials and marched out. The classroom emptied, no one saying a word. I beelined it to her office. Poking my head around the partially open door, I saw her standing motionless, facing the window with her back to me. Barely audible, I knocked.

She jumped and turned all at once. With flaring nostrils and fire in her eyes, she appeared ready to scorch the next straw figure, me. "What do you want?"

Her fierce attack didn't deter me. "I'm concerned about you. You seem strained, like you're dealing with something. And your treatment of Lukas disheartened me."

She doused whatever flames she had almost unfurled at me. Her stern face relaxed. She took a breath. With a restrained tone, she said, "I'm going through some personal upheaval right now. I don't want to get into it."

"Okay. I feel bad about whatever you're going through. I hope you find peace about it." Not knowing what else to say, I said, "Let me know if you need anything." Then I turned to go.

Her voice softened. "Thanks for checking and for saying something about Lukas."

I looked her in the eye. "You're welcome. We all have value." I headed out the door, and let out a long breath, glad that she saw it as helpful. *Strange, I felt on equal footing with her.*

Further down the hall, I couldn't go by the department's library without checking on Lukas. Like I was compelled. He usually studied and did homework at a conference table in view of the hallway. Not there. I looked down the other rows, finally spotting him at a desk in the back corner.

His head stayed down as I approached him. "Hey, Lukas."

He looked up. "Hey," he said with a breathy, hollow tone.

"I felt bad about Sailhammer ripping into you. She was ripe for lashing out at someone, and it happened to be you. But it was wrong, even if she's the prof."

Putting on a weak smile, he muttered under his breath. "Thanks."

"I told her what I thought. Hopefully, she'll come clean with you about it."

He tilted his head. "That was brave. What the hell compelled you to do that?" Then, before I answered, he said, "Thanks for saying something. But as far as her, I won't hold my breath."

I gave Saanvi a ring the next evening. After we greeted each other, I asked, "Anything new for you?"

"I went bowling with a friend and had a blast."

"Cool, I haven't done that since the day I met Dean."

The phone went silent for a moment. "I'm sorry for raising that sore subject."

"I'm chill. It was an awesome day. The upheaval came much later. How'd you do?"

"Up and down. Chatting with my friend was the best part. She's honest, the way we are, and I learned about how I tackle things I've never done."

"What do you mean?" I asked.

"She mentioned how tenacious I am when I'm trying to understand something. What advantage does a hook have over a straight ball and why? I always need to understand the foundations."

I reacted, words flying out of my mouth before thinking about them. "I just threw the freakin' ball down the lane and hoped for the best."

She chuckled.

"Something new happened yesterday," I said. "I talked with my prof about her snapping at a classmate. She reamed out the student, and I couldn't rest until I told her what I thought."

"That's difficult to do, like me with my boss. How'd it go?" she asked.

"I expected some flack, but she responded better than your boss did." We laughed. "And I did it out of concern for her, too—just came to me last minute, how to say it. Then I found the student and made sure he knew it was her problem, not his. But I keep shaking my head about how compelled I felt to do it. I felt fearless."

"That's your conscience at work. Moving you to take action."

"My conscience?"

"It moves you to care for whatever you're connected to," she said as a matter-of-fact. "Everyone's conscience works that way, unless it gets buried under pain or lies."

"I never thought about it that way. I just know I want more of what happened—standing for something bigger instead of cowering around people like an abused puppy. I felt sick seeing my classmate shrivel up to nothing. I did that most of my life with Mom, but I tapped into something bigger yesterday."

Then Lukas' comment came to mind. "After I told the student that I called her out on it, he asked what compelled me to confront her. And that's exactly how I felt. Compelled. It reminded me of my wild experience the night of the hospital. I just hadn't thought of it as tied into conscience."

"You know I'm research and science oriented," she reminded me, sounding ready to say more.

I joked. "That's right. You're an unusual combination of science and abstract things."

She gave a slight chuckle but didn't miss a beat. "The word conscience comes from 'con' and 'science.' It means to connect knowledge into a greater whole."

The silence over the phone must have told her I didn't get her point.

Saanvi elaborated as if instructing a Psych 401 class. "Con means to connect and condone, and to come together. That's the first part of the word. You following?"

"Okay. I think so."

"Science, the second part of the word, studies facts, principles, or truths and brings together scientists' hunches, intuitions, and hypotheses about the info."

I waited, still not sure what to make of it until she said her punchline. "Our consciences, when we follow them, continually teach and connect us."

I ragged on her. "Glad you got to the skinny about it. Why didn't my program put more emphasis on learning about my conscience? So much seems to hinge on it."

"It's difficult to research, and even to talk about, but it should be central. We're meant to learn from conscience within ourselves and others. That awakens the unique beauty in everyone. The diversity. And it connects us like a symphony playing a beautiful song. Do you see how your actions would have encouraged your professor to pay attention to her conscience, like my honesty did with my boss? That honesty awakens us and pulls us together if we let it."

I repeated her words, taking them in. "It awakens us."

"Yes, people can't live in their true self without awakening to their conscience and following its lead."

I kept reflecting on it as she asked, "Didn't honesty with your classmate help him pay attention to what his conscience knew about how she treated him, rather than believing lies about it? Conscience always cares for both ourselves and others. Our pain doesn't."

Letting that sit for a moment, determination rose up in me. "I want to learn to follow my conscience."

Living In Sacred Awareness — Gene

Isabelle got up early, her voice more upbeat than usual. "Hey G, smells great!" She stopped and took a long, exaggerated breath through her nose, then straight-lined it for the coffee pot.

"Good morning, Isabelle. If I had to guess, I'd say that you seem focused, maybe even tenacious, today."

She poured some steaming coffee into a mug and plopped into a chair across from me. "Yeah, something's at the forefront. But it's funny that you saw me as tenacious. Saanvi just said that someone described her that way, too." She took a sip. "Hmm. That's the ticket." Then Isabelle told me how she had felt compelled to be honest with Sailhammer and Lukas.

After her story, I smiled. "Holy LISA!"

"Lisa? Are you getting senile?" she asked. "Your wife's name is Hanna. What does she have to do with this?"

"I'm not talking about Hanna." I spelled it out. "L.I.S.A.—Living. In. Sacred. Awareness."

She frowned. "Are you being serious, or is this your dry humor again?"

"When you live in sacred awareness, you honor your conscience and its leading above all else. That's what happened. With that higher awareness, everyone is valued; everything has its place. You see purpose in all that is. LISA means tuning into and caring about all that's valuable and life-oriented, beyond the rough edges. Then your conscience moves and leads you better." I waited for her to catch up. "You've been growing in LISA."

She wagged her head while her eyes searched for something. "Okay. Saanvi said my conscience moved me to do what I did. Have I been clueless to mine? I don't get why I felt so compelled about it, beyond normal."

"Nobody understands these things fully," I said. "But you're listening more inwardly than outwardly compared to your past. For inner leading.

That's sacred awareness. And you have less pain and clutter in the way than you used to. That increases your ability to be aware of your conscience."

She nodded, as if that registered.

"Sometimes it's bold like that. But usually conscience is a faint voice—a peaceful voice that's difficult to hear amongst all the loud ones. You have to really want to hear it because it's a whisper compared to all the other, overpowering, voices and thoughts."

"Have to want to hear it," she said aloud.

"When you pay attention to the whisper and pause about it, when it's from conscience, there's peace. You know that you know. Learning from that voice and following it is right for you, and in line with what you value."

She shook her head and wrinkled her face. "I used to rag on you about getting caught up in some unseen universe. Now I'm stoked about it. I feel like a kid trying to snatch up the next mystery prize with one of those mechanical arms. The idea of being compelled by my conscience opens up a whole new world about why I do what I do. My true self seems more attainable now. I can be more intentional."

I couldn't stop grinning. "You're giving a sip to a lush! I drink this stuff nonstop. I told you Saanvi would be a great mentor. You're both thirsty for inner learning. She's just been at it longer. You'll be a heavy drinker before long!"

She rolled her eyes. "She said conscience keeps drawing people into unity, yet with diversity, as long as we hear and follow it." Then she sped up, her questions pushing and pressing for more. "But how do we know for sure if we're following conscience or not? Pain moves us, too, like it did with Sailhammer. And what about false guilt? False conscience?"

Keeping my words slow and deliberate, I wanted to give everything time to sink in. "True. Other things often move us if we don't remain awake or aware." I paused. "That's why LISA is necessary. Especially with decision-making. I ask myself if I feel peace about a decision—if it's a good path for me or not. That's sacred awareness about conscience and its peace. It keeps me centered."

Her eyes lit up. "Conscience. That's what you call GUS, isn't it? Gut Understanding and Sensitivity."

"It is."

She spoke with authority. "Chill a minute!" Her eyebrows lowered, concentration filling her face. "So, being aware, especially of GUS, or you could say conscience, helps you follow his lead and doing that keeps you in your true self?"

"That captures it well."

She put her hands to each cheek, her head going back and forth. Then peering off to the left, she tilted her head. Her voice sounded far away, as if speaking to herself. "Now I get it—how higher presence or inspiration works—what I asked you about in the old days. People label it in different ways: God, higher self, Allah, Christ. Or Buddha and other names, like the Force or the universe. But, whatever it is, it comes through GUS, through everyone's conscience." She paused. "With Sailhammer, I felt more calm and confident. Like a higher presence moved me when I followed my conscience."

I prodded her. "Ask Abdul Hakeem the next time you see him. He's clear about it."

"I will. Following conscience makes all the difference. It was ridiculous how secure I felt with Sailhammer." After stopping, she said, "I want to make decisions about Carlos that way. I just need to pay attention to which choice gives me more peace. But what if every direction makes me anxious?"

"Good question. You want to pay attention to what path gives you the most peace, even if you're anxious to carry it out."

She jumped up from the table and turned to go all in one motion. "Button and I will be in my room contemplating. Thanks." She marched off and closed the door behind her.

I shook my head at her spontaneity. It never took her long to act once she made up her mind.

Half an hour later, someone knocked on the front door. I opened it and found Carlos standing there. "Hi, Gene. Could I speak to Isabelle if she's available?"

I tilted my head. "You found us?"

He made a face. "I'm sorry. I knew you lived on Maple Street, and I waited on a bench last evening until I saw you come in here."

I nodded and smiled. "Persistent. Step inside and hold on a minute. I'll check."

I tapped on Isabelle's door. "Someone's here to see you." Just as she started opening the door, I mouthed the word, Carlos. Her jaw fell and eyes widened. She whispered. "Tell him I'll be right out." Then she turned toward her mirror as she closed the door. I grinned.

Returning to the living room, I saw Carlos showering Button with attention. Crouched down and petting him, he pointed at the counter. "Is that Button's tooth-marked Frisbee sticking out of the pack?"

Eager to brag about the best disk-catcher in the land, I said, "Button's incredible. Only if I make a bad throw does the Frisbee ever hit the ground." I trailed off when he stopped listening and looked past me.

He had that dazed look in his eyes as Isabelle sauntered across the living room with her shoes already on. I said, "I'll head back to the den with my cup. You're welcome to coffee if you want, Carlos."

Silence. Then, as if an afterthought, he said, "Uh, coffee. Uh, no thank you, Gene. I had some earlier." He only took his eyes off Isabelle for a second and then turned back to her, speaking in a quiet voice. "I've been wanting to connect. You up for brunch at *The Big O?*"

Sitting down at my desk, I heard her ask, "I, uh, how did you find me?"

More hushed this time, he said, "I only knew Maple Street. So I snagged a bench last night, a block and a half down. Then I saw Gene get home. I didn't know how else to find you. I'm sorry if that's a problem. I can just leave if you want."

Isabelle yelled to me. "G, we're stepping out. I'll be back soon."

She didn't say we would be back. I stayed at my desk to do bills.

Twenty minutes later, I heard the front door squeak open. Hoping to hear how she made out, I hollered to Isabelle. "Let me know if you want to talk." Nothing.

Finally, she gave a loud sigh. "I'll come in and chat."

With pursed lips and colored cheeks, she shuffled through the doorway. I wondered what happened.

"You can sit if you want." I pointed to the chair.

"No. I need to stand." She shifted her weight back and forth, her feet unable to stay planted. "I just want to say one or two things and then go to my room and think."

"I'm all ears."

"I thought if I paid attention to what gave me peace that I'd feel clear and confident like I did with Sailhammer. And I did beforehand in my room with Button. But I lost it as soon as Carlos got here. Everything got jumbled. On the bench outside with him, I fidgeted like a, well, never mind. But I couldn't focus. I could hardly talk. I think he just caught me off guard."

I fought off a smile and knew not to joke. "It's not always easy following conscience or its peace. Maybe you settled on a decision that made sense, but just fumbled a little carrying it out."

She shook her head. "I just hadn't expected to act like a babbling idiot."

"Here's where kindness, instead of judging yourself, helps you to grow."

She nodded, still bouncing around in place.

"You don't have to tell me if you conveyed what you wanted to with him. Just wondering."

Her face tightened, her answer sounding more like a question than a statement. "I think so? At least we didn't go to brunch like he wanted. I told him to think about what I said, and we'd talk again later."

"I'm not following. What did you ask him to think about?"

She still looked dazed. "I think I told him I only want to be friends. And for him to think about whether he's okay with that or not."

"That's good."

She groaned, and made a pained face. "I don't remember for sure what came out of my freakin' mouth."

"It probably went better than you thought. You might have really high expectations. New situations are stretching. Be gentle with yourself."

She gave an eyeroll, her voice flat. "I guess. But now he has my cell number. I'm gonna go to my room with Button." She turned, shoulders slumped and a tail wagging by her side.

Inflated to Deflated — Isabelle

Sitting in my Interviewing Skills II class the next day, I squeezed a finger. Nope. Not dreaming. Dr. Sailhammer had just given me a nod and said, "Someone made me aware of my short temper last class. I apologize to you for that. Especially to you, Lukas, for my poor treatment of you." She paused, then continued. "My behavior had nothing to do with you or anyone here. I'm going through some personal difficulties. I won't divulge the details. But if you need to talk about anything that happened here, please stop by my office."

To the point. Unswerving. No fluff. Sailhammer had the market on that, but I had never heard her apologize. I looked around the room, probably the only student no longer focused on her. My classmates just gaped, as if two different worlds had collided—one being an unflappable professor always portraying the picture of total competence, and now the other, a regular, fallible human having to say she's sorry. Sailhammer waited. She scanned the seemingly vacant faces, probably for reactions. "If there are no other immediate concerns, let us move on to today's topic: counseling ethics and causing no harm." She chuckled, not normally one for humor. Then she shook her head and added, "Well, that's great timing." Students fidgeted and gave breathy laughs.

Half-way down the hall after class, Lukas waved me into the department's library. He shook his head, his face wrestling and searching. "I owe you one. I never thought I'd see her apologize. She did yesterday in private and told me she'd talk to the class about it today. I thought I was toast when she asked to meet with me. She still scares the hell out of me. But maybe this'll take the edge off."

"She used to scare me, too. But I'm more centered lately thanks to some good friends. Seeing a counselor has helped, too."

We parted ways. I smiled as the words "used to scare me" lingered. Admitting my personal counseling to Lukas, rather than hiding it, stood out, too. A new move. I would've wanted to know that in his place. *More able to care; hmm.*

With no assistantship hours after class today, I went home and painted another rock. This one, flat and shaped like a stop sign, required little imagination from me. After I painted it red with a white border, I formed words in white.

Gardens Give Generously
STOP
and Smell the Roses

The first set of words across the top, the last phrase across the bottom, with the large upper-case letters, S T O P, screaming to onlookers. Then I dabbed a white splotch in the lower right as background for the three red roses I painted next.

As I finished the green stems, my mind drifted to Joe's Pizza in the mall on the other side of Landsburg. I hadn't been to Joe's in months because of the twenty-minute drive. For some reason, their pizza was calling my name, and giving Val a ring came to mind. We hadn't gotten together since the day I helped her with gardening, so I clicked on her number.

Normally a fast, high-pitched talker anyway, Val's pitch rose several notches when she heard my voice. "Hey, Izz!"

"You up for Joe's?" I asked.

"Hell, yeah. Can't leave for 'bout fifteen 'cause of family things. But if you hang, I'm game for hitting the pizza king. See you there, about forty?"

As soon as I agreed, silence. She had shut off her phone.

The call with Val reminded me of the first time I tried a fast-paced video game. *Everything's a blur. There's no space to think! Is it getting worse or do I keep changing?*

After putting my paint supplies away, I rechecked my red and white creation sitting on the chair. Dry. The paint had already soaked into the rock's pores. I could give Val either of my two stones. Placing them in separate boxes, I lugged them out to my car and put them in the trunk.

Opening the fridge, I grabbed the water pitcher and saw the sparse shelves. G had bought food the last time. My turn. Seeing I had time, I jumped in the car and headed for Giant. After shopping and filling the cooler with food, I drove to the mall and sat on a bench not far from

Joe's Pizza. On the wall in front of me, a large, colorful poster advertised an art competition. I read it aloud. "Prescott Gallery Gala and Art Competition: Paintings will be displayed in the mall's square for one week. The gallery's curator, James Fontaine, will be among the judges. The Angelica Ann Ainsworth will head the judge's panel."

I made big eyes. Just like AAA is to travel, Angelica was the Triple "A" Artist for over a decade. An icon. We studied her painting style in my Advanced Art class at LU. The ad, in smaller print, continued. "Best in Show and Judges' Choice will be displayed in Prescott's Gallery for two weeks following the gala and then sold in auction. Half of the proceeds go to the artist and half to the gallery for future events. After the two overall awards, judges will select first, second, and third places."

I took note of the deadline. About a week to submit it. My painting of the woman looking into the lake came to mind.

Still studying the details of the competition, I heard a woman on a nearby bench telling two people "an often-told story in India." Everything started fading. The story took center stage. She described a man who sought a guru to ask him for the secret to wisdom. Instantly, GUS came to my mind.

Sounding passionate now, the storyteller went on. "The guru told the questioning man to look into the large basin of water that sat in front of him. As the man peered into the basin, the guru pushed his head into the water and held it under until he struggled for air. After the guru finally let his head out, the shocked man gasped. 'Why did you do that?' The guru answered, 'You will find wisdom when you seek her more than air itself.'"

I don't remember if the story continued. Or if the people talked further. Their voices waned. Then the shops and their merchandise exploded with color and texture. The mall lights beamed with brilliance, and something similar to electricity surged through my whole body. The timing felt crazy. Bigger than life. The guru's words hung motionless in my mind like a portrait. I sat still and reflected for several minutes.

I nodded to myself. *Wanting is the secret. Thirst for, and learn from, GUS' leading more than all else.* More than money, more than a marriage that actually works, or more than an easy life and even more than my health. Of course, I'd always want health and life's good things. But, at the moment, I had no doubt that if I wanted those things more than learning, I wouldn't learn when life didn't turn out how I wanted. G's words about listening for GUS' voice vibrated through me: "You have to really want to hear that voice because it's a whisper compared to all the other, overpowering, voices and thoughts."

The whole experience felt epic, even though nothing outwardly had changed. Life seemed clear, as if I had nothing to be afraid of and everything to gain by listening for that faint voice within.

I shook my head at the whole ridiculous ordeal. The same as my hospital experience, I didn't know how or why this happened. It seemed to happen *to* me. The only recent change had been my passion to hear and follow GUS. My conscience.

Although fading, I still felt weightless—like a helium balloon floating in space. I waved at Val coming through the mall, hoping that no stupid grin showed. She studied me as she walked over to the bench where I sat.

Her words fast-paced, she asked, "What's up? You look like you're spacing out."

"Just caught up in thought."

"Snap out of it. Let's do some pizza."

We ordered two slices each and grabbed a table near the opening to the mall.

Val usually kept life about what you could see and touch; maybe that's why she liked gardening. Her response threw me, possibly because I had just been floating in some unseen world. Or maybe because I valued inner experiences now, and it was becoming more apparent than ever that she didn't.

As we settled into place and tore into the pizza, I asked, "How's life been?"

In her no-frills fashion, a flurry of words streamed from her mouth. "Same old, same old. MedCheck squeezes the life out of us. But the money's good. I hang with the old gang, bowling on Wednesdays, drinking on Fridays. You ought to chill with us this Friday at Fitzpatrick's. Been a while."

Her comment about the money being good reminded me of what I said to G in the hospital about B & F Warehouse. "Yeah, it'll be cool to reconnect with everyone." Swallowing a bite, I took in her words and imagined myself not tuned into the inner life. I sagged into my seat. "Anything new happening for you or the others?" I asked, hoping for something more.

With double-time staccato speed, she blazed away again. "No, that's it. Other than Jackie hooking up with a new guy. You?" She shifted the focus back to me as quickly as the six-thirty news returned to commercials. Only then did I realize that I had been shoveling in pizza like someone might snatch it before I finished—probably caught up in her fast-paced energy.

Still catching up, I inhaled another mouthful. *How could she be satisfied with the status quo? With nothing changing?*

I felt a disconnect. I tightened, but tried to ignore it. "Actually, I've changed a lot. You know I fell into a dark hole after my grandma and dad died. But life is good now. I'm in LU's social work program. And some friends pulled me out of the hole. They get me."

"Give. What'd they do?" she asked.

She sounded interested. So I described my new friends and how they had been mentoring me about being true to myself. She listened and nodded. Her matter-of-fact way always made her a little hard to read. She leaned forward, so I kept going.

"It's about inner learning, like my professors and mentors focus on." Then I began telling her about my insane experience earlier, trying to make it sound less ridiculous. The peering-through-a-fog look on her face made me feel crazier the more I talked, so I cut it short.

Val reacted like her research-minded dad. "Izz. That stuff sounds like believing in fairies and gnomes. Am I right?"

I fizzled—inflated to deflated.

She barreled ahead. "Our minds play tricks on us sometimes. I believe in logic. What I see. We're born. We die. Make the most of it while we're here. Am I right?"

I cringed each time she said, "Am I right?" Her blunt and callous characterization of what I experienced left me feeling empty.

Instead of getting louder to defend myself like I would have done in high school, I slouched. "Val, it makes me sad to hear you describe life as that clear cut. Life gave me a raw deal, and I felt lost until I learned what was happening inside me."

Hardly budging, Val went on another tear. "Great it worked for you, Izz. Still sounds crazy to me. But I guess some people need that. Others don't. I take life at face value. Deal with what's in front of me. With reality."

Stinging from her comment, I managed to hold my ground. "Dealing with the cards we're dealt makes sense, Val. I just couldn't have done that without the support to learn from it."

Still not buying it, she changed the topic. "Heard Dean got hauled off to the slammer. What a piece of work!"

I reacted. "No way! I didn't know."

"Just happened. Jackie got the scoop from a friend earlier today. She had pressed charges after getting worked over by him. Then flipflopped and dropped them. He still got locked up. Not sure why."

I knew why. G pressed charges. So did the Potbelly Deli manager. And so did I. Now I felt bad for Dean again. And guilt.

Val shifted the conversation to sports, then to gossip about our high school classmates. I lost energy after our disconnect and hearing about Dean. She didn't even notice that I needed the table to hold me up. I told her that I had school work and needed to call it a night, so we headed out to the parking lot.

Giving her the flat-arrow rock about true self made no sense. I liked it far better, but, of course, she'd want the one about gardening. So I opened my trunk, blocking her view to the arrow rock. I reached in the other box and handed her the stop-to-smell-the-roses one. Giving it to her still felt right in spite of our disconnect.

I held it out for her to study. "It seems to fit you."

As soon as she saw it, she said, "Thanks a billion. You need to sell these! Just saw garden stones at a country store. Almost bought one. But didn't want to fork out the dough. Their prices were criminal."

"I'll think about it. Selling them." Something clicked about it, although I didn't know how I felt about making money on something artistic or maybe even inspired.

She tilted her head. "What a coincidence, giving me this one. Gardens make me stop. They're my therapy. They unhook me from all the head stuff. Your stones would sell as good as half-price IPAs at happy hour. I'm telling you, find unique stones. Add your flair. Like this saying—I get that. Just don't write about fairies or gnomes."

Her jab hung in the air, ready to drill me like a yellowjacket. But I zeroed in on selling garden stones, instead. It had possibilities.

Val called her stone a coincidence. I almost commented that

coincidences were part of something bigger. But I dropped that thought as quickly as it came to mind.

She had been a loyal friend back in high school, but talking about emotions never clicked for her. As if inner experiences didn't exist. That showed big-time today. Lies from my past pulled at me: *Be different than you are, or there'll be hell to pay. You're not enough of this. You're too much of that.* The taunts used to come from not pleasing Mom, but today they're from Val dismissing what I value.

The dark cloud lifted as I drove home. Judging myself gave way to reflection. I had changed the last two years, more than I had given myself credit for. I felt more in touch with my inner experiences and emotions than in the past, and more sensitive to Val disregarding them. Fortunately my new friends' support kept me grounded even though her comments had initially shaken me. If anything, I felt more determined to stay the course. A great future job or not, people liking me or not, a successful marriage or not—all of that mattered less to me than being true to myself. Valuing who I am. Especially by following my conscience. Like Saanvi, I wanted to continue that dance with life.

People Over Things — GENE

I parked my car in the lot and grabbed my briefcase to go inside. Since retiring, presenting at conferences and workshops still satisfied me, but cutting back made sense at this point. The two-part, four-hour presentation and three-hour drive back from Ridgefield University took its toll. Hunger pangs rumbled in my stomach. Isabelle emerged from her room as I opened the front door. Button ran to my feet and greeted me.

"Hey G. I just got in from school. I went next door to Joan's and got Button a few minutes ago. She said he did great and would love to have him anytime."

"That makes life easy, having a good neighbor. You give her the twenty?"

"Yep. She declined at first. But I laid it on the counter and said we need to feel okay about asking in the future."

"She okay with that?" I asked.

"She put her hands on her hips, but then nodded. I got groceries last night. What are you up for? Salad, soup, chicken, pasta?"

"Before leaving this morning, I saw you filled the fridge," I said.

"Thanks, but I'm in the mood for Thai. You want to go? I'll buy."

Her mouth hung open. I thought she might drool like Button waiting on a treat. "I haven't eaten Maya's pineapple fried rice for months!"

Within minutes my old blue Ford was lurching onto Maple and weaving through the back streets toward Maya's. On the way, Isabelle asked, "How was your presentation?"

"Very interactive. The impact of conscience and ego on identity development sparked a lot of interest. Standing room only."

"We've talked about conscience, aka GUS, but not as much about ego. I don't know a lot about it from school other than Freud's version."

"Unholy ED!"

She flattened her eyes. "You gotta be kidding. Who's Ed?"

"I use the name ED for E.D., or Ego-Driven, or as Abdul Hakeem would say, Ego Drama." After a pause, I glanced over. "So it's not confused with the E.D. on the TV commercials."

She shook her head and wrinkled her face. But then her whole body tilted forward as if she couldn't wait to hear more. "Okay, you have LISA and GUS; and now there's ED. How many freakin' people do you have in there?"

I smiled. "LISA, or we could just say sacred awareness, centers on GUS, who values people over things. You learn about yourself and others. True identity develops. But ED values things over people, and he comes with many voices. Even disguised ones, to manipulate you to not be authentic."

She took that in as I continued. "ED never learns, except for how to get what he wants, even at the expense of people. With ED driving you toward things, fight or flight happens anytime failure seems likely."

She put her finger to her chin. "So even obsessing about goals, that's ED?"

My eyes widened as I gave a nod of approval. "Yes, ED is consumed by outcomes, never taking his sight off the thing you should do to get a particular thing. Performance and results always overshadow how you treat people. Even yourself."

"I get that. But how does identity development relate?"

"How can you have personal growth when you're driven by things? It's like toddlers who simply learn what to do to get what they want from Mom or Dad. They stay developmentally stuck in the areas that ED dominates. They don't learn about themselves or their parents. They mainly care about the thing they want. That's ED. People don't grow personally when ED runs the show."

"So it doesn't mean letting go of a goal because you could do it in LISA's way, not ED's? Then you still grow?"

"Exactly." I couldn't believe how quickly she got it. Her learning seemed to take off since meeting with both Abdul Hakeem and Saanvi.

"It seems similar to the voice of the angel on one shoulder and the little guy with the pitchfork on the other—LISA's care versus ED who wants the thing at all cost. Always those choices?"

I wagged my head. "I couldn't have summed it up any better myself."

Five minutes later, we strolled into Maya's. Pictures of fish and elephants hung on the walls, and two fountains of water descended into pools with lotus flowers floating in them. Dim, low-hanging lights created a peaceful atmosphere—shutting out the chaos of Landsburg as the restaurant door closed behind us. The hostess led the way toward a table in the corner. After settling into our chairs, Maya, herself, greeted us with several nods and a smile before the waiter came to take our orders.

After ordering, I asked, "How was your day? And how was your time with Val last night?"

"School's been awesome, and I'm stoked about something uncanny that happened at the mall. I told Val about it, but that bombed."

"What happened?"

Isabelle beamed as she described her experience about the guru story. I reacted. "Holy visitation, the timing of that."

"I know. It's like the universe said, 'Here, I'll make it plain as day for you.' Everything clicked. I won't ever forget it."

"Don't assume that profound coincidences like that happen regularly. They don't, but they seem to happen more often when I tune in at that level. You know, LISA."

I asked how things flopped with Val. Before she could answer, the waiter returned with our meals. Isabelle's eyes lit up. Pad Thai for me. Pineapple fried rice for her.

In between bites, she moaned. "This is ridiculous. I gotta be crazy to wait so long to come back here again." After a few more bites, she continued. "She was clueless to the inner world. No interest at all in it. Was I like Val when I first met you?"

"Pretty much. You showed interest, but my words seemed to bounce off an invisible shell."

She shook her head. "Life hardly means anything when people act as if the inner world doesn't exist. When they don't even give it a chance. That's what she acted like."

"It hurts having your genuine experiences thrown away. It feels empty when others don't value LISA."

She half-smiled and sighed. "It did." She took another bite of rice and swallowed. "It's a total disconnect—me changing personally and hanging with someone from my past who hasn't. It was discouraging. Other students mentioned before that you can't go back after growing. At least I didn't get mad like I used to when people didn't get me. And I didn't sell out to get her approval either."

"When you feel more, you hurt more. But you're also more awake to the joys and wonders of life, too. That's all part of LISA."

She gave it time to settle in, and then moaned. "Yeah, like this pineapple fried rice. It's the bomb." Her eyes looked up, searching. "Everyone's on their own journey."

"You remember what I said about identity development before? How healthy development comes from being authentic and at peace with yourself?"

She nodded and took another bite.

"You stayed centered better last night. You were more authentic even when Val dismissed your experiences. The support's helping. You're growing in LISA."

She shrugged. "But it wasn't with a guy."

I raised my eyebrows. "You're quick but just negated the positive affirmation I gave you. Not wanting to lose yourself with Carlos makes sense. Just make sure you take in support rather than judging yourself about what you haven't yet achieved. That's ED."

After grabbing our doggie bags, we headed for the car in silence. Isabelle appeared lost in some unseen world like she always razzed me about. As I drove home, she peered into the distance. Mist began forming on the windshield, so I turned on the wipers.

Crossing Fifth Street, I glanced to the right and saw Carlos holding an umbrella with his left hand and a woman by the arm with his right. Isabelle had been looking that way too. Her head immediately swiveled in my direction. She wrinkled her face and rolled her eyes.

After waiting for a moment, my voice cut the silence. "I only caught a glimpse. And it's rainy. Maybe it was his sister."

She spoke through gritted teeth. "A blond-haired white woman?"

"Oh. It's still possible that it was just a good friend."

She gave another dramatic eye-roll as her voice spiked. "Are you his defense attorney or what? She wasn't a casual friend. They were connected. I know the difference."

I gave her space, but didn't let it drop. "You're right. Maybe he's seeing someone. At the same time, the other day he wanted to date you, and you're the one with the brakes on."

Her pursed lips told me something more. I voiced my thoughts. "So, you don't want to date him right now. But you might after spending time as friends?"

She groaned. "I would've. But not after seeing that. I don't trust him."

GUS said, *Let it go*. I stayed quiet the rest of the way home.

In the morning I waited for Isabelle to talk about Carlos if she wanted. She had taken coffee to her room, informing me she wanted to contemplate a while. A half hour later she came around the corner of the hallway for more coffee when her phone chimed. She looked at it and did a one-eighty toward her room. I heard, "Hey Carlos." Her voice disappeared when the door went shut.

Five minutes later she strolled into the kitchen, poured another cup of coffee, and plopped down across from me. I almost chuckled. She reminded me of a little kid—lips pressed together, elbows on the table, and hands lodged under each side of her jaw to hold up her head. She grunted. "I don't know what the hell I'm doing. I just don't want to screw this up."

"I can just listen. Or I can tell you what I see and hear as you talk. Let me know what you need."

Her right hand thumped the table. "I don't even know what I need. I don't feel peace about any of this. I don't know if it's him, me, or what."

I waited.

After a long sigh, she explained. "Carlos said he wants more if I do. But he also said he's cool with just being friends if that's what I want. Then when he asked about getting together today, I froze. I blanked out. After a long silence and whatever else I blathered, I told him I needed more time to think."

"And?" I probed.

She crinkled her face. "He said to take whatever time I needed. That he was willing to wait."

"That sounds good. It works with how I see him. Very accepting."

Desperation in her voice, she asked, "But what if he's a player?"

"That doesn't fit for me. Did you say you saw him hugging a woman?"

She frowned. "Of course not. You don't just accuse a person of something like that."

I tilted my head. "Accuse? We're only talking about saying what you saw and asking about it. How can you have peace or move forward when a big question like that hangs in the air?"

"Maybe Dean warped me, but men just have a one-track mind."

I tried to lighten up things. "Oh, thanks."

She didn't laugh.

I started again. "That may have been true with Dean, and your history with him would naturally cause you to worry about that. But the way you grow is by communicating. Then you learn. Maybe I'll find I'm wrong. But my gut tells me that Carlos lives more in LISA than ED—he cares more for the person than what's in it for him."

Silence.

"One other thing. I don't see how you can make good decisions without an honest conversation about what you saw. You'll flounder without LISA's awareness. Check if you feel peace about being honest. Even if you're nervous about doing it."

She chewed on her lip. "Being honest makes sense. I'm just afraid I'll blow it."

"Give yourself permission to make mistakes. And give him the benefit of the doubt about being mature enough to handle imperfection. We're all diamonds in the rough. Communication is the polish."

She shook her head and got to her feet. "You and your sayings. But I'm swiping that one for a rock."

Under Lock and Key — Isabelle

Flying high lately thanks to great talks with G and Saanvi, I considered touching mom issues during counseling next time. I initially told Abdul Hakeem I wanted to face the mom baggage "soon." But the fallout from the scene at Potbelly Deli took time to process. It opened up grief about my marriage and overflowed into losing Grandma and Dad.

With only four days left until meeting with Abdul Hakeem again, I still couldn't commit to taking the plunge into the mess about Mom. Strange. My mind battled back and forth about it, as if my whole life depended on the decision. But I needed to let go of it and focus on the task at hand: preparing for counseling my own client—one of the program's first-year students who chose, from among three options, to go for personal counseling to fulfill course requirements.

Our department used one-way windows for faculty to observe our counseling sessions—state-of-the-art equipment for an undergrad program because of a grant. Sailhammer sat behind the window when we counseled. Being observed usually gave me butterflies. This was worse. Today I could scarcely breathe. That shook me.

After reviewing confidentiality and the necessary logistics with the student in front of me, I prompted her to begin. She jumped right into things, mentioning that it had to do with her mom. My throat tightened. I braced, my left hand clutching the chair's arm. *Intuitively, somehow, I knew what was coming. Hmm, that life connection beyond logic?*

My client, Julie, told me that she had avoided talking about the abuse from her mom for far too long. My heart skipped a beat. I gulped, my jaw tightening now, too. Then I fidgeted in my chair. I thought I said, "That's something you likely have a lot of feelings about." Whatever I said, it probably sounded robotic.

Details and actual words swirled as we talked. I couldn't focus. I reminded myself, *Keep trying to describe her experience. But say things tentatively so she can feel safe and correct me if needed.* But my own memories ambushed me—the very thing Sailhammer had criticized.

I felt more tuned in at one point, right when she described her mom shoving her against a wall and calling her disgusting. I shook. Wanting to hide it, I crossed my arms in front of me. *Why am I shaking? Is it trauma?*

I berated myself for not facing my mom baggage sooner, as other destructive thoughts assaulted me: *You can't even stay present with your client. Mom told you that professors would only pass you because of pity. Or give you the boot.*

I tried to shrug off the attack. I caught the last part of her story and said, "That would've been terrifying, maybe even causing you trauma. Like help or safety was nowhere in sight."

Julie burst out bawling, gasping for breath in between wails. I froze, not knowing what to do. I had never been around anyone in that much pain. I didn't want to distract her, but I'd have wanted a tissue if I were her.

I mumbled something about the tissues on the stand by her chair. She grabbed them, said thanks, and started wiping.

Sailhammer hadn't run into the room. I took it to mean that she hadn't panicked about the session. *What would I need? What would Abdul Hakeem, Saanvi, or G do with me?*

As soon as I paused, I knew. They'd just be with me. Not trying to get me away from the pain. They'd let me cry it out. I only needed a safe person knowing the real me. Then I wasn't alone in that pain. In that out-of-control place. I nodded to myself, *that's what heals trauma.*

"I'm sorry," Julie said, crumpling lower in her chair with her head and hair hanging down.

"It's okay to feel what you're feeling. And it helps to have someone just sitting with you and knowing you in that place."

I gave her time, her head still down. I watched as her eyes searched for something, probably deciding whether to keep hiding or to venture into the land of the living. Her head inched up, braving the uncertainty of safety and finally looking at me. Studying each other for a moment, I saw the rigidity and shame on her face melt away. Her body relaxed.

We sat silent for what seemed to be several minutes. It probably lasted a minute.

Finally, Julie let out a big breath. "I never told anyone what I lived through, and you said exactly how I felt. I never thought of it as trauma where no help seemed available, but that's it." Her eyes gave me the impression that she was still processing, which gave me time to consider what direction made the most sense.

I almost mentioned my own struggle with Mom, but hesitated because of professors telling us to avoid self-disclosure if it takes the focus off clients. Something inside told me to tell her anyway. A GUS-voice? If I did mention it, she could feel less alone and go forward with more connection—which happened for me after G told me about his trauma. I thought Sailhammer might reprimand me, but I kept it short and said, "I got it—what it was like for you—because I've experienced it with my mom. It made me feel as if I had no value. I wondered if that's how you felt."

Moving to the edge of her seat, the young woman's eyes lit up. "That's exactly how I felt. I always thought something was wrong with me. That I was defective. I'm glad I'm not the only one, and that regular life is still possible. I mean, you made it."

"It's been a battle. I have further to go, but life can become good again." Then I told Julie that we were out of time. I summarized the key points from the session and checked to see if she felt okay to leave. After letting out another big breath, she nodded and smiled.

As we hopped up from our chairs, she asked if she could see me again next time. She had initially signed a document stating that she would come for two sessions, each one with a different clinician-in-training. I said I'd check with my supervisor. I told her that someone would call her if the contract could be changed. Otherwise, it would be as prearranged.

After Julie left, I shuffled into the observation room expecting backlash. My prof sat in her chair grinning and shaking her head. I couldn't get a read on her. Intuition told me I nailed the last part of the session. But my self-disclosure went outside normal responses, and I had lost focus earlier in the session.

Sailhammer usually wanted interns to say what they thought first. But she jumped up from her seat and gave me a high five. I didn't see that coming. Ever. I had never seen her give anyone a high five. I didn't know she had it in her. I all but missed it; my hanging jaw almost got in the way.

Overriding her usual logical and emotionally measured self,

Sailhammer's energy and fast-paced words poured out, even as she described some initial apprehensions. "I got concerned when your client talked about abuse from her mom, because of similarities. You appeared lost initially, but you kept trying to understand her experiences, and it uncovered the pain that's been under lock and key. Her reactions told me that she obviously felt known."

My face probably blank, I nodded.

"Then you hit a home run when you described her experience as trauma. You went into it rather than pushing it away. You allowed her to feel her experience and be understood about it. You stayed more present at that crucial place than in the rest of the session."

I couldn't find words.

She shook her head again and continued. "You responded effectively in spite of countertransference issues. Your defenses initially caused a loss of focus and caused you to protect yourself by putting your arms around your body. But you kept going into the pain with her. I've never seen that in all my years—an intern going beyond her defenses."

"I give credit to my counselor, even though we haven't even talked about the mom issues yet. That's supposed to happen at my next appointment. Losing focus early in this session shows I still need that."

"Isabelle," she started, "that's true. But the personal work you've done shows. It's worth it. Keep going like this, and you'll make a profound difference in people's lives. And, just so you know, I'll be recommending you as one of the six students for the Landsburg Health Services internships next year. I'll also call your client so she can meet with you again this coming week."

I sauntered out to my car in the dark. I wouldn't have been surprised if I had been beaming like a lamppost. As I started the car, Sailhammer's words rang in my head—words about my client's pain having been "under lock and key." How locked up was I about Mom? I wanted to unravel that mystery with Abdul Hakeem. Experiencing the total loss of focus for the first part of the session with my client motivated me.

Feeling spent, but still buzzing about the awesome session, I drove to Fitzpatrick's Pub to meet Val. I hadn't touched a beer since the night the ambulance raced me to the hospital. Tonight I wanted to celebrate my counseling victory. I also wanted to see how my old friends are doing, not having seen them for over two years.

Three blocks from Landsburg High School, Fitzpatrick's was the favorite hangout for local grads. The Irish pub had a great reputation for cleanliness, good food, and trendy beers.

Strangely feeling out of place, I scooted around the heavy front door and made my way inside. Little had changed—hardwood floors, four solid oak beams, the same ten round tables in the front section, the bar with its five taps, and big Dan with his friendly smile, still standing behind the counter, bartending. *Val was right, same old, same old.* I just hoped I wouldn't throw an attitude at the group if I felt disconnected.

Dan looked over, eyebrows raised, and gave his long-familiar greeting—a half wave with fingers pointing toward me. "Long time, no see. Thought you fell off the face of the Earth."

My eyes widened. "I did for a while. It took time, but I rejoined the living. Just been carrying a lot of school work at LU the last two years."

He pointed to the back, toward one of the two long, rectangular tables, knowing that I'd be joining the old gang.

I'd told Val that I'd probably meet her at the pub. I don't think she thought I'd show. Well, I didn't either. But here I was.

The gang jumped to their feet, eyes and faces lighting up when they saw me across the room. They all held up a glass and cheered as I walked over to the table. I hadn't experienced feeling wanted by a group for years. I felt warm inside, and I hadn't even started drinking!

Before I sat down, Val motioned with hand signals to Terry, the waitress, who stood behind the bar. She practically flew across the room and placed a Thunderbolt Double IPA in front of me. Val said, "It's a killer."

"How'd she know what you ordered?"

She laughed. "We read minds." Her words poured out as fast as an auctioneer. "Then after more beers, we'll move on to gnome and fairy stories."

I just nodded, not up for more jokes at my expense. At least it felt that way, and I didn't want to lose my high from nailing counseling.

My friends pumped me for info. None of them, except Val, had kept in touch with me after I stopped coming to Fitzpatrick's. I stuck to the nuts and bolts about school work and where I lived, hesitant to open up after meeting Val at the mall.

The beer rocked, but I told myself to stop at two after my last experience. I asked Jackie about the new guy she was seeing. She looked starry-eyed and couldn't stop talking about him. Other than that, her life was the same—working as a hair stylist, bowling, and drinking on Fridays. The more I asked questions about her and the others, the more I felt empty.

I zoned in and out. Coldplay songs echoed through me. I wanted to get lost in the music. Not because of drinking; I just wanted to be. But people's loud voices, or maybe the topics, grated on me. I slid into a funk. It grew as I nursed the second beer. The void felt unbearable.

I was glad that they were having fun. I liked fun, too. But it felt like meaningful conversations were off-limits again, like with Val at the mall. Even when I tried to go there, to know them more as persons, nothing penetrated some invisible shell. It'd glance off. I didn't need to do serious talk all the time, but I wanted more than one-dimensional chit-chat. A balance kept me in touch with what mattered.

I decided to leave. The group pressured me to stay when I got up. I knew that nothing could sway me. I gave a big smile. "It was great catching up again. But I need to split. You know, after the long day at school, I'm out of it."

They all put their glasses in the air and toasted me as I shuffled out. In spite of their cheers when I left, I felt heavy as I sank into my car seat. Driving home, it dawned on me: they kept focusing on things. That's why I felt as if I couldn't connect with them. Meaningfully. How did I not see that in the past? I kept reflecting as the invisible battle continued. But why is this gettin' under my skin? They're good people. Had I changed that much? I couldn't relate to anyone. No one appeared interested in growing personally. How can we know one another without understanding each other's feelings and inner experiences?

The agonizing abyss inside wouldn't stop. As if some big need in me couldn't get met. Maybe being with my old friends triggered the emptiness and pain I had lived with back then—being around people every day but never really knowing them. Or them, me. *What would have happened if I hadn't met my new friends? How would I have survived without being known by them? That emptiness would have destroyed me.*

Unlocked — Isabelle

Strange. I planned on talking about mom issues with Abdul Hakeem today and felt unusually calm. Even Freud's eyes in the picture didn't appear to follow me when I walked past it. I strolled into the familiar room, as if dropping by to chat with a best friend.

After Abdul Hakeem gave me a warm smile, we took our seats across from each other. I told him about my experience with the old gang. He pressed his lips together. "When you know the value of learning about inner experiences, others' lack of interest in it can discourage you. That's how you sound."

"I got in a total funk. I felt alone in a room full of friends."

"Many counseling and social work students have shared similar stories with me. Their programs open their eyes to richer communication. To fuller connection. Then they feel as if they've found a key to life and others don't care. Or understand. It's discouraging."

"It definitely took me down from the high about counseling my client. But I feel less crazy knowing that it's normal for clinicians-in-training."

"So counseling went well for you?" he asked.

"It did. I nailed it when I kept trying to understand her experiences. That's what I would have wanted if I were her. Mom flashbacks got in the way at first. I shut off at points. But I guess I did okay because my advisor said that she'd recommend me for one of the internships at Landsburg Health Services next year."

"That's wonderful news! Her recommendation shows that you must have done very well in spite of detaching initially."

"Yeah, it was unexpected."

His eyes peered off to the side for a moment. "Just like unrestricted breathing helps your physical well-being, unrestricted expression of your inner experiences frees you to live authentically. Whole and full of life instead of bottled up."

I nodded.

"But memories of your mom bottled you up a little?"

Maybe I had pushed down how difficult taking the plunge with Mom might be. Now fidgeting, I tried to joke. "Being mum about Mum definitely choked out life."

He appeared not to get it at first. But then he tilted his head and grinned.

I put my toe in. "I never told anyone about what really happened. Talking about family feels like betraying them. It was a mess."

"It's normal to protect your family. But hiding your story when you want growth betrays your true self. It restricts it. That's the greatest betrayal; the worst emptiness. There's nothing wrong with genuinely describing what you've experienced."

Through shallow breaths I talked, trying not to topple some unseen house of cards. "I had no siblings. Just Mom, Dad, and me. Mom was an addict. High and mad at the world all the time. Dad gave way to her. She ruled. I dreaded coming home from school every day—Mom high as a kite laying sprawled out on the couch, TV blaring."

Talking about my home life felt the same as spewing garbage across my front lawn for neighbors to see. Back there again, I started sweating and gulping down feelings. But I wanted to do this.

"It made me sick to my stomach to see Mom like that. I could never reach her. After school one day, I tried to talk with her about the drugs. She screamed and hit my face with a magazine. The corner cut my cheek. I dropped it after that. But about a year later, I found her in my room stealing money. I had been saving it for a car. I had wondered once before if money had disappeared from the jar in my closet. The thought of Mom scarfing some for drugs crossed my mind, but I always felt guilty for thinking that. Just in case, I moved the jar to a dresser drawer and hid it under clothes. But here she was, stealing right in front of my eyes."

"How shocking that must have been, and not what you'd expect from a parent."

I nodded and went on. "After it finally registered, I yelled at her that it was my money. She jumped about a foot in the air. Spinning my direction, she shrieked that she wasn't taking it, just borrowing it. Then her eyes narrowed and she asked how I could accuse her of such a thing. I told her that she didn't have any money to replace mine, and that I had already found money missing once before and had wondered if I somehow misplaced it. I said I was careful with my hard-earned money and thought the drugs caused her to do it."

Abdul Hakeem's compassion showed. "You were trying, even then, to give her the benefit of the doubt—that she wouldn't have done it if she were in her right mind."

I shook all over, tears welling up as I told him what happened. "Mom got in my face and knocked me to the floor. She screamed that I had always been selfish. That I didn't care about anyone but myself. I froze. I laid there, glued to the floor, as she kept spouting that only a cruel daughter would accuse her own mother like that. Then, with a wild look in her eyes, she kicked me in the side and said I was disgusting. I'll never forget her look. Or what she said. As suddenly as that whole shitstorm started, Mom turned and left the room. She never said another word about it. My mouth just hung open. I didn't move for a good five minutes. I replayed what happened over and over. Then I vowed never to question her again."

With watery eyes, Abdul Hakeem spoke softly. "That must have been terrifying. No wonder you hid the real you. She devalued and shamed you."

I got emotional after his words and gentle voice started reaching into hidden places. I waited until I caught my breath. "I thought my life was normal. It's all I knew. The reality of it didn't hit until recently."

I took a moment, and then started. "Telling G I couldn't live up to Mom's and Dean's standards felt good. But I needed someone to know what I actually lived through with her. What I told you was one of the worst. It didn't happen all the time, but she snapped a lot and pushed me around whenever she felt like it. It's a wonder I never pushed back when I got older." Hurt showed in Abdul Hakeem's eyes.

My story kept pouring out. "A few days after her stealing, Dad tried to be honest with Mom. He seemed mostly invisible to me growing up. So this was totally not him. Maybe he was trying to stick up for me after I told him what happened. I can still picture it as if it was yesterday. I peeked from my bedroom as he told Mom, while she lay on that freakin' couch, that he wanted to talk about something."

"Like a whip hitting him between the eyes, she snapped, 'Well, spit it out.' Her sharp comment told him to keep his place. I'll never forget seeing his face change—the terror spreading across him in the snap of a finger. He babbled and stuttered about wanting to talk with her about the drugs."

I let out a big breath and continued. "He never finished. To this day, I can't tell you what she screamed. But it lasted ten minutes. My eyes burned when I saw an ashtray and a folding chair flying like missiles at my dad. He backed away with his arms up, guarding himself. Then her drinking glass and two vases exploded like gunshots against the wall. Millions of pieces peppered the kitchen floor. That night and the next two days, my dad ducked to avoid mugs or framed pictures hurled at him. And hateful comments. Nobody messed with Mom."

Tears came to his eyes. "There aren't words for that. It's heartbreaking. I feel sad and appalled about what you lived with. How could you ever talk about your feelings after horrendous treatment like that? You lived with no safety. You had to wear a brave face to survive."

I was silent. He was silent.

His tears, like his earlier response about the terror I experienced, cut through whatever defenses I had built up inside. I said, "My head told me that Mom treated me atrociously. But, somehow, my heart didn't get it until now." I paused. "I know she wasn't in her right mind when she got that way. I was always on the alert and felt the vibes anytime she was about to attack. Then nothing would stop her until she was spent."

His soft eyes stayed centered on me. "It's one thing to understand logically that your mom wasn't in her right mind. But don't stop there or you stay in your defenses, detached from the pain. Not touching some of it keeps part of it locked up."

I bit my lip. His comment confused me. "Didn't I just feel the pain? I felt a shift after talking about it, too. So, I thought I faced it."

He tilted his head. "That means it helped, but I suspect there's more."

"What do you mean?"

He leaned forward, appearing more serious. His passion touched my heart. "Her not being in her right mind doesn't take away from the fact that a person who was most supposed to love you treated you like rubbish. You lived on edge, never knowing when she'd strike—when she'd treat you as if you had no value. That's the loss. You were cheated out of a real mom who could care for you. Value you."

Pain seized me. Waves of grief washed over me. Afraid it wouldn't stop, I closed my eyes and covered my face with my hands. My only thought was to hide.

Then I heard Abdul Hakeem's soft voice from the chair beside me. "Let yourself be where you are. You're experiencing trauma that needs support. Nod if you're okay with me putting my hand on your shoulder. It will help you to know that you're not alone in that place."

I nodded.

He rested his hand on my shoulder. It felt right. My whole being relaxed and let go of all restraint. More of the pain that had been hidden and held back for years—the vulnerable, childlike feelings, memories, and shame—poured out of me. Waves of it kept gushing out, but this time the grief relaxed me, as if some kind of rigidity poured out of my body.

After the experience subsided, Abdul Hakeem moved back to his chair across from me. I saw the sincerity in his eyes. No walls between us. No fear or shock evident about the humongous pain I unleashed. He never retreated one step emotionally. I could feel that. He let me sit quietly, waiting on me to start when ready.

Head down, I began. "I didn't know how much I hid. Not just the pain. I hid from people. I never invited friends home. I was ashamed of Mom and how she was. I could never please her. She never gave compliments. She acted as if she didn't want me. Like I was an inconvenience. Looking back, I was ashamed of myself, too. I blamed myself—thinking if I were just different or did some great thing, she'd have been there for me."

"Like you should have been able to reach her. As if her being drug-free should have been in your hands to make different. And you blamed yourself for not reaching her?"

I nodded.

"So you used shame as a weapon against yourself." He waited, then said, "It ends up destroying you when it smolders inside, unchecked. Or destroys others, like your mom's did."

"I never thought about the shame. Running in both of us. Just differently."

After pausing, I shook my head. "I don't know what I'll be like tomorrow. But I feel lighter now that all of that poison came flooding out."

UNLOCKED

He waited.

"I can't make sense of all of this yet," I said. "But something got unlocked. I feel more whole. G started that for me, but I never talked about the reality of living with Mom, not even with him. Always being on edge and living with shame. I could tell you got it. You knew, and you didn't look down on me."

He grinned. "I'm glad you felt both—being known and accepted. Acceptance without being known still leaves you empty. And alone. Or locked up, like you said."

Then he summarized key points before I left. Exhausted, but thankful, I made a follow-up appointment to process the session. I knew a breakthrough had happened and I wanted to learn more from it. I expected ripple effects. And I wouldn't forget Abdul Hakeem's statement: Acceptance without being known still leaves you empty and alone. *That's going on a rock.*

Reflecting about it on my way home, his hand on my shoulder acted as a catalyst. The comfort during the pain seemed to fortify me to face more of it. And to learn better in that safety. It reminded me of a professor's lecture about healing trauma through corrective experiences—how counseling provides comfort during the pain where there had been none. Comfort to face the truth about the pain. That happened for me. Through it, my prior episodes of useless anger had shifted, instead, to a healing grief. In that desolate place, I went from feeling like a down-and-out orphan in a room full of strangers to feeling known and valued. As if a long-lost friend treasured my story. And me.

Chaperone — GENE

In my office writing notes for an upcoming presentation, I heard Isabelle's bedroom door open, then her voice calling. "G. You up for the park? Carlos said he'd meet us there."

Tuesday evening, just after supper. "Sure," I yelled back.

The voice from beyond came again. "He's wondering if you could bring Button and his disk."

"Button could use a run. Sounds good."

On the way, I asked, "What's up? Why do you need me?"

Isabelle fumbled her words. "Well, it seemed Carlos wanted to see Button play catch."

"Oh." I flattened my eyes at her.

Nothing. Only the wind whipping through the windows. I waited. Just more wind.

"Are you avoiding being alone with him? You need a chaperone?"

Silence. I gave her time.

Short and choppy, she said, "I want your eyes and ears. I don't trust myself. To know what I want. Or even to know what's real."

"I thought you didn't trust him."

"Both, I guess." She didn't expand.

"Because you might want certain outcomes too badly? And that messes things up?"

She shook her head and berated herself. "Making outcomes bigger than people again. When will I learn?"

"That's a daily occurrence for people. Go easy on yourself. But I can be eyes and ears today."

We pulled into the park and saw Carlos in the distance pushing Emily on a swing. I razzed her. "Apparently he needed a chaperone, too." She frowned.

Button on a leash, Isabelle speed-walked down the path toward the playground. I followed.

As we approached them, Carlos said, "Emily wanted to come along. Adelina had errands to run."

I lifted my eyebrows at Isabelle. Her face told me that she was already floating in lalaland. She quickly turned toward Carlos, maybe breaking eye contact with me so as not to react to my jab. I looked their way, too. "Hey Carlos. Hi Emily." Isabelle said hi to both, as well. After they returned the greeting, Carlos bent down, petting Button who leaned into the attention. I said, "Button really takes a liking to you. He's not usually that way with men. I'm curious about what you do for a living."

"I manage Have a Heart, Give a Start, an animal relief shelter out on Route 56. Don't know if you're familiar with it. We bring in all kinds of animals that need help: horses, pigs, dogs, cats, birds, donkeys, deer. You name it, if it needs help, we give it. Then we find good homes for them."

"Well, that fits. You seem really natural with Button." I gave a look of approval to Isabelle as Carlos stood to push Emily on the swing again. Then Isabelle appeared to come out from under her spell. "That's gotta be satisfying work."

"It is," he said with a big nod. "I look forward to work every day. Animals are awesome. They know when you respect them and when you're there to help. And it feels good to make a difference."

Hearing his passion about his work verified my gut instinct about him: a big heart. I studied Isabelle. Her head, tilted to the side, made me think his response resonated with her too. She and Carlos got quiet and returned to gazing at one another. So I said, "Feel free to take him for a walk. That'll loosen him up for playing catch. I'll push Emily on the swing if you two want to go. That okay with you, Emily?"

"Yay. I wanna go higher!"

After they left, I asked Emily, "You really like your uncle, don't you?"

She nodded, her eyes and smile lighting up her whole face. "He takes care of Mommy and me. And Aunt Mary."

"Aunt Mary?" I asked.

Her high, sweet voice hid nothing. "She lives by herself. After Uncle Sergio went to heaven."

"Oh. That's sad that something happened to Uncle Sergio."

"The doctors didn't fix him in time. I was very sad. I'm scared something will happen to Mommy or Carlos, too."

I went with it. "I felt as if my heart broke when doctors couldn't fix my wife, Hanna. And you're scared that something will go wrong with your mom or Carlos?"

Her lower lip pushed forward. "Maybe no one will tell me. I knew something bad was happening to Uncle Sergio. But no one told me the truth until he was gone."

"Not knowing what was going on probably made it scarier. You had to go through it by yourself."

Her head and whole body bobbed back and forth with each nod as she swung. Kids. They're so open, honest, and expressive until they're treated like they shouldn't feel. I hoped Isabelle would be honest with Carlos as I watched them strolling with Button on the far side of the lake. Meanwhile, I asked Emily about her mom, friends, and school.

She gushed after my next question. "Mommy said I can go to a sleepover at Janine's house on Saturday. It's her birthday." Her words poured out with little prodding.

When Carlos and Isabelle came around the bend and into view, Emily jumped mid-swing. As soon as she landed, she sprinted to them. Carlos opened his arms as she raced full blast into them. I grabbed the red disk and moseyed their direction.

Carlos said, "Can't wait to see Button in action."

"Yippee," Emily cheered, now running over and smothering Button with a hug. He stood upright, as if posing for the cover of *Dogs Quarterly*.

We all moved into the open area as Isabelle unhitched Button's leash. He immediately came to my feet and sat down. Carlos gave a nod, looking impressed.

I gave the disk a sharp snap. After sailing across the opening for about forty yards, Button chased it down. Timing it just right, he lunged three feet into the air and snatched it with ease. Head held high and disk in mouth, he trotted back to my feet and sat waiting. Emily rewarded him with another bear hug. His eyes glued to the disk, he hardly noticed. As soon as Emily let go of him, I turned to my left, throwing it again. Button took off, making a beeline for it. Leaping into the air with grace, he grabbed it, landed, and turned in one continuous motion—as good as a star ballerina in *The Nutcracker*. After returning, Carlos threw several times. Button lived up to his reputation. Even Emily threw two, only about ten or fifteen steps away. But Button managed to reach them before they hit the ground. We all talked and laughed about what a champ he was.

On the way home, Isabelle asked, "So what did you think? What did you see?"

I played up my not-going-to-give-much role. "Confirmed what I already thought about Carlos and Emily."

She zeroed in on me while I drove. "Well?"

"Well what?"

"What did you think—especially taking into account that he hugged that woman?"

GUS said to wait for learning. "I don't think it's prudent for me to answer."

She mocked me. "I don't think it's prudent to answer." Then her voice skyrocketed. "Prudent? Cut me a break!"

I stayed matter-of-fact as GUS gave direction. "You didn't ask him about the woman, did you? What's that about?"

She frowned and pursed her lips. Then she tilted her head and shrugged.

"What a load of body language for not saying anything."

She rolled her eyes and hesitated before confessing her dilemma. "I'm afraid that asking will just confirm what I think."

My tone softened. "It's okay that you're afraid. You have a history that makes it understandable." I gave her a moment and asked, "What did your heart tell you when he talked about his job?"

She threw her hands up in the air. "I don't know. He sounded as if he cared." She got silent for a minute. "Alright, cared a lot. I wanted to believe him. It's just that Dean was such a player. I can't trust guys now."

I nodded. "Consider telling him that. You don't have to date him in the end. But let him know you, and try to know him. That's putting people over outcomes. Watch how he responds. That's how you make informed choices."

She let that sink in. Then, putting on a sweet smile and syrupy tone, she asked, "So, can't you tell me what you learned about them?"

I smirked. "I'm going to be prudent. I'll tell you after you ask him about the woman."

She punched my shoulder.

"Owww. I'm going to start wearing shoulder pads."

Two days later around 5:00 P.M., Isabelle came in the door. I put my book aside. "Something good must have happened, the way you're smiling."

Her smile changed to a sheepish grin. "You can say 'I told you so.' I asked him about the woman."

I wanted a reaction. "What him? What woman?"

Her face wrinkled. Then her voice spiked. "Carlos, about the woman he hugged. Who the hell did you think I meant?" Her mouth hung open.

I gave a gotcha smirk. "Getting that reaction was better than winning the Olympics—way better than an 'I told you so.'"

She half growled and grunted as she grabbed a pillow from the couch and threw it at me. I pulled my book up again without looking at her. "It was still worth it."

She stormed off to her room. "Now you'll just have to wait for the details."

Half an hour later, she came out as I finished getting Brussels sprouts and chicken ready for supper. Didn't even have to call her. The aroma must have drawn her.

"Brussels sprouts," she said, studying them. "The burnt edges always make them better."

"I love these things. Except they give me gas."

She shook her head. "Doesn't anything embarrass you?"

"Not much. I hope that pulling your leg earlier didn't bother you too much. It makes life interesting."

"Nah," she said. "I was mostly jazzing you, too."

After we sat down to eat, she swallowed a bite and started. "I told Carlos that I have a difficult time trusting men because of Dean. Then I said I saw him hugging a blond-haired woman on Locust and Fifth."

"Did you watch how he responded?" I asked.

"He didn't get defensive. He just said, 'That would've been Mary, my sister-in-law.' Then he told me his brother, Sergio, had died from lymphoma. That he looks out for her now. His eyes teared up when he told me. I think it's true. Even Dean couldn't have pulled off an act like that. Or pulled at my heart strings with something made-up."

"It's true."

Her eyebrows lowered as she studied me.

"Emily told me," I said, nonchalantly.

"You learned that just from the time at the swings?"

"She jumped right into it. How sad it made her. She needed to talk." Then I cut to the chase about her update. "So talking with Carlos went well overall?"

Lalaland blanketed her face again. "It rocked. I need to keep saying what's on my mind with him. He's so easy to talk to."

I acted as if I didn't hear well. "What's that? He's so dreamy to talk to?"

She made a face and shook her head. Fortunately, I sat across the table from her. Too far away for another shoulder punch.

The Queen of Hearts — Isabelle

Sitting in a chair across from Abdul Hakeem, I went for it. No hesitation at all. "Thanks for last time. A load lifted after that."

"Wonderful. I'm sure that would be a relief for you."

"I even had my second counseling session with the first-year student, the one with mom issues like me. It went awesome and my professor was thrilled with it."

Warmth radiated from him. "I'm so happy, Isabelle. Things are really turning around for you."

"They sure are, and I want to keep learning. Personally. But also for understanding counseling better. G said that you can tell me more about how conscience works. How did the last session about Mom fit into following conscience versus ego?"

He paused. "You described your mom as attacking until she was spent. Nothing would stop her. Because?"

"She wasn't in her right mind?"

He probed. "True, but why?" After I made a blank face and shrugged, he explained. "Ego ran her life, not conscience. Think about it. What pushed the urgency in her? What caused a catastrophe in her mind?"

His point registered at the same time G's description of ED came to mind. "Mom's need for heroin. Only getting the thing mattered. Everything else, including me, was an inconvenience. That's ego—things over people! Desperation for her fix lashed out at anyone who might interfere."

He grinned. "Yes. Ego devalues people because it prioritizes things and outcomes over individuals. When ego's desire for its prize dominates a person, rigidity starts and care stops. The greater the threat, the more it'll react like the Queen of Hearts in *Alice in Wonderland:* 'Off with your head!'"

I laughed at how he said the queen's words. Then memories flashed through my mind. "No joke. That's a picture of my mom when she felt threatened."

"Addiction makes ego's voice stronger. More demanding. An addict's actions illustrate how ego chases its desires at the expense of people. How too much of it causes destruction."

"So, ego valuing things over people caused my pain?"

He asked, "Can you see how your mom's obsession with her prize devalued you? And how it shaped your own pattern of valuing things over yourself?"

That washed through me, until a related thought jolted me. "Damn, my panic attacks. Getting results felt catastrophic. I put constant pressure on myself, 'shoulding' on myself, like a counseling theory calls it."

"Isn't it amazing how ego keeps pushing for its way in life? In place of valuing yourself, which following your conscience would've done?"

I nodded. "That's crazy how much life looks one way or the other, depending on whether you put things over people or not. And G, Saanvi, and you keep helping me to get the order right, putting me as a person over things."

He beamed. "You catch on quickly."

I hesitated, not sure if I wanted to venture into the topic coming to mind. "I just met a guy. He's interested. I guess I am in him, too. He seems to focus on people, not things."

"Wonderful!" He kept studying me. "But you're uncertain of something?"

"I'm afraid of losing myself. And of trusting someone again only to get betrayed."

"That makes sense, given what you've been through. Recovering from betrayal takes time. You've already grown to value yourself more, but losing yourself with Dean may also have been from loving him too much."

"What do you mean?" I asked.

"Too much, meaning ego's way." He explained. "By catering to his desired things above either of you as a person, you betrayed yourself. Lost yourself. That would have increased the chance of him betraying you."

"So staying true to myself and not bending too much cuts down on the possibility of someone betraying me?"

"Yes, the other person learns to honor your core values when you're clear about them."

"I need to sit with that," I said. "Can we just listen to the running water for a minute or two?" Abdul Hakeem had recently purchased a bubbling fountain for his office. Hearing the trickling water helped me to relax and learn better.

After sitting in silence, I breathed a few long breaths. "I'm ready."

He asked, "Isn't it soothing?"

"That's for sure. It reminded me of Saanvi and me sitting by a waterfall at White Pine Trails. I was filled with wonder, like a curious little kid. I didn't have my normal empty, alone feeling. I felt that again here, listening to the water. Is the emptiness disappearing because of putting people over things more?"

"Yes, and also because of getting support from people who prioritize that. I'm oversimplifying a bit, but your build-up of pain came mostly from ego chasing things. As if you didn't have worth because value was always 'out there' somewhere. In some outcome."

"Okay. I think I get it."

"That treats you like there's a constant gap between you and value. That's the emptiness."

"That's what it felt like. Out of reach."

He continued. "And the pain you carried kept you on that chase until you felt cared for as a person about it."

"I get it. You valued me about the pain with my mom—where ego slammed me the most." My thoughts formed as I spoke. "That would have caused the biggest emptiness."

Abdul Hakeem's eyes widened. "Very good. Ego gathers things. Conscience gathers hearts." Then he added, "And things can't value you. Or fill you."

"Tell me about it; I lived it. But what does fill a person?" I asked.

"Belonging. Your most valuable asset is who you are. We're all valuable, connected, and meant to make a difference in this world. When you understand that, you know you have place. You know you belong to a cause greater than yourself."

Fascinated, I said, "You sound like you lived this. I realize that therapists are supposed to keep focus on the client, but I'd like to hear your story."

He looked at his watch, his face tightening for a moment.

I tried not to plead. "It might help, and I don't have anything else I'd rather do with the time that's left." I sat on the edge of my seat with my eyes wide and expectant.

He put his finger to his chin. "I'll keep it brief. But, yes. I lived in what some call 'the ego drama'—living for my own little world."

"Ego drama?" I asked. Then I remembered G mentioning that Abdul Hakeem referred to ED as ego drama.

"That world is the one we direct. We play the starring role and all other pieces are merely props for our agendas. For our things, like I said about you with Dean. But I lived that way just for myself, speed-chasing after my goals in the glass factory where Saanvi, my parents, and I worked. I strived to be the hardest worker there. I wanted to get rich. My parents weren't financially successful like some of my friends' parents, and I looked down on my mom and dad. I didn't show care for them well." Tears filled his eyes. "Suddenly a furnace fire took them from me, caused by neglect. I couldn't let it go. I was mad at the world and disillusioned with religion, but mostly mad at myself. I poured myself all the more into work, ignoring the fact that I was spiraling out of control. That's when company neglect of the truck I drove caused another accident and I lost part of my arm. I was totally bitter at the time. My parents had been two of the most loving people I knew. They didn't deserve what happened. And, after all of my striving, my hard work didn't equate to success. Are you following?"

The sobering reality of his words hit. Not wanting to interrupt, I just nodded.

"I couldn't make sense of life when my scripted ego drama no longer worked. I could no longer control my world or achieve what I wanted. Living right didn't guarantee good outcomes. Life was bigger than me. Beyond my ability and understanding. I saw no way out of the suffering. Then everything came together after moving to America and hearing Gene's story about gaining what he could through suffering. I had never thought of that. Suffering formed who he is now—a well giving water to others in the desert. You with me?"

"Go ahead. I'm chill," I said, wanting to hear everything he had to say.

"I learned that I couldn't control life and didn't have to. I saw that in Gene. He showed a different path than control for personal gain."

"And what path was that?" I asked.

"A path that lets go of 'I' and learns for 'we.' Ego lost power in me through that."

"I get that," I said.

"I awakened to the greater story of conscience that cares for the betterment of all. For everyone's good. That story keeps taking me beyond my ego's limited win-lose personal agenda and, instead, to a win-win, collective story about establishing true self in all."

My whole body reverberated. "A collective story?"

"My conscience shapes the real me to keep touching and establishing the genuine you. We touch each other. All of us belong. All are valuable and meant to play a part in a larger story than ourselves."

I was speechless.

He said, "I hope I didn't go on too much."

My voice cracked with emotion. "No way. That was beautiful. I wish the whole world lived like that."

I couldn't contain it anymore when I left the room. Tears ran down my face as I walked down the hallway. His story touched and filled me in a way that not much else in life had. I just wanted to let his words keep working. I didn't know why—other than the fact that he, as much as Saanvi, lived the life I most wanted. I never had words for that before. But now I did: living a life of conscience instead of the ego drama. Following GUS instead of ED.

Three hours and one boring Social Welfare Policy class later, I glanced back on the way out of Bigler Hall. Lukas picked up his pace to catch me. I waited.

After reaching me, he said, "Just wanted to say thanks again for telling Sailhammer what you thought that day. She's treated me extra nice since then."

"You're welcome. She pays more attention now when I say something, too." I pushed the door open to head out.

He asked, "What did you do to your arm?"

I forgot about the scratches and brush burn on it. "From carrying a rock."

His voice spiked, as if no reason on earth could justify that. "Carrying a rock?"

"I've been finding unique rocks and painting sayings on them. For garden stones."

"That's cool. Never thought of using them for that. If you need more, I got tons."

My don't-inconvenience-people rule hijacked my reply. "I just find one here and there. I'm chill."

His tone got insistent. "Remember. I owe you. It's no sweat off my back. My parents moved into Landsburg a couple years back and left me the old farm house on seventy acres. I swear there's a million rocks just in the two hollows alone."

Selling garden stones came to mind again. He caught my hesitation. "You look like you could use them. It's easy access. A dirt road goes up each hollow. And my place is only five minutes outside Landsburg."

"For real?" I asked. "I might need lots of rocks. Eventually."

"Like I said, no worries on my end. I'd just be glad if it helped. Seems meant to be—you need rocks and I got loads of 'em."

Half an hour later, Button greeted me, wagging body and all. G had gone for a presentation. My phone interrupted Button's kisses. "Hey, Saanvi. What's up?"

"You up for painting?"

"Just got home and thought about that. Why do you ask?"

"We missed getting together last week," she said. "What do you think about tag-team painting?"

"You serious? I didn't know you painted. You never said anything, other than encouraging me to take it up again."

"True. But I was speaking as much to myself as to you. Now, don't expect much. It's been a while. I want to explore it again, maybe do a surrealistic painting. What do you think?"

Still wrapping my head around this, I asked, "You know about surrealistic painting?"

"Not much. I took three art courses at LU the year after I got here. Plus, you said you painted one that excited you. I want to see it."

"No way! I probably missed you by a year or two. Might be the same three courses I took. You would've had Old Fuzzy, because I came after you. That's what they called him."

She chuckled. Rays of sunshine and warm feelings always filled me when she laughed.

Twenty minutes later, she followed me into my room with her paint set, Button at her side this time.

She cried out as soon as she saw my painting leaning against the far wall. "That's incredible!" She began studying the woman peering into the lake with a young girl looking back at her. "The colors are extraordinary. They draw me into it. And the symbolization of true self couldn't be clearer. I don't know how you made their eyes so clear and lifelike."

"Thanks," I said, still not used to letting compliments sink in. "It got me pumped about art again."

Saanvi made a face. "Now I feel anxious. And self-conscious about painting with you."

She sounded accepting of herself when she said it. "You're so open about how you feel. You seem comfortable in your own skin. That makes me feel freer. Not sure why."

She smiled. "My mom always said that authenticity has authority, and shadows don't. She told me it bridges gaps and unlocks doors."

I stared at her. "That went boom in my heart. I got honest with Abdul Hakeem about my locked-up mom issues the other day. The steel vault finally opened. Sounds like you learned a lot from your mom."

Saanvi closed her eyes for a moment. "She wasn't perfect. But I'm grateful for how she raised me."

A pang of jealousy hit me. "I'd have given anything to have a mom like yours. Mine was 'gone' all the time because of addiction. I probably missed something foundational. And I avoided talking about it forever because of how big it felt. But after getting it out with your brother, I only feel sad about it now."

She put her hand on my shoulder, similar to Abdul Hakeem doing that during counseling. "I'm glad you were able to get everything out with him. I bet now you'll be more comfortable in your own skin too."

Ready to jam, I said, "Well, let's see how painting goes. No pressure. I already stretched the canvas and primed it. How do you want to start?"

"Why don't you paint for about two minutes—whatever comes to mind. Symbolism of something deeper. Then I'll create for two minutes. We'll keep doing that without saying what we're doing."

UNLOCKED

"Let's go for it. You're cool with doing an underlay first?" I asked. She nodded.

Button lay against her feet. I told him no and patted the floor along the wall. I did it twice before he listened. We giggled like two eight-year-olds during the underpainting. After finishing it, I painted the beginnings of an upright ladder with a solid base on the right side of the canvas. Saanvi watched.

I stepped back while she painted a ladder on the left. It laid on the ground. "You don't paint like a beginner," I said as I watched her work. "You mix your colors really well."

"Thank you. I have a lot to learn. But I enjoy the creativity."

We kept taking turns. I painted the ladder on the right that disappeared up into clouds. Then I outlined a young girl climbing the ladder—a cartoon figure with a big smile and bright eyes. Saanvi similarly painted a girl running on the ladder that laid on the ground. Beads of sweat dripped from her head. She had no mouth, perhaps to indicate no voice or identity. I smiled at how our pieces connected.

Next, I moved to her side. Button started getting up, but I told him to stay. At the far end of Saanvi's ladder lying on the ground, I added a goal post. Around and above it, I painted dollar signs, several pairs of hands clapping, a woman in a business suit, a shiny car, and a huge house.

In the meantime, she moved to my side of the painting. Beside that girl, she painted three doves, several pairs of held hands, and a few hearts.

Shifting from side to side, we refined the painting for another hour. With fewer additions as we went, she finally asked, "Are you about finished? I am."

"Definitely. This turned out awesome!"

Saanvi summed it up as she studied it. "It's always this choice: the ladder of ego or the ladder of conscience. Chasing value outwardly or developing your true self."

We cleaned up while looking over our work for several minutes. After numerous glances back and forth from the painting to each other, we made big eyes about what just happened. I said, "I saw an art competition advertised at Wellington Mall. We need to enter this."

Climbing Ladders — Isabelle

The morning after Saanvi and I did our surrealistic creation, I sat in my room preparing to paint. Rocks this time. G had gone out of town to visit a friend for the day. Our lives ran like two trains on different tracks, rarely intersecting at the terminal.

I felt drawn to contemplate before getting creative. That c-word was normal for me now. Not feeling empty or alone like I used to, I looked forward to time with no expectations. I liked sitting still and letting my heart draw me to whatever it did.

Button, as usual, snuggled against my feet. I sat and breathed deeply, hoping for inspiration about the rock in front of me. A round flat one this time. I had decided to sell my rocks to garden shops like Val had mentioned. Not for big bucks, but to cover my time and draw people's attention to what matters.

During the quiet, G's recent words kept coming to mind. He had said, "Pain and love awaken authenticity." How true that was for me, and the statement felt relevant to my recent counseling experience—feeling Abdul Hakeem's compassion that made a way for dealing with the pain from Mom.

Then other words hit, which I started painting: *Without love and pain, only ego will remain.* I chuckled out loud, thinking that G would be proud of me. Button let out a big breath. Maybe I disturbed his beauty sleep.

I paused when I came to the word "ego." A ladder flashed in my mind with the big letters E G O at the top of it. *I see. It wants attention, and to be above others.* So I painted a circle around those three letters. I formed the G as the nose, slightly lower, and put eyes in the upper part of the E and O. Then I painted a self-satisfied smirk below the nose—all at the top of a ladder. Finally, I added legs, feet, arms, and hands below the face, similar to the M&M candy characters. *Cool.*

Feeling hungry, I cleaned and packed my brushes, ready to head to the kitchen. I glanced down at the rock, feeling drawn to sit and study it again. After admiring it, I slipped into a trancelike state. I had never experienced anything like this.

I had no awareness of anything except the vision in my mind, not even the fact that I was sitting in my room. I think my eyes were open; I'm not sure. A vivid picture of me back in high school climbing a semi-visible ladder appeared. I instantly recognized the chase for value. Mouth open and panting, I took step after step, as if I might keel over any moment. But no matter how fast and furiously I climbed, I never went higher. The upright ladder might as well have been lying down like the ego ladder Saanvi had painted—the bottom kept going down and disappearing into the ground as I strived upward. I shook my head in exasperation while watching my empty life all over again. Because of ED!

Then a partially visible ladder materialized on the right. I saw its solid foundation like the one I had painted with Saanvi. As I watched, I had no doubt that it was a ladder of conscience—of knowing inner peace, value, and identity. The elementary-aged kid, me, beaming with joy, slowly climbed the ladder. This young girl showed a pure, powerful presence while she took lengthy pauses between new steps. Suddenly I felt sad as I watched, knowing that for the most part I got off that ladder sometime during childhood. I abandoned LISA, and stopped listening to my GUS voice, although I wouldn't have called it that back then.

I waited until Saanvi got home from work to call her about my vision. After listening, she said, "It played out what we painted!"

"Yeah, I buzzed all day after that. I couldn't stop thinking about it."

Her voice sounded far off. "Abdul Hakeem says that ego's weeds hog all the attention until we pull them out. Then our conscience blooms like a flower."

"That's an awesome way to put it. I felt that way after talking with him. The mom-weeds finally stopped choking out the flower!"

Saanvi asked, "Did you enter our painting in the art competition?"

"Not yet. I found out that if we win one of the two grand prizes, they auction those paintings at their gallery. Half the money goes to the artist and half to the gallery for future competitions. You okay with that? I'm still deciding if I'm cool with them selling my other painting. Probably won't come to that."

"I am if you are."

"Great. I'll swing by Wellington Mall tomorrow to drop it off. Maybe my other one, too."

⊂D

I decided to enter both paintings. After morning classes, I dropped them off with a Prescott Gallery representative at the mall. Then I stopped by Hamm's Hobby Shop for more art supplies. Coming out to get in my car, I heard someone up the street yell my name. I looked up and saw Carlos in front of Mamma's grocery store. The stores sat half a block from one another.

He jogged over to me. "Hey, Isabelle. Almost called you. You have time to tour Have a Heart today?"

"I still need to eat, and I have homework. But around three works."

"Great. Not much happening at work. Just grabbed groceries for my sister and some supplies from Outdoor Life for the animals. Pick you up at three, then?"

⊂D

Right on time, I heard the doorbell ring. I grabbed my purse and opened the door to Carlos' warm smile. He led me around to the side parking lot. Hmm, a blue Chevy Malibu. A regular car. Not some flashy look-at-me center-of-attention Corvette convertible like Dean's.

Carlos held the door open for me as I got in. After he sat behind the wheel, I asked, "Do you do that for all your non-dates?" My distrust again. I couldn't help myself.

He searched for words. "Do what? I'm not following."

"Open the door for women you're not seeing."

He looked at me with sad-puppy eyes. "Ouch! I do. No offense, maybe I'm old fashioned, but I just believe in treating women with respect."

"I'm sorry, Carlos. It's just my distrust of men throwing a tantrum. I'll cool it."

"No problem. Just be you and I'll be me. No other expectations."

He appeared so easy-going. He made life seem simple.

Approaching a crossroad, Carlos slowed down and wrinkled his face as he went through the intersection. He leaned forward, glancing both ways as he proceeded. "Route 10 has stop signs. We don't. But the tall corn right up to the shoulder of the road unnerves me. The other day someone flew through here without stopping. A few seconds difference would have been bad."

As he got back up to speed, he asked, "Anything new for you lately? Classes going well?"

"I'm on a high about school right now. Better than I ever imagined. And art gets me pumped lately."

He glanced over. "Art? What kind? You mean painting?" His eyes lit up.

"You're not going to tell me that you paint, too?"

"I wish," he said. "I just like looking at paintings. At what they capture. Similar to photography."

"You're into photography?" I asked.

"I am. Pictures bring out a moment in time. Significant events in people's lives. Their expressions take you right back to that day. With animals and birds, too, you capture what many people never see. Their world, even their personality, comes alive in a snapshot."

"That's how I feel about painting. You bring out more dimension, beyond what people see at the surface."

Different than with Val, his face showed that he understood. My stomach jumped.

Passion showed in his voice. "Even the colors and designs on birds and butterflies are awesome when you see them up close."

"Butterflies! My grandma loved butterflies. I miss her. Seeing them always makes me think of her."

"She must have meant a lot to you," he said. "Did you ever hear of the town called Hedgerow about four hours from here? People from all over go there to see their butterfly house."

"Cool. Never heard of it."

"Apparently the town got its name from all the hedges and gardens, and they call the butterfly house The Gatekeeper. The name came from the kind of butterflies that hovered around the flower clusters at the gates."

That piqued my interest. "Grandma would have asked me to take her there had she known."

"You might want to check it out sometime."

I got chills. I didn't know why. Already imagining it, I emphasized each word as I said them. "Yeah, something seems right about it."

"You sounded like there was more to that. I think we need to make a pinky promise that you'll at least consider going there."

I shrugged and chuckled as we hooked pinkies, still confused about my unexplainable reaction. I made a mental note of it for future reference.

Then he asked, "Do you paint often?"

"Just getting back into it. I've only done two paintings lately. Other than that, I paint sayings on rocks for garden stones. But I want to paint more pictures. That's what I'm most into. Just don't get the time."

"Pictures of what?"

That caught me off guard. I didn't know how to answer. "I'm not sure what I most want to paint. The one I did that I'm stoked about is a woman gazing into a lake. In the reflection, a little girl looks back at her."

"No way. That's deep. We all have a kid inside wanting to get out. Emily's spontaneity and honesty remind me to keep things simple. My job responsibilities and having people to support make that more difficult now."

I couldn't speak. *How crazy that we relate like this!* I started freaking out, knowing I could give in to these overwhelming feelings pulling at me. Afraid this was too good to be true, I needed to keep guarding my heart.

He asked, "Could I see the painting when I drop you off back at your place?"

"I'm, uh, still catching up, here. I'm just finding it difficult to believe that we have so much in common."

"The distrust again?" he asked.

"Not that." I shook my head. "I just met up with a group of high school friends, and they kept all our conversations superficial. As if they didn't want to go past that. I guess I changed and they didn't. What a total disconnect."

"Bummer. You probably felt empty after that."

As we got out of the car at Have a Heart, I said, "I just realized that I didn't answer you about showing you the painting. I don't have it. I dropped it off at Wellington Mall for an art competition."

"Well, maybe I'll get to see it sometime soon."

"I hope so. I don't really want to part with it. But if it wins one of the two overall prizes, the art gallery auctions it off." I shook my head. "Winning's not likely."

"You never know," he said thoughtfully.

I looked up, taking in the scene. The place, built as a one-story ranch with numerous out-buildings, opened up to endless pastures with small groves of trees that shaded the animals. The length of the central building caught my attention, although I couldn't see how deep it was from where we parked. It appeared clean and well-kept, especially considering all the animals that came through those gates and doors.

Carlos opened the front door for me as we entered.

"Thanks, I guess."

An elderly man stood to one side, cradling a baby pig in his arms. He nodded at Carlos and gave a toothless grin. A young woman behind the desk lit up when she saw us. "Yancy's doing better!" I wondered if she had eyes for Carlos.

"I told you he was a fighter," Carlos said. "This is my friend, Isabelle. This is Amanda." After we greeted each other, he walked over to check on Yancy. I followed. "Hey, Russ. Thanks for taking care of him. You have the touch. He looks about back to normal." The man's face beamed.

After Carlos introduced Russ and me, we went through another door. The place appeared much bigger than I had thought from the front. Unending stalls, similar to dog kennels, lined each side of the hallway. That was only the first of seven hallways—all clean but homey, not sterile-looking like past dog kennels I had seen.

Carlos appeared at ease as he introduced me to numerous employees, volunteers, and animals. Their eyes brightened when he approached them. After going through the last hallway, we stepped through an open doorway and into the first of several fenced-in fields with horses, donkeys, and cows. Carlos said, "That about does it. Who wouldn't want to hang out here every day? Fantastic staff and awesome animals that eat up attention?"

I asked, "Are you always this positive?"

"I have down days like anyone. But I try to be thankful for what I have. Nothing's guaranteed. Love it while you have it."

"Their eyes lit up when they saw you."

He smiled. "Yeah, the animals like anyone who shows them care."

"I meant not just the animals, but the people. You don't see that every day with employees and their bosses."

He shrugged. "I like them and I guess they like me." Then he changed the topic. "I need to drop by my office and get some forms for Amanda. Then we can head back." He hadn't shown me his office during the tour. It only appeared to be an afterthought. The people and animals consumed his attention, not his position of authority.

Myriad pictures tastefully queued up two of his office walls—candid, balanced ones that captured special moments. One wall displayed animals in their settings. Horses stood majestically in the fields. Goats clung to the top of rock piles. Pigs wove their mud-splotched noses through the fences, probably for handouts. Dogs and cats cuddled with one another. The second wall showed employees or volunteers feeding, brushing, and hugging animals. Then I scanned the series of pictures lined up on two long shelves—colorful birds and butterflies. I lost my breath at their unique detail and beauty. Maybe he's the real deal.

Perfect Timing — Gene

Reading mail at the table, I glanced up when Isabelle came in the door. "You look flustered. What's up?"

"You catch everything."

I flattened my eyes. "That was about as hard as spotting purple elephants sashaying down the street."

She rolled her eyes. "Nothing. Just lots on my mind. Flying in all directions."

"Wouldn't happen to be about Carlos, would it?"

She hesitated. "Just spent the last hour and a half with him. Where he works."

I widened my eyes, putting on my expectant face.

"He gave me a tour of the place." Her voice shrugged off the words. She grabbed an orange but fidgeted without peeling it. Then she snapped. "What's your damn smirk about?"

"Nothing."

She shot back. "Nobody smirks about nothing. You always say that I'm hiding what's real. What the hell's up?"

"You look like your insides went topsy-turvy over Carlos."

She scrunched up her face. "Nobody says topsy-turvy anymore except history books about the Great Depression."

I shouldn't have, but my words squeaked out like a rusty seesaw. "Just saying."

She fired the orange onto the table. Then she marched to her room in a huff, slamming the door behind her.

Oops, I went too far. I tried to let it go and started preparing dinner.

An hour later, Isabelle emerged from her room. She made her way to the counter and waited until I rinsed my hands and looked up. "I'm sorry for losing it. I hate throwing things like my mom did. The anger caught me off guard after the awesome time hanging with Carlos. I had just been pinching myself about how cool he is. The meltdown blindsided me."

"Thanks for saying so. I'm sorry, too, for teasing. I saw you had a lot of energy whizzing around. But it hadn't registered as fear under there. If it had, I wouldn't have teased."

"Thanks for seeing the perfect timing of it," she said, her spontaneous sarcasm giving me a slap on the back of the hand. "I thought I had grown a lot."

"You have. The 'perfect timing' just touched a sore spot."

She nodded. "While I was painting after going to my room, a memory of Mom screaming at me lit up in my mind. She said I'd fail with any man who'd have me. It played out with Dean. Since then, I keep picturing it happening with Carlos."

"Glad you got awareness through it," I said. "And be kind to yourself when you blow it. You learn more. It's usually ED when you're mean to yourself."

"Yeah, I need to keep paying attention to that. I'm nicer to myself when I paint. More insights pop in then, too. And I don't have to work at it."

"What do you call that GUS-sense now?"

Her eyes searched for a moment. "Just conscience or GUS, I guess."

"Hmm. what about IS?"

"IS?" she asked.

"Yeah, short for Isabelle, for your true self. Or it could be for Intuitive Sense. You used to think about it that way when we first started talking."

She grabbed another orange from the counter and lobbed it at me as a joke—slow enough for me to catch, but I flinched because of earlier. As she walked away, I tossed it and hit her in the middle of the back. Not hard. She turned, putting her hands on her hips. Then, taking a breath, she started talking again.

"I couldn't believe how pissed I got. It seemed like it came out of nowhere. I felt out of control. I kept moving to distract myself, but some incessant whirlwind took over. Being still made sense, but it felt impossible. That's when painting came to mind."

I bobbed my head several times. "It's hard to be still with a ton of energy swirling around inside."

"When I went into my room, I put one of my fifteen-inch-long stones on a chair. I sat and waited, just looking at it while my mind whirled. I told myself repeatedly, 'Take space and be still.' Then it struck me, that's it! After painting those words, more hit, 'Then you know what's real.'"

"Interesting." I said. "Because what's meaningful emerges from stillness. Your priorities show. Is that it?"

"Exactly. That's when I pictured two children on a log looking at a waterfall—what Saanvi and I did. So I painted that scene above the words. Then I remembered that Saanvi had said before just to observe experiences without judging them. So you can learn better. That's what started happening as I painted."

I smiled. "Holy padawan."

She crossed her arms and frowned. After giving me my token reprimand, she went on. "While I painted, I felt fear under the anger. Everything started connecting. I've treated Mom's prediction about me and men like a self-fulfilling prophecy, when it was really about her—how she failed my dad and me. I don't want her fear making me afraid anymore. All the evidence tells me that Carlos rocks."

"I agree about Carlos. That's a lot of learning. And humility, facing it. Do you mind showing me your artwork?"

She led me to her room. On the way, she prepared me for what I'd see. "I'm meeting with a man from the Green Acres shop tomorrow about the garden stones. I met him yesterday and showed him rock pics on my phone. He's coming over to get a dozen, along with a contract for me to sign. He sells them and gives me fifty percent."

My mouth dropped when I saw her room. "Holy rollers! You're going into business?"

She shrugged. "Hardly worth calling it a business. I could probably make more money doing other things with my time, but this could help people stop and think about what's important in life. We'll see if they sell or not."

"I didn't know you had a fortress in here." I studied them. "The pictures and sayings are great. I especially like the diamond-shaped one and the saying—'We're all diamonds in the rough; communication is the polish.'" I grinned, remembering that she got the saying from me. "You're not just talented, you're a chip off the old rock."

She shook her head.

"GUS just gave me a picture of a beer truck with *Stone IPAs* printed on the side. People lined up for them. I bet you'll sell more than you think. The Landsburg area is known for gardens and shrubbery."

"GUS got it wrong this time," she said. "Or maybe you heard what you wanted. That country store is off the beaten path."

"Sometimes GUS' messages have several possible meanings. Your stones could soon sell fast. Or maybe later. Or I just heard what ED wanted. But I've gradually gotten better at sensing what comes from GUS versus ED."

She widened her eyes. "Of course I hope GUS nailed it. But not likely this time. Either way, painting them feels therapeutic. Beaucoup bucks or not."

Hot Cakes and Flutters — Isabelle

G called it—the stacks of rocks in my room had created a small fortress. But they were already gone. I had only contacted the Green Acres guy, but a week after he loaded twelve of my stones onto his truck, two other local shop owners called. They each wanted a dozen, too.

After the last guy left, I told G how things came about. "Each store offered me sixty percent. I asked how they got my name. They both said the Green Acres' owner couldn't stop talking about the unique garden stones—that he went on and on about the talent and creativity of Isabelle Vasquez, the artist."

He smirked.

I rolled my eyes. "Okay. GUS got it right. You can say I told you so."

He shrugged as if it happened every day. "No need. When awesomeness fits, just wear it."

"I'll wait till your ego crawls back inside." After giving him a time out, I started again. "I agreed to give a dozen rocks to each shop owner the first Monday of every month. I don't have classes until the afternoon that day. So on the hour starting at 9AM, each shop's person will come to collect their rocks. That'll keep me hustling. I trekked out to Lucas' farm twice last week alone. Even though I paint quickly, I called it quits at B & F Warehouse so I have more time. Plus, I only have three weeks until the end of the semester. Then summer will be freer until my senior year."

"I'm glad you trimmed back. Too much busyness leaves you empty. Something had to give and I hoped it wouldn't be you."

He was right. Contemplation had taken a back burner. Fortunately, the occasional talk with him, the once-a-week woman time with Saanvi, and counseling with Abdul Hakeem every other week refilled my tank.

After meeting the Monday rock demands, my packed-but-uneventful week flew by. Last night and this morning, I couldn't stop thinking about the Prescott Gallery Gala later today. And Carlos. He had called yesterday about going together. When I hesitated, he clarified. "Just as friends." So I agreed.

The flutters continued through the morning. If G noticed, he didn't say so. For a change. He gave me space, at least until after I ate lunch and changed for the gala. His eyebrows rose about an inch when I came out in my favorite yellow dress with blue trim. He said, "You look classy. What's the occasion?"

"Today's the gala."

"Holy festivities! I thought that was next Saturday. Best wishes with it. Is Carlos going with you?"

I nodded and said with a bit too much energy, "And Saanvi. She'll meet us there." I didn't want him to see it as a date, and maybe I didn't either.

He studied me. Longer than usual.

"Why the once-over look?" I asked. "And don't play games."

He hesitated, perhaps measuring his words this time. "I don't think he stands a chance. You're stunning. He'll respect your wish to be friends, but he already has eyes for you."

I considered changing just as the doorbell rang. I opened the door to find Carlos. He took my breath away. I hadn't seen him decked out before—a dark jacket with a light-blue shirt and navy tie.

He appeared to be at a loss for words. Finally, he said, "You're beautiful!" His sincere expression and tender voice pulled at my heart. I went blank. My legs almost gave way.

G's voice brought me back to reality. "Hey Carlos. Hope you two have a great time at the gala."

He took a moment to respond. His gaze never left me. "Uh, thanks. I can't wait to see Isabelle's paintings."

After we headed out to Carlos' car, he opened the door for me. I ribbed him about it. "And you'd do that for any friend? Right?" He grinned.

He slid in behind the wheel and looked at me for a long moment before starting the car.

I pleaded. "Don't look at me that way."

He shook his head. "That's not so easy."

On the way, he asked questions about the gala and my feelings about it. Talking about it was refreshing. I felt known and valued as compared to my time at Fitzpatrick's. Wanting to know him like that, too, I said,

"I'm curious. We never talked about what happened at the deli. Were you scared of Dean? And where did you learn to fight? Nobody ever stood up to him, as if people knew that they had no chance. But at the deli, he had no chance."

Sadness washed over his face. He hung his head. "That's a part of my life I'd rather forget."

"You don't have to talk about it."

"No," he sighed. "I'd rather you know my history. With no secrets." He took a breath. "Because of my past, I wasn't afraid of Dean, just sad that it had to happen. I was the boxing champ in the Marines.

"One day I found out that Hugh, a guy who constantly watched for the next conquest, had raped a good friend of mine. I called her my little sister. She saw me as her big brother. When I heard what he did, I beat him to within an inch of his life.

"The Marines discharged me when they found out. They didn't slap me with a dishonorable discharge. I think they knew what Hugh had done and they didn't want the bad publicity. So, they kept it under wraps. But it changed me."

My heart melted. His simple honesty amazed me. Nothing appeared hidden.

He went on. "A few guys, one of them my best friend, found Hugh barely alive. After getting help, he suspected me and came to me about it. I'll never forget his words. He said, 'I get that you wanted to beat Hugh to a pulp. I felt like it, too. But I didn't, because by doing it, you dished out the same disrespect. Just in a different way. You're no different, then.' I saw the hypocrisy in what I did. I almost killed someone, thinking I had the right. So I went to my commander and confessed."

My mind drifted to the night I ended up in the hospital. I said in a distant voice, "Something bad changed your life for the better because you learned from it."

Carlos nodded. The brokenness showing on his face moved me. Dean never broke about anything. I teared up. I wanted to hold him, but he was driving.

Ten minutes later we strolled down Wellington Mall toward the square. Saanvi sat on a bench near the action and waved when she saw us. The mall's hub pulsed with activity—people milling around, some talking and pointing at paintings from a distance, others scrutinizing them up close. The judges huddled with one another off to the side, maybe already discussing their thoughts about stand-outs. Their body language showed deference to Angelica Ann Ainsworth and Prescott Gallery's curator. Those two likely held the most weight for selecting awards, which they'd announce in forty-five minutes.

I told Saanvi, "You look beautiful." Two long, gold earrings shaped like feathers shone brightly against her black hair. She wore a maroon and black dress with a slender golden belt.

"You do, too. Yellow's a perfect color for you. And this must be Carlos?"

After introducing them, we began studying the pieces of art as we walked. She looked my way and widened her eyes about Carlos while he studied a landscape painting. I shook my head, then pointed at our tag-team surrealistic piece with the ladders. "There it is," I said, mainly to shift the focus.

Carlos took longer strides toward it. He looked back and asked, "You did this?"

"Both of us," I said, proud of Saanvi's work too.

Saanvi smiled. "I haven't painted much. But I'm happy with it."

Carlos examined it. "I don't know much about painting. But photography taught me how to capture moments. This does that. Your piece contrasts two ways of living, right?"

Saanvi nodded. "It does. Living for what matters or chasing material things."

Carlos' settled tone conveyed he had lived it. "The one gives you life. The other eventually sucks it out of you." He tilted his head. "I periodically crashed emotionally until I started giving back to the world."

Saanvi looked over at me and lifted her eyebrows to indicate approval.

"You're as bad as G," I whispered, hoping Carlos couldn't hear me in all the commotion.

He said, "I hope you don't mind. But I wanted to get a picture of you two beside your painting. Wish I had brought my big camera. Didn't want to lug it around everywhere. I only have my phone. What do you say?"

I looked at Saanvi and joked. "Guess we ought to get some record of this before winning a prize." Saanvi and I laughed as he snapped several pictures.

After appreciating more paintings, Carlos' eyes lit up. "Cool. Here's your reflection painting. I'd have recognized it, even without your initials in the lower left. There's nothing here like it."

Saanvi said, "I bet you'll win one of the overall prizes. I still can't get over how lifelike this is."

Carlos joined in. "I agree. You can't look at this and be passive. The only other painting that draws me into it like this is the old woman getting water at a well. Her strained face shows the wear and tear of a hard life. With those two pictures, I'm part of the story."

I wagged my head. "I don't want to get my hopes up. Unestablished artists usually don't win the grand prizes. Besides, they display them for two weeks at their gallery and sell them at auction. I don't really want to part with the painting. It mirrors my life."

Carlos studied me and nodded. The compassion in his eyes caught my attention. So did the flutters inside. Then he asked me to step beside it while he snapped more pictures. He gave a once-over look and widened his eyes at me right before he did.

After the pictures, Saanvi kept studying the painting. "IV—how creative," she said, "incorporating your initials into the water. Did you sign your name on the back like they taught us at LU?"

I laughed. "Of course. Ol' Fuzzy hammered that home."

Saanvi tilted her head. "IV gives life. That's catchy. The Triple A of Painting's got nothing on you."

I shook my head.

With fifteen minutes to go, we careened through the crowd to the awards ceremony. The gallery temporarily set up operations in an empty storefront. Nothing fancy—a podium with a mic, cushy chairs on a platform up front for the judges, rows of folding chairs for the audience, and tables at the back with wine and hors d'oeuvres. An artificial ficus tree stood at each stage corner beside a splashy billboard displaying their name and logo, along with their hours and contact information. We each grabbed a glass of wine and a small plate of fruit, crackers, crab dip, and cheese.

Carlos asked, "Matter where you sit?"

Saanvi and I looked at each other and shrugged.

"How about here on the left side? You two can slip out easily for your awards."

We all chuckled.

"I'm buzzing inside," I said. "Reminds me of watching the Kentucky Derby at a party once. I had ten bucks riding on the outcome. Didn't win, but had a blast."

We watched the judges proceed up the aisle to the front at three minutes until seven. Five minutes later, the gallery curator approached the mic. "Good evening. Welcome to our fifth annual gala. We are pleased to see everyone and are excited about this unprecedented turnout." Then he introduced the judges—the last one, of course, being Angelica Ann Ainsworth. She stepped to the podium and took charge.

"I am honored to be here this evening at Prescott Gallery's wonderful gala." She looked over at the curator and beamed. I wondered if they were an item.

She turned back to the audience, launching right into the awards. "While the gala's paintings show exceptional quality, two masterpieces captured our attention. One of those artists has gained recognition recently and has shown superior work again today."

I finally took a breath.

"The other artist, to our knowledge," Angelica said, "is completely new. We always appreciate discovering new talent."

Carlos touched my hand. I looked over, jittery from all the excitement. He nodded, as if she meant me.

I gave a tiny shake of my head, not wanting my imagination to go crazy. Still torn about parting with the painting, my heart pounded, wild with hope for the validation this award would mean as an artist.

Angelica scanned the audience. "I personally look forward to meeting this new talent. We will announce Judges' Choice first, and then Best in Show." She gave a lengthy pause.

The suspense was killing me.

The announcement echoed throughout the room. "Judges' Choice goes to," she paused for emphasis. "Wilfred Clancy."

Everyone applauded as he strolled forward to receive the award for "The Woman at the Well." After shaking hands with Angelica, he returned to his seat.

She again scrutinized the audience, and then declared the next winner. "Best in Show goes to." Taking a deep breath, she said "Isabelle Vasquez."

Carlos put a big arm around me and squeezed. Saanvi squealed. "I knew it!"

I almost blacked out.

Finally, I pushed off the seat with my hand to keep my balance and wobbled to my feet. Everyone stared as I shuffled forward. I remember Angelica shaking my hand, but not what she said. Or what I said. I think I nodded a lot and sounded appreciative.

The next thing I knew, I collapsed into my seat. Hitting the chair snapped me back to reality. Saanvi whispered, "What did she say? I couldn't hear over all the commotion."

I shook my head. "I have no clue." She gave a belly laugh, almost as loud as the lingering clamor of the crowd.

A little later, Saanvi and I approached the stage as people clapped again—our surrealistic painting took third place. That came with a two-hundred-dollar gift certificate for art supplies at Hamm's Hobby Shop. Angelica handed us the award, greeting Saanvi and then saying to me, "I told you, with your painting style, I'd see you again." Saanvi beamed on stage, appearing to enjoy the moment. I felt numb.

After the awards ceremony, I slumped into the car seat. Carlos hesitated before starting the engine. Turning toward me with a puzzled face, he asked, "What's up?"

"I know I should be excited about getting Best in Show. I am."

"But?"

"I talked myself into letting go of the painting. But it felt bigger than me. Maybe inspired. Parting with it feels like betraying myself. That probably sounds messed up. I don't even want to go to the auction."

His eyes told me he got it. "I wondered about that. Some of the pictures I take feel like they're part of me. If I had painted your masterpiece, I wouldn't want to let it go either."

I nodded.

"One look at it draws me more into who I'm meant to be," he said. "It's a gift. Maybe you can talk to them about it."

I hung my head. "I wish. It's too late. To enter, we all signed a contract agreeing to auction our painting if we won one of the overall awards. It's cool. I just won't go and watch it sell."

The concern on his face touched me. "You really care. You get me."

Life's Cruelty — Isabelle

The next morning, I sat in contemplation for half an hour with Button at my feet. I finally felt peace about selling my painting. But I probably wouldn't sell another one that felt uniquely inspired like this one did. I still felt sluggish, but able to let go of it, although I wasn't about to go to the auction and see it snagged by some stranger.

I jumped when my phone chimed.

I clicked on it. "Hey Val."

Silence. Then, choppy and forced, she said, "I'm not doing so good. I need to talk."

Calling me instead of someone else from the old gang threw me. "What's up?"

"I'm in a dark place. 'Cause of MedCheck. Tomorrow's Monday. Can't go back."

"Something big must have happened for you to feel that way." Her silence and slower, choppier words alarmed me as I waited for her to continue.

"My supervisor rips into me. For everything. Nothing's ever good enough. I can't take it anymore."

"That sucks, Val. I know you. You're conscientious and good at almost anything you do." Logic took over. "If that's a pattern of hers, it's her issue. Not yours."

"I usually roll with it. But she's like a wild animal lately. Last time, she called me a dense bitch."

I gasped. Childhood memories came to mind. "That's degrading, Val, her treating you like that. And unprofessional. She shouldn't get away with it."

She let out a prolonged sigh. "Yeah, I know."

Then her history dawned on me. "You remember Pete, Repeat, and Sidekick in high school? They always got on your case like that. Until I got in their face about it."

After several seconds, she dragged out her words. "Damn. That nails it."

I waited.

"They trashed me all the time."

"As if you were the scum of the Earth," I said.

"Uh, huh."

"And so far, it sounds like you've acted the same as back then—as if you have a kick-me sign on your back." After pausing, I asked, "You said a minute ago that you can't take it anymore. How badly can't you take it? Enough for a new move?"

Silence at first. "So it means quitting? Or being point blank with her?"

"That's the reality," I said.

"It's pathetic, but I don't think I can tell her. I always just went with things. That's always worked for me. Until now."

"And yet she disrespects you, like my mom did with me. I finally told her I'd split if she kept lashing into me. And I did when she got like that. I hated doing it. But I've started valuing myself now."

I wondered if the phone went dead. "You there?"

"Yeah. Just the irony of it. At the mall, I told you to deal with reality. I thought I was the queen of that. What a joke."

"Don't turn against yourself," I said. "Then the harshness continues."

After talking another fifteen minutes, Val seemed to settle. Before hanging up, I told her to give me a call sometime on Monday if it worked. She didn't. I had called a few times to check on her. With it being late the following week now, I was getting worried. I had just decided I'd drop by her place to check on her if we didn't connect by phone. I called one last time.

She answered, her pace quicker again after I asked how things went. "I didn't go there with my boss when I went back on Monday. I just went through the motions at work, and after a few days, I thought that things might go back to how they used to be. Less stressful. But then she ragged on me one day. I blew up at her and walked out. Probably shouldn't have screamed at her, but she's backed off since. Didn't even dock me for the hours I missed that day."

"Even if you could've handled it better," I said, "a new move causes change. Keeping everything the same doesn't."

After we finished talking about her work situation, she said, "I can't thank you enough for your help. It helped me to see how the same thing from the past was happening all over again. That got my attention. I knew there was something more about it."

"You're welcome. I needed to learn the same kind of thing, too. Somehow my past was going to keep playing out until I learned a new move about it. That's why I always ask myself what I'm supposed to learn in those situations. But it still doesn't make it easy."

"No it doesn't," she said.

After getting off the phone, I smiled. *She's finding her way through the mess now. And I didn't feel empty after talking with her!*

Auction night for the paintings came and went. I stayed home and worked on rocks to distract myself. Unsuccessfully. Even Button against my feet didn't help. Restlessness, after crawling into bed, mushroomed into battling with the covers. I kicked and turned and tried sleeping in every position imaginable. Something felt wrong. I questioned my decision to let the painting go. But this nagging ache—whatever it was— felt deeper. I couldn't make sense of it. *Maybe exhaustion.*

I woke up in the morning in a cold sweat, a nightmare still on my mind. One of those never-ending ones. Trapped in a foggy maze with an ominous presence following me, I screamed for help. No one heard. I felt alone. Unreachable. Every time I thought I had found a way out, the maze turned inward again. The dark presence pursued me with a vengeance, its echoey sounds increasing and closing in. I couldn't keep running. I could no longer escape the onslaught from this creature's inevitable attack. So I stopped and turned to face it, watching for it to come around the last turn and swallow me up. Then I awoke. G would've barreled right into the symbolism had he been here.

After coffee, I trudged out to my car. My world felt dark for some reason, and I half-expected my old bomb to churn without starting. But it kicked in. I headed over to pick up Saanvi and get rocks at Lucas' farm. She had asked to come along.

Sauntering out of her apartment, her bright smile faded as I pulled up to the curb. After crawling in, she asked, "What's wrong? Your whole face shows it."

I opened my mouth to talk and cried instead. Finally, I told her about the inexplicable ache and my nightmare. My head went from side to side as I talked and drove. "I don't know what's wrong. Could it be grief from selling my art? But it feels bigger than that. I'm scared and I don't know why. Maybe I'm just warped."

Saanvi looked me in the eyes. "No. I believe you. Your feelings don't seem attached to selling your painting. Or to anything tangible at the moment. But big experiences don't happen for no reason."

We drove in silence until the turnoff. After coasting up to the large expanse of rocks, I parked and asked, "The piece represented me—you don't think that this is about letting go of it?"

"No. I don't." Then she reached across and gave me a long hug. Her embrace reminded me I wasn't alone. And that, hopefully, I wasn't just going mad.

Staying busy and lugging heavy rocks to my trunk helped. "It's amazing how much lighter I feel. It's still there. But I feel less alone because you didn't act like I was crazy."

"Someone understanding your honest emotions makes a difference," she said.

"I still wonder if it's about selling the painting. Nothing else makes sense."

"You could call the gallery and ask about it," she said. "Then learn from your reactions to their answer."

"That's a great idea. It can't hurt."

Sitting by a new rock pile in my room an hour later, I called the number on the gala brochure.

"Prescott Gallery, Jill speaking."

"I'm Isabelle Vasquez, calling to find out about my painting that was sold last night at auction."

"Oh, Best in Show. What gorgeous work! You must be proud. Unfortunately, the person who bought it wanted his name and details kept anonymous."

I asked, "I can't get any info at all? I thought I'd at least be able to see it again."

"I'm so sorry. I'm afraid not. We're required to honor the recipient's wishes. But you'll receive your check for half the selling price when everything clears. That'll be in a few days."

After hanging up, I paid attention to my feelings like Saanvi said to do. I felt down. Melancholy, like before. And disappointed that I wouldn't see that special creation again. But no gut-wrenching pain about it. That seemed illogical. Then Carlos came to mind. *Jill said 'his.' Maybe he bought it!*

I lost my breath at the thought of Carlos buying it, but within seconds the awful ache started again. That deeper, unexplainable throb scared me. Feeling out of control, I reached down and petted Button. He snuggled tighter against my feet.

I picked up my phone. Not knowing why, I felt compelled to call Carlos. Just to chat. We only talked twice on the phone since the gala because of how busy we were. *Hmm...am I calling to ask if he knows anything about the painting? Or about wanting to spend time with him after he tenderly touched my hand at the gala?*

I almost selected his number when I saw a voice-mail. An unknown number. I usually ignored them, but for some reason I clicked on it.

Silence at first. Thinking it might be a telemarketer, I considered hanging up and deleting it. Then I heard sobs. Someone in anguish. Finally, words: "I'm sorry. I'm Carlos' sister, Adelina. Something's happened. Please, give me a call."

The message ended. Chills rippled throughout my body. Not the good kind. The ache grew more voracious.

I hesitated, fearing the worst. But I hated not knowing.

I clicked on Adelina's number.

Sniffles. Silence. Then, "Isabelle, could you stop by to talk when you can? I'm at 633 Hawk Street."

"Did something happen?" I held my breath.

Silence.

Faintly, I said, "To Carlos?" The ache in my heart pounded wildly, shaking my entire body.

Her voice wrought with emotion, she suddenly burst open with words that I'll never forget—words that shot through me. "A drunk driver blindsided him at the crossroad. He's gone!"

Stunned, my mouth fell open, her words still echoing like some nightmare from hell. Dazed, I slowly shook my head back and forth in disbelief. Then I doubled over, my whole body convulsing as I wailed in anguish.

Shut Down — GENE

After my two-day workshop, I looked forward to relaxing this evening. I stepped inside and hung my hat. No Button running to greet me. No Isabelle on the sofa with homework, razzing me as a distraction. Instead, she sat slumped on the end of her bed with Button not leaving her feet. One look told me that the sun had gone behind the clouds for a season.

I watched her as I walked toward her room. The empty, lost gaze on her face conveyed utter devastation. That look reminded me of how broken I felt when Hanna died—one of those soul-shattering events where recovery feels impossible. Words offered no hope.

I approached Isabelle slowly and put my hand on her back. She didn't move. Button didn't move.

I asked, "You okay if I sit down with you?"

Nothing. She just stared at the floor. So I sat beside her and put my arm around her. It took a minute, but her head finally sagged against me.

After fifteen minutes, I said, "I don't know what happened. But you can talk with me when it feels right. Let me know what you need when you're ready."

Just a blank, barely-noticeable nod. I gave space.

I poked my head in her doorway on my way to bed an hour later. She hadn't moved. Her gaze never left the floor.

The next morning, I heard her calling in sick to the department secretary. "I won't be at classes or my assistantship this week. My boyfriend passed. I'll drop off my assignments for the week. I already have them done. You'll let my professors know? And you'll let me know if I still have anything incomplete for the semester?" Then, only sobs.

I sank in my chair, a lump in my throat and tears streaming down my face. I could feel the same weight of helplessness and despair as when I lost Hanna. Carlos had been such a bright light for both Isabelle and me. I felt a deep pit of emptiness wanting to swallow me up, and I couldn't imagine the horrendous hole Isabelle was experiencing. I kept shaking my head in disbelief at this sudden turn of events.

A few minutes later, she trudged out of her room, slower than a ninety-nine-year-old woman. Her face, lifeless and her arm moving at snail speed, she poured coffee into her "Human Being, Not Human Doing" mug. Every movement labored as if under heavy weight.

"I don't want to talk," she said, the words forced and strained.

"No pressure to do that. But I'm not going anywhere today or tomorrow if you feel inclined at some point."

She plodded back to her room without a word. Button tagged along.

Feeling heavy, I sat in my recliner reflecting on the loss of Carlos. Tears kept trickling down my cheeks, both for him and Isabelle. I couldn't stop my head from wagging back and forth. *This must be an enormous blow to her on top of all her other losses.*

After sitting still for half an hour, I reached for *The Hobbit*. I don't know how many times I reread Bilbo's escape from Gollum after finding the ring. Nothing could distract me from the deep chasm I felt. Even reading an action chapter didn't help. Then Isabelle's door opened. She still moped as she walked, but I felt hopeful when I saw the easel standing in front of her bed. Painting might help her express what she couldn't in words.

I always went for walks and talks with Button to get through intense times after Hanna died, but Isabelle needed him more than me. I kept glancing over as she grabbed some veggies from the fridge, put them on a plate, and poured ice water into her bottle. Then she turned and moseyed toward her room, Button with her every step of the way.

After hopping up and making a sandwich, I carried it to the stand beside my recliner. I eventually dozed off. The click of Isabelle's door awakened me. I looked at my watch. Three o'clock. Isabelle strolled over to the sofa and sagged into it.

"I don't even know if I," she mumbled, "can talk about it."

"No have to's. We're only starting to touch this pit of emptiness. Whatever you're able."

She hesitated, then took a breath. "A drunk driver never stopped at the crossroad on Route 56. He blindsided Carlos. Hit him on the driver's side, crushing him. I don't want to believe it's real!"

She pressed her lips together, fighting to hold in the mounting pain.

Her words came out faster. "Carlos' sister, Adelina, told me that he went to the auction and bought my painting. She said he leaned it against the wall on top of his dresser and sounded so proud of it. She had never seen him so pumped—like a kid who couldn't keep a secret."

Her voice broke. "He couldn't wait to show it to me. Then he got a call about an emergency at Have a Heart." She sobbed for a minute. "That's when it happened."

After more cries forced their way out, she shook her head. "Losing Grandma. Dad. Betrayed by Dean. Now this. And I never told him how I felt."

My eyes blurred. I could scarcely see. Emotions kept spilling out as I tried to talk. "Oh, Isabelle, I can't believe it either. It must be devastating, losing Carlos."

Her neck tightening, she raised her voice. "It's not just devastating. It sucks! It's unfair!"

"It does feel unfair."

"Not just for me. But for Adelina. She lost her younger brother and now Carlos. And he took care of Sergio's wife, Mary. She lost both of them. Then there's Emily. She lost two uncles. And how can Adelina care for her daughter if she can't function? How can people recover from pain like that?"

Isabelle broke. After letting her wail for several minutes, I moved to the sofa to put my arm around her, but she jumped up. She cut off the tears as suddenly as they started. Anger took over again. "This is too much. What does the universe want from us? It can shit on you over and over and we're just expected to take it? Well, I can't. I'm going for a drive."

I wanted to tell her to be safe, but I knew better. She grabbed her keys, blazed past me, and slammed the front door behind her. At the thud, I closed my eyes and shook my head. My heart ached for her.

What could I say? I fought it, too, when Hanna died. I needed time to be mad. To fight that unwanted reality—that harsh reality. I only hoped she wouldn't reject care for too long. Anger had a way of doing that. I needed to let out my own feelings with Abdul Hakeem and Saanvi. If I didn't, I, too, could slide down that tempting path of fighting life like I did about Hanna.

Over a hundred people attended Carlos' funeral at Brickerhome Cemetery. Many from Have a Heart gave testimony of Carlos' endless generosity and care for those around him. "He brought out the best in the lives he touched," replayed from one person after another. Tears ran from most everyone's eyes. Except Isabelle. Saanvi embraced her afterwards, but she stood like a dead tree. No expression. Little Emily cried and asked her mom unanswerable questions. Isabelle's face turned redder as she watched. Adelina and Mary appeared dazed as they held Emily's hands and tried to explain the loss of Carlos. Seeing their raw-pained faces and empty gazes tore me apart. Almost as much as Hanna's funeral.

Two weeks passed. Isabelle emerged from her room with her jaw set. Nothing had changed since that first day she told me what happened. I felt shut out of her world. Just like when her grandma passed. She even kept Button out of her room since the funeral. That frightened me for her.

I had to say something. "I feel cut off from you. Like before. You even ignore Button when he runs to your feet. That makes me afraid for you, for the path you're going down."

She stayed silent, her blank face not changing in the slightest.

I let out a sigh. "I understand that anger is part of the grief process. But I'm concerned that you're not just angry—that it might be rage against life, shutting you down like in the past."

"What if it is?" she asked, as if nothing mattered anymore.

"You can't fight life and win. When you shut off life, you hide yourself in a prison. And you prevent people from caring for you."

She shrugged.

"You remember the day Button pushed open the bathroom door and I talked about your new journey of being naked? Being authentic about your inner experiences?"

Her left shoulder lifted slightly. "Apparently you do."

"Being naked, known, and valued heals you." After pausing, I said, "Hiding invites the darkness."

Ego Drama — Isabelle

Early in the evening, my phone vibrated. I kept the volume off after Carlos passed. I looked. Saanvi. Hesitating, with a flat tone, I finally answered. "Hey."

"Gene told me you're having a tough time. I left three messages. I hope you got them."

I breathed out a long slow, "Yeah."

"Sometimes life makes no sense," she said.

I couldn't find words. I had nothing to say.

"Isabelle." She waited for a moment. "Coming to terms with losing Carlos will take time. Let me know what you need. Just don't pull back from talking for too long. You need support."

I grunted.

"I hope you're managing and getting help somewhere. Maybe from friends at LU?"

I said, "Only got to LU once. The department secretary called me about turning in one more assignment. I saw a few classmates when I got there. I just told them I lost someone close and they backed off."

"You act as if you want that."

I chewed my lip, hating the thought of admitting it. "I guess I do. I'm not ready to deal with it."

"Make sure you open up with someone soon. You may want to talk with Abdul Hakeem. If a person wants to grow and heal, he works miracles."

I gave a robotic, leave-me-alone reply. "Thanks. I'll keep it in mind. Talk to you later." Then I hung up.

Saanvi nailed it—*if* a person wants to grow and heal, *then* a counselor like Abdul Hakeem works miracles. I threw my phone onto the bed.

I sat and stared at the floor some more. Ten minutes later, I pulled out the easel to try painting. I gazed blankly at it. With no energy to do anything, I laid on my bed, numb most of the day. Then I brushed my teeth and crawled into bed at seven-thirty.

The next morning, I dragged my feet but eventually called the receptionist's number to set up a session with Abdul Hakeem.

"Holistic Health, Patsy speaking."

"I'm Isabelle Vasquez. I'd like an appointment with Abdul Hakeem, this week or next if he's available."

"What a coincidence. He's usually packed. It's 9:30 right now. Someone called a half hour ago and cancelled for 10:00 this morning. Can you make it by then?"

"Hmmm." I shuffled my feet several times and rubbed the back of my neck. My disheveled hair hung as if I had spent weeks in bed. I didn't feel ready to let anybody in, even Abdul Hakeem. But maybe I'd feel differently when I got there. I figured I should take advantage of the opportunity. "I'm only fifteen minutes away. I guess I'll drag myself over there."

Patsy sat at her desk smiling as I trudged up to it. "Nine fifty-five. You made it!"

I sighed. "At least my body did."

I slogged into Abdul Hakeem's office. Looking up, he made a pained face. "Gene and Saanvi told me you're going through a lot. Tell me about it."

After we sat down, I explained, my voice sounding hollow. "I told you about Carlos before, the guy interested in me. We started spending more time together. I was falling for him. Or, I should say, fell for him." I let out a breath. "A drunk driver smashed into him broadside, crushing him. Gone in one freakin' instant."

His eyes watered. Then he closed them and lowered his head. "Isabelle, you've already experienced more than your share of loss. This probably tore things wide open again."

I didn't say anything. I didn't feel anything. Except fire. A raging fire inside.

"Tell me what's happening—what you're going through."

My face and neck tightened. "Not much to tell. It's too much. For me. For Carlos' sister who lost both brothers now. For his sister's daughter, Emily, who lost both uncles and now has an unable-to-function mother! That's the worst. Emily has no one there for her and has to live through this alone. It's not right. End of story."

"How heartbreaking." He moved his head slowly back and forth, not taking his eyes off of me. "For you, and when you have to watch those you care about suffer."

I said nothing.

"I feel the anger radiating from you. And your helplessness about no one being able to care for Emily." He paused. "The same as you with your mom about that age. Getting no help. No wonder you're angry."

I stayed silent, my lips pressing together even tighter.

He waited.

I had no intention of budging at this point. He might as well have just said an amen to my point.

After waiting another minute, he started slowly. "Your silence gives me the impression that you're intensely angry about what happened. I would be, too, in your shoes. It's natural and valid to feel anger and even rage at injustices." After pausing, he said, "You'll need to go at your pace. But, in the end, anger hides you from deeper emotions. If it doesn't give way to those more vulnerable feelings at some point, it prevents you from healing."

I stared blankly.

"You don't seem ready to let go of it right now. That's okay. The choice to let go of anger, and when, is always yours."

I snapped back. "But it's wrong, what happened! Senseless suffering because of some drunk is messed up."

He put his head down. Then he tilted it. "You know that I'm not just saying empty words when I talk about suffering?" He held up his partial arm.

That caught my attention.

"It is messed up," he said with a raised tone. "My past employer's neglect caused this, as well as my parents' death. It took me a long time to let go of anger. To accept the injustice of what happened." His eyes locked onto mine more intently after his words.

I nodded, taking in his point more fully.

"I suffer intense nerve pain daily because of something unfair." His eyes searched for a moment. "But we have two choices when we suffer: Stay stuck in anger about our losses or gain valuable insights for ourselves and others. I'm not certain that the timing is right to say what

I'm thinking. But my best sense is to add to what we already talked about once. Anger is fueled by the ego drama. The world you want and the way you want it. If, instead, you want to live the life of conscience—for the collective story bigger than you—let go of the anger when you're ready. And allow comfort during your suffering."

He studied me. "If you allow me to care for you, to treat you with value during your worst struggles, you awaken to an inner sense of value and wholeness that not many people attain. That's your true self awakening—the self that knows we all have value. Then you're more able to take part in the larger story—continually awakening what's genuine within you and others. And one final thought. You have the chance through this tragedy to live the life of conscience. To care for Emily, for example. To give her what you always needed as a kid. To be truly known and valued in spite of the world's violence and suffering."

I don't recall if I responded. But I remember him saying, "It's early, but let's call it a day. I don't want to add anything that will detract from your life and death choice: choosing between the ego drama or the life of conscience—between the little story you want to control or the bigger collective story that advances everyone's good. With one, you always find purpose and value. With the other, not so much when you suffer."

I exited Holistic Health in a daze. Not angry. Not emotional. Just numb.

Driving home, staring at the road, I missed Maple Street. Already three streets past it, I almost turned when I heard the word cemetery. Clearer than other spontaneous thoughts that came to mind, it propelled me forward—not to Brickerhome Cemetery where Carlos was buried, but to Newsome's Cemetery to talk with Grandma.

I pulled into the empty lot, my eyes leaking and nose running. I grabbed tissues from the box on the passenger floor, started wiping, and hopped out. Sobs started pouring out. The closer I got to Grandma's gravestone, the louder my primordial screams of anguish pierced the air.

"Why, Grandma? Why does the universe always make people suffer? Why do Adelina and Mary have to go on alone? Losing both Sergio and Carlos! Carlos dreaded that intersection, and it happened! And why does Emily have to suffer like this? She was afraid something would happen to Carlos or her mom. And it did! How can a little girl go on after that?"

I don't remember what I screamed after that. Or how long it took before I stopped. But I sat there on the ground, a total mess.

In a strangely calm voice, I said, "Grandma, I need your help again. I loved Carlos. My heart was already his and I never told him. I don't know if I can go on."

Sitting four feet from the gravestone, I stared as a monarch butterfly landed on a clover just in front of it. It sat there looking at me. Grandma came to mind; always pointing out butterflies. I felt warm. Then, from somewhere inside, a current of air surged and filled me, along with a soothing, vibrant whisper: dance with life. It reminded me of Saanvi's words when we saw the butterflies moving back and forth in harmony, as if tied by an unseen string.

That evening I called Saanvi to see if she wanted to talk while we got rocks. I picked her up on the way. She hopped in, saying, "You sounded different on the phone. Something budged."

"I talked with Abdul Hakeem. And with Grandma at the cemetery."

She widened tear-filled eyes and leaned forward as she studied me.

"I screamed a lot with Grandma. Afterward I saw a butterfly land on a clover right in front of the gravestone. It chilled there for a minute or two, just looking at me. I heard the words, 'Dance with life,' just like you said before. Then it flew."

Her eyes lit up. "That's amazing. No way that's a coincidence!"

"I still feel devastated about Carlos after screaming. But I know there's more. I felt a burst of life in me when I heard Grandma's words. I felt connected to her, like the butterflies with an invisible string. And to you, and to Carlos at the same time. The night of the hospital came to mind, too."

"None of that's by chance. Similar to the butterfly strings, I think connections continue after we pass. At times, I feel my mom's presence when I get insights. Almost like she's part of that."

"I never considered a connection with Grandma after she died until I first went to her gravestone two and a half years ago," I said. "And this time, with the monarch, I had no doubt that we were connected."

She saw my head tilt and asked, "What are you thinking?"

"Your brother talked about the collective story versus the ego drama. I wonder if that bigger story is not just here, but beyond here. At LU, we studied research about people sending positive thoughts and care to hospitalized patients, and how it helped them even when they weren't aware of it. Some studies called it prayer; others didn't. The research showed that healing increased in those patients compared to others not receiving it. And the care was invisible."

She gave a long, slow nod.

"Everything felt connected when the butterfly kept sitting and staring at me. Like the night above the ICU."

"I think it is," Saanvi said. "Think about how insights work. They connect things that were previously unseen. Each insight reminds me that life is connected."

I finally turned off the car. "I didn't realize we were here. I came to get rocks to distract me from focusing on Carlos. But I haven't felt as angry since the cemetery and, now, talking with you."

After we got out and gathered some rocks, I found a rock shaped like a heart. "Saanvi, look. I want to paint this for Carlos. With Emily."

"That gives me the chills," she said.

Living for Conscience – Isabelle

In a session with Abdul Hakeem a week after our last meeting, I waited for him to sit down. After settling and looking into my eyes, he said, "You started your journey to live for conscience, haven't you?"

I smiled. "Yeah, I screamed things out at my grandma's grave after I left you last week. I've felt a lot more peace since. I'm still angry at points, but the peace is growing."

"That's a quick turnaround. I'm happy that you're moving in a positive direction."

"Looking back, your comment about not distracting me from my life and death choice seemed right, somehow. Ending on that caused it to keep cycling back through my mind, and it felt exactly like that: a life and death choice."

"And? Your face looks as if something more is happening."

"Are you okay if I learn a few things for being a therapist before I dive into the heavier stuff? I need to go a little slow getting into the pain."

"By all means," he said. "You saying what you need is already paying attention to care for yourself. Wonderful."

"Are ego and conscience opposites, like life and death? It felt that way when I was down and out last time."

"Yes. They're counterparts. I see them as two psychological systems for choice. Ego limits you because it's totally individual-based and, therefore, selfish at its core. Conscience is collective and keeps expanding and connecting you."

"They're like two different realities."

He grinned. "I believe that they are."

"Ego sure makes you feel like an orphan," I said. "So, getting afraid, that's my ego?"

He explained. "Yes, ego is the root of fear and oppression. It isolates and divides—one versus another because it sees resources as limited.

Why? Because you're on your own. Conscience connects us, caring about both me and you; it recognizes that we're all interconnected and need each other to be healthy and whole."

He waited, then asked, "You brought up being afraid for a reason?"

I told him my idea, painting a rock with Emily. Shaped like a huge heart, it'd remind everyone of Carlos. My head drooped as I talked. "I'll check with her mom to see if she's okay with it. But I'm scared I'll mess up with Emily. Even if it goes okay, what then? Carlos was basically her dad. And I have my own pain about him. I'm so broken I feel like I have nothing to give."

"This may seem unrelated, but it's not. What did you need from your mom or dad when your grandma died? Didn't you go through the pain alone?"

"Yeah," I said. "But Dad had just found out he had cancer, and Mom couldn't care for anyone."

"That's my point. You had no support. It doesn't matter who you are, you get stuck in pain when you have no help. In America, adults tell children to pick themselves up by their bootstraps—something like that. Then when someone dies, parents try to be 'strong' and show no feelings to their children. What happens? Children suffer alone. They have no care during their pain. Other cultures know the value of grieving together to go on together."

"You mean, cry with her?"

He nodded. "You're a friend, not a counselor to her. Your gift to Emily, and to others, is fully being you. Whether that's your grief or your learning from it."

"I keep thinking my life has to be completely together to be able to help someone. As a therapist-in-training, I should know by now that's not true."

"Many people think that," he said. "As long as your pain doesn't dominate and overwhelm Emily, your courage to touch loss helps her to be brave too."

"At the grave, I didn't feel alone. I felt Grandma's presence. I couldn't scream and get rid of the pain anywhere else. I think that's when I let go of what you call the ego drama, enough to want to help Emily."

"I'm glad. I don't know of another effective way to move through devastation apart from letting go of the ego drama. That means getting healthy support so you can express the anger in helpful ways, move through it, and accept what is. That starts the healing, and the learning for the collective story."

I nodded. "I get it. You can't learn when you stay pissed."

He leaned forward. "Living for conscience means paying attention to how your part contributes to bettering the world. Your abilities, gifts, and accomplishments. Your struggle through pain, and the comfort and learning you receive through it—it's for more than your ego. It's meant to enhance this world. You recognize your value when you know this. You find greater purpose. No matter what difficulties you face."

"I'm still afraid to touch that pain. Maybe I'll get stuck in it. What good will I be for Emily then?"

"You get stuck in grief when you resist what is. Especially when you have no supportive person at your side. You grow through it when you accept it and let it shape you for making a difference in the world. To give others what you needed for getting through it—a comforting presence."

The next day, my heart pounded as I clicked on Adelina's number.

"Isabelle, I," her voice broke, as she answered. She sniffled.

I mumbled. "I didn't know whether to call or not."

Her voice raised several notches. "I'm glad you did. Everyone's afraid to talk about it with me. Mary's the only one—she gets that you have to go through the pain. That there's no shortcut. And you had feelings for Carlos. I knew you'd get it."

No words came.

After silence, she said, "At least he said you had feelings."

A wave of grief poured out of me. After catching my breath, pain-filled words came out. "I'm sorry. I wanted to be there for you." My voice broke.

"Don't apologize. I know it sounds lame, but it helps when I'm not the only one suffering. I need someone who knows. Someone who doesn't just give stock answers."

"I feel sick," I said. "I never told anyone how I felt. I never told Carlos and now it's too late."

"Isabelle. He knew. He lit up when he talked about you."

More raw emotions found their way out. "This is what I was afraid of. I didn't want to wail in front of you. Or Emily. You two have enough grief without mine adding to it."

"I need this. Everyone except Mary tries to protect me. Hearing you helps me feel less crazy. Not so alone. It shows he was important."

That clicked. "That's what I needed when I lost my grandma and dad. But isn't that too much for Emily? Breaking down like this with her?"

"I've been a wreck in front of her every day. She's doing better than me. At first I was scared about Emily getting stuck, too. I had tried to keep a lid on the big emotions when Sergio passed—hers and mine. I couldn't do that this round and I've been amazed that she just says how she feels. I don't correct her because I feel it, too. Kids are resilient when they find a listening ear."

"Are you cool with me painting a rock with her? For Carlos? It's shaped like a big heart."

She sniffled again. "That's touching. She calls you Aunt Isabelle. Painting together would thrill her. She's in her room, probably hearing every word."

"Do you want to ask her?"

"Hold on." She checked. A little voice cheered. "You must have heard that."

"I sure did. Does Friday evening at 7:00 work? I can pick her up. Or I can come there with my paint set."

"What do you think about painting in Carlos' room? And maybe leaving the rock there for Emily? Just for a week or two."

I couldn't talk at first. "I'd like nothing better."

Friday 7:00 P.M. couldn't come soon enough. But at 6:45, my legs almost gave way as I grabbed my paint set. *It's cool; just be you. That's what she needs.*

On the way to Adelina's, I started biting my lip three times and told myself to stop. Coasting up to the curb, I admired the collection of daisies at each side of Adelina's front steps. The beige, one-level ranch house appeared well-kept in spite of her loss. As soon as I parked, the screen door flung open. Emily charged through it and out to my car screaming. "Aunt Isabelle! Aunt Isabelle!" I jumped out to greet her with a hug. She grabbed my hand to lead me inside.

"One minute, Emily," I said. "Let me get my paint set and backpack." I shouldered the straps, working to get the weight of the rock to the middle of my back. Then I grabbed my paint set with one hand while Emily took the other.

Adelina stepped out, tears on her cheeks. Some trickled down mine as I walked over to her. We embraced like longtime friends. "Thank you for coming," she said.

I half-smiled, both happy and sad thoughts running through my mind. I turned to Emily. "Do you want to show me Carlos' room? You can carry my paint set if you want."

Her eyes lit up, almost as much as her cute smile. She spoke as her little hands reached for the paint set. "Puffy talks to Carlos. Sometimes she's happy and sometimes she's sad."

I looked back at Adelina. She explained as she followed us into the house. "Puffy is Emily's horse. Carlos got it for her. She plays with her in Carlos' room. I'll let you two be."

As soon as we entered the room, my lip quivered. I looked around through blurry vision. Pictures from Have a Heart hung on two walls. Emotions gushed out of me when I saw my painting sitting on his dresser. At each side stood the two pictures he had snapped at Prescott's Gala—the one of Saanvi and me beside our surrealistic piece, and the other of me beside my reflection painting.

Emily sat the paint set on Carlos' bed and moved beside me with her lower lip sticking out. She never said a word but just reached out to hold my hand as I cried. After I semi-recovered, I pointed. "He took those pictures of me at the art place."

"I know," she said in her sweet little voice. "He told me about a million times when he put them there."

I chuckled, shaking my head at her simple honesty. "And that's my painting he bought." My words trailed off.

"He told me that, too. He couldn't stop staring at it until he got the phone call." Her eyes filled with tears.

I started crying again. She grabbed her fluffy horse and held it up. "Here's Puffy."

My voice wavered as I shook her foot. "Hi, Puffy. Nice to meet you." Sobs sneaked out. "I'm sorry, Emily. I still get very sad about Carlos." I sat my backpack on the floor.

"Me, too. Puffy gives me a hug when I'm sad." She gave her a squeeze and held her up again. "She wants to hug you."

I pulled her against me. "Thank you, Puffy. I needed that." A long breath flowed out of me. I actually felt relief after squeezing a stuffed animal.

Grabbing old newspapers from my backpack, I laid them on the floor. Then I placed the rock in the middle of them.

Emily yelled. "It does look like a big heart! That's what mommy said."

I put some paint pots on her side of the newspapers and some on mine. "Do you have something you'd like to paint on it? Or do you just want to start and see what happens?"

She looked up at me with her big, green eyes and flashed a mischievous grin. "I'll just paint."

I watched as she painted orange. I refrained from asking, "Is that an orange heart?" She had formed two humps that almost came to a point as they narrowed at the lower end. But she added little orange strands to each side at the bottom.

She asked, "Can I use black? It's on your side."

"Of course. Use any color you want."

She dipped her brush in black and added a thick line down the middle between the two humps. My jaw fell. My eyes watered as she formed short thin lines bending outward at the top of the black.

"A butterfly!" My whole body felt warm.

"Puffy wanted to show Carlos the one we saw on our flowers yesterday."

I shook my head in disbelief. I came here to help Emily but she already helped me more. I blew my nose with one of the tissues from my pocket. "I'm sure Carlos loves your butterfly. Are you okay if I paint some, too?"

She gave quick, excited nods. We painted seven colorful butterflies on that big heart.

After painting and cleaning up, I said, "I think Carlos would like you to keep his big heart here. That way he can see the butterflies on it whenever he wants."

Her beautiful grin told me she liked that idea. After showing Adelina our masterpiece, we cried a little more and then walked together to the front door.

Adelina said, "You're welcome to stop by whenever you want."

Emily put her arms out to the sides. "Group hug!" All three of us embraced.

As I walked out, I said, "Feel free to give me a buzz, too. This helped me, being here. I hope it helped her, too."

On the way home, my head kept going back and forth at the wonder of it all—the coincidences and the relationships I hadn't expected. Abdul Hakeem's words came to mind about the ego drama versus the life of conscience and how it expands us. ED versus LISA.

My mind drifted to Grandma, so I talked with her. "A butterfly again. Somehow, you're a part of all of this. And the cool time with Adelina and Emily wouldn't have happened if I had continued fighting the universe about what I wanted. None of us would have received these gifts."

Acknowledgements

Many people contributed to this work.

Starting with my wife.

Kathy, you believed in me. Encouraged me. That made a tremendous difference. You also carried more household responsibilities at points, allowing me the time and space to write, and then to refine, refine, refine. Thank you for your unending love and support. That was, and is, a gift.

The Charles Bruce Foundation for publishing *Unlocked*. Pat and Chad, thank you for your special talents and tireless work. Thank you for your important life mission through the organization, all of that contributes to many with dreams just like mine.

My editor, Cheryl; during a later stage of revisions, you gave invaluable input that upped the level of the whole novel. You helped it go way beyond the original concept – being helpful supplemental reading for counseling courses. Then you polished it with your incredible insight and editing skills. What a gift. Thank you.

Illustrator, Jeremy Ruby, thank you for the breathtaking book cover that perfectly captures the essence of the novel. I really can't find enough descriptors for how captivating and remarkable it is. Thank you so much for your time and phenomenal talent and insight.

My writing group—Sherry, Pat, Jody, Phyllis, and James—you poured your years of wisdom into a rookie. Creating a realistic novel to make a difference in people's lives couldn't have happened for me without you. Your generosity is beyond measure. Thank you for your long-suffering patience and expertise.

My friends and family who read and gave input about earlier versions of *Unlocked*, thank you. Your time and thoughtful comments made a difference. Also, my skills as a counselor and educator came through countless interactions with counseling professors, students, and clients, especially at Shippensburg University (you know who you are!). Your contributions were inestimable.

So much of what got poured into this novel came from beyond myself. You've heard many times before that no person stands alone—that one's accomplishments come from standing on the shoulders of others. Through the gifts of others. *Unlocked* symbolizes that to me—many gifts coming together in a work that has a chance to transform people's lives. I sincerely thank each of you who poured a piece of yourself into *Unlocked*.

www.ingramcontent.com/pod-product-compliance
Lightning Source LLC
Chambersburg PA
CBHW070614030426
42337CB00020B/3789